A Confederacy of Dunces
COOKBOOK

A Confederacy of Dunces
COOKBOOK

RECIPES *from* IGNATIUS J. REILLY'S NEW ORLEANS

Cynthia LeJeune Nobles

LOUISIANA STATE UNIVERSITY PRESS   BATON ROUGE

Published by Louisiana State University Press
Copyright © 2015 by Louisiana State University Press
All rights reserved
Manufactured in Canada
Second printing

Designer: Michelle A. Neustrom
Typeface: Sentinel
Printer and binder: Friesens Corporation

Library of Congress Cataloging-in-Publication Data
Nobles, Cynthia LeJeune, 1954–
    A Confederacy of dunces cookbook : recipes from Ignatius J. Reilly's
New Orleans / Cynthia LeJeune Nobles.
        pages cm
    Includes bibliographical references and index.
    ISBN 978-0-8071-6191-3 (cloth : alk. paper) — ISBN 978-0-8071-
6192-0 (pdf) — ISBN 978-0-8071-6193-7 (epub) — ISBN 978-0-
8071-6194-4 (mobi) 1. Cooking, American—Louisiana style. 2. Cooking—Louisiana—New Orleans. 3. Toole, John Kennedy, 1937–1969.
Confederacy of dunces. I. Title.
    TX715.2.L68N63 2015
    641.59763—dc23
                                                        2015006263

CONTENTS

PREFACE

· ·

> "Personally, I have found that a lack of food and comfort, rather than ennobling the spirit, creates only anxiety within the human psyche and channels all of one's better impulses only toward the end of procuring something to eat. Even though I do have a Rich Inner Life, I must have some food and comfort also."
>
> —Ignatius J. Reilly, entry in *The Journal of a Working Boy, or, Up from Sloth.*

Satire, of course, is the focus of John Kenney Toole's Pulitzer Prize–winning novel *A Confederacy of Dunces.* But as Ignatius J. Reilly wages his fight against the modern world, the lampooning extends to the novel's setting, that "City of Romance and Culture," New Orleans. And since the elephantine Ignatius is a glutton, ridicule naturally spills over to the city's fabled cuisine. So as scenes unfold through clouds of doughnut sugar, rivers of Dixie 45 beer, tangles of spaghetti, and mounds of empty erster (oyster) shells, the reader quickly realizes that food, like New Orleans itself, becomes a character.

For those who haven't read this brilliant observational comedy, imagine the plot twists associated with an over-educated, thirty-year-old ideologue who abhors work and lives in a minuscule urban house with his overprotective mother. It's the early 1960s, money is tight, and anything akin to intelligence is even more scarce. The two are surrounded by a cast of starkly colloquial supporting characters, most of whom, by today's standards, come off as blatantly politically incorrect, with many helping define themselves through their eating habits.

At the time Toole wrote *Dunces,* also in the early 1960s, food trends were in transition. After World War II, the United States saw an explosion in the invention of kitchen appliances, along with the consumption of processed foods. TV dinners were coming on the scene, orange juice was sold in powdered or concentrated frozen forms, salad dressing came in bottles, and most sauces started with a can of soup. Sales of boxed cereals and pizza kits were also on the rise. And, of course, there was lots and lots of junk food, mostly aimed at baby boomers.

Conversely, this was also the time when vegetarianism went mainstream. Soul food was getting a serious look, and forward-thinking restaurants were dabbling in Japanese. The 1960s also saw a movement toward the lavish. In particular, first lady Jacqueline Kennedy was wowing gourmets with sophisticated French fare at the White House. On television, the classically trained Julia Child was trying hard to endear the watching public to French cooking, and in homes hosts were heating up fondue pots, lighting up backyard barbecues, and setting entrées and desserts aflame.

In New Orleans, a city often slow to change, the decade started out with much of the old, with grocery stores still selling unshelled beans in barrels, and milk, Creole cream cheese, and Coca-Cola still delivered to homes. But by the end of the 1960s, home delivery of groceries was virtually gone, in part due to Schwegmann's, the mega-giant chain that introduced the region to self-service discount shopping, and which offered just about everything, including garden supplies, live frogs, oyster poor boys, and cocktails from in-store bars. But, even with the trend toward supermarket shopping, corner grocers abounded and were the anchor of many a neighborhood.

Toole's character development touches on many of these food trends. For example, sophisticated dining definitely bypasses the fictional Reilly house on Constantinople Street, and convenience is king, with most of Mrs. Reilly's dinners coming out of a can. Representing the traditional is Santa Battaglia, whose life revolves around cooking Italian food. Mr. Watson and Burma Jones are African Americans who discuss their problems while surrounded by a corner store's pickle meat and sausage. Officer Mancuso's wife owns all the latest kitchen gadgets, and, of course, there's Ignatius, who's addicted to just about every junk food imaginable.

The use of food as a character device began, naturally, with Toole's familiarity with his beloved city, a place that still hasn't forgotten its European and African ties. Keep in mind that, from 1718 until 1803, the French and then the Spanish owned New Orleans. The colonial landowners, many of whom fancied themselves European aristocrats, naturally thought eating sophisticated food was a sign of status. Some even brought their own chefs from their home countries. But the majority of newcomers had to settle for teaching what they remembered as being elegant to skilled, inventive African cooks, who proceeded to mix haute cuisine with their own spicy, stew-based traditions. Add to that the herbs, corn, and game of Native Americans, a large dose of the produce and dairy products from a small but significant group of German farmers, and waves of Irish and Italian immigrants and their hereditary food habits, and, *voilà,* you have the seeds for one of the world's great cuisines, Creole, meaning "born in America," and a way of cooking unique from any other.

As a side note, food known as Cajun (short for Acadian) is more rustic and robust than Creole. And, although many modern New Orleans restaurants bombard tourists with boudin; dark, thick gumbo; chicken and sausage jambalaya; alligator; and a myriad of spicy "Cajun" specialties, none of these dishes are mentioned in *Dunces.* But that's not surprising. Unbelievably, New Orleans and the Acadian parishes to the city's west had very little culinary interaction until the interstate system connected the two regions in the early 1970s. Chef Paul Prudhomme, specifically, is credited for introducing New Orleans to Cajun food, and he wasn't hired at Commander's Palace until 1975.

Although Toole's characters often eat what was then new, they also have a deep connection with mainstays of old Creole cuisine, such as crab and oysters, along with pralines, long-simmering beef daube, cakes soaked in wine, and chicory coffee with milk. And for those of us who are food obsessed, it's a little disappointing the book does not mention any of the city's actual historic cafés and restaurants, or any of their iconic dishes. But this oversight is understandable. Even if the Reilly household had enjoyed a higher income, they probably would not have dined out like we do today because during the 1960s, most folks still ate at home. Back then, eating out anywhere was reserved for special occasions, with the high-end, coat-and-tie places strictly attracting tourists and wealthy diners. On that note, imagine *Dunces*'s Gus Levy, owner of Levy Pants, and his wife, who had "given herself freely to . . . gourmet foods," and you've got the typical patron who frequented Arnaud's and Antoine's.

With all that in mind, this cookbook is meant to memorialize the foods, both the nutritious and the wickedly unwholesome, that are important to the book's characters, as well as to introduce new classics that spin off from what the characters ate. Aside from recipes and a little food history, I'll also take you on a tour of Ignatius's favorite haunts. So get ready to learn about the D. H. Holmes Department Store, the Prytania Theatre, and Bourbon Street's bars. You'll also be introduced to Lucky Dogs, the real-life template for Paradise Vendors. Then there are quick detours to the city that scarred Ignatius for life, Baton Rouge, as well as Lafayette, the southwest Louisiana city in the heart of Cajun country, which left a lasting impression on Toole.

I signed on for this book when Alisa Plant, acquisitions editor at LSU Press, asked if I knew anyone who might want to tackle the project. I've always been a fan of *A Confederacy of Dunces,* and in no small part because of the novel's rich use of food. So, without missing a beat, I volunteered for the job. And after a year of writing and experimenting in the kitchen, I not only came up with recipes for the expected macaroons and cheese dip, but also for dishes that would have been popular in Ignatius's New Orleans. Many are for delicacies I serve at my house today. A good portion are also drawn from my experience as a cookbook author and food columnist for the *Baton Rouge/New Orleans Advocate,* and from years studying New Orleans food as a member of the Newcomb College Culinary History Writers Group. Too, some recipes were inspired by New Orleans cookbooks from the 1960s. And a smattering come from restaurant chefs and from generous friends who live in and around the city, and whose names appear along with their recipes.

Another influence has been my lifetime of cooking gumbo, okra, jambalaya, crawfish, crabs, oysters, strong coffee, and pralines. This love of stirring in pots started in my hometown of Iota, Louisiana, where I grew up on a rice and crawfish farm, and it followed me to New Orleans, where my husband and I owned a house in the Uptown neighborhood on Broadway Street, just a block behind the house on Audubon Street where John Kennedy Toole had lived with his parents. Then Hurricane Katrina forced us to move to Baton Rouge, and my main residence remains in the city Ignatius lambasts as a "whirlpool of despair." But I do keep one foot in New Orleans.

And as I step out of my apartment in the French Quarter, also known as the *Vieux Carré,* the "old square," and I stroll down Bourbon Street, St. Peter, Chartres, and Royal, I rarely pass up a restaurant with an outdoor display menu. There, on the same streets where Ignatius once lumbered, I find delicacies such as crab cloaked in creamy ravigote sauce, P & J oysters, Chicken Pontalba, Café Brulot, and inventive dishes with okra. And it always strikes me that, as with this spoof's quirky characters, much of the food New Orleans takes for granted would seem foreign anywhere else. But such is Creole still, in people as well as cuisine, born and residing in America, yet flaunting whispers of an alien, exotic, and unforgotten past. So, after reading these pages, hopefully you'll understand why Ignatius never wants to leave New Orleans, why the food the characters cook and eat is a parody in itself, and why *A Confederacy of Dunces* could not have been set in any other city.

LIST OF CHARACTERS

Ignatius Jacques Reilly. The book's unsympathetic protagonist is an overweight, buffoonish, overeducated savant, with one blue eye and one yellow. The thirty-year-old is also an enthusiastic student of the medieval philosopher Boethius and, therefore, abhors anything modern, including canned food. Yet throughout his fight against the contemporary world, the enigmatic Ignatius gorges on pastries, candy, and cookies and, of course, hot dogs.

Irene Reilly. Ignatius's overprotective mother. The long-time widow is in love with Dixie beer and Gallo muscatel, but not with cooking.

Santa Battaglia. Newfound friend to Mrs. Reilly and Sicilian through and through. In between trying to hook Mrs. Reilly up with the retired Claude Robichaux, Santa cooks specialties that, in New Orleans, are known as Creole-Italian.

Claude Robichaux. An elderly widower with a Cajun surname, who's constantly looking around every corner for a "communiss." Robichaux woos Irene Reilly, and he likes to cook.

Myrna Minkoff. Ignatius's former Tulane University classmate and on-and-off-again love. This Jewish "minx" now lives in New York City, and she and Ignatius tortuously exchange love letters. From her correspondence, it's clear Myrna is more interested in sex than food.

Lana Lee. The stone-hearted proprietress of Bourbon Street's Night of Joy nightclub. Lee is so money hungry, she dilutes the alcohol she sells with water.

Darlene. B drinker and an exotic dancer hopeful at the Night of Joy nightclub. Darlene doesn't cook much, but is a fan of juicy wine cakes and canned Spanish rice.

Burma Jones. Chain-smoking, world-wise African American janitor at the Night of Joy. Jones stays with the demeaning job to avoid jail time on the false charge of pilfering cashews. When not sweeping floors, Jones hangs at Mattie's Ramble Inn, a combination bar and grocery store.

Mr. Watson. The "quiet, tan, café au lait" owner of Mattie's Ramble Inn grocery store and giver of advice to Burma Jones.

Patrolman Angelo Mancuso. Santa Battaglia's bumbling nephew, whose wife, Rita, has the latest kitchen gadgets.

Gus Levy. Owner of Levy Pants, Inc. A "nice" man who can certainly afford to dine in New Orleans's best restaurants. His shrew of a wife, Mrs. Levy, has, over the years, given herself to, among other self-serving pursuits, correspondence courses, the sun, saving the ancient Miss Trixie, and a love of gourmet foods.

Miss Trixie. Elderly bookkeeper at Levy Pants. When not napping, Miss Trixie demands that her employer hand over the holiday turkey and ham he's been promising.

Mr. Gonzalez. Ignatius's timid boss at Levy Pants.

Dorian Greene. A flashy homosexual who drinks martinis and daiquiris, and who throws lavish parties.

Mr. Clyde. Cranky owner of the hot-dog company known as Paradise Vendors, and Ignatius's eventual boss.

George. A high-school dropout in cahoots with the sinister Lana Lee, and who tries to hide porn in the bun compartment of Ignatius's hot dog wagon.

Betty Bumper, Frieda Club, and Liz Steele. A rowdy beer-drinking threesome of lesbians who badger Ignatius.

Dr. Talc. History professor at Tulane who still has nightmares from the time he taught Myrna Minkoff and Ignatius. Talc, therefore, drinks a lot.

Miss Annie. The Reillys' grumpy neighbor who's always complaining about Ignatius's lute-playing.

A *DUNCES* GLOSSARY

Banquette. A sidewalk.

Big Chief Writing Tablet and Blue Horse Paper. Ignatius records his philosophical ramblings on the wide-ruled lines of Big Chief writing tablets which, even today, are constructed of pages made of newsprint. With distinctive red covers featuring line drawings of Native Americans in flowing feather headdress, Big Chief tablets were trademarked in 1947 by Western Tablet Company in St. Joseph, Missouri. Use of the product peaked in the 1960s, when spiral notebooks started becoming popular. Blue Horse was the trademark of Atlanta's Montag Brothers Paper Company, whose loose-leaf paper was sold in packs with a wrapper stamped with a Blue Horse head icon, which could be clipped and redeemed for prizes. Montag eventually merged with Westab, the new name the Western Tablet Company took in 1964.

Boethius. A Roman philosopher of the early sixth century who, while jailed for treason, wrote the philosophical work *On the Consolation of Philosophy,* a satire based on the teachings of ancient Greek philosophers.

Charity Hospital. Mrs. Reilly wants to commit Ignatius to Charity Hospital, in the 1960s located at 1532 Tulane Avenue. The huge Art Deco facility was built between 1936 and 1940 with funds from the Public Works Administration. The Charity system had originally started in 1736, and has been closed since Hurricane Katrina hit in 2005, making it one of the longest continuously operating hospitals in the world. Charity had been governed by the Louisiana State University hospital system, and not only cared for the indigent, but was a premier teaching institution, with one of the best level-one trauma units in the country. As of this writing, the building on Tulane Avenue, the sixth Charity structure, is now empty, and construction for a replacement, called University Medical Center, has begun in Mid-City.

Constantinople Street. A narrow street in the Twelfth Ward (division) of the New Orleans neighborhood known as Uptown.

D. H. Holmes Department Store. At the time, one of the glitziest department stores on Canal Street. And the clock is real, too.

Dixie 45. One of Mrs. Reilly's favorite adult beverages, Dixie 45 beer was produced in New Orleans by the Dixie Brewing Company at 2401 Tulane Avenue. Dixie started brewing beer in 1907, filed for Chapter 11 bankruptcy in 1989, and reorganized in 1992. After suffering through flooding and looting during Hurricane Katrina, the brewery shut down in 2005. Dixie beer is still available, however, and is currently contract brewed in Wisconsin.

Dr. Nut. The soft drink Ignatius craves was an intensely sweet almond-flavored product sold in a seven-ounce bottle and produced through the 1940s by the World Bottling Company at Chartres Street and Elysian Fields Avenue. Along with its familiar squirrel logo, the drink was known for its catchy advertising phrases, such as "It's a Food—Not a Fad," "The Sure Cure for Thirst," and "Calling Dr. Nut." In 1951, the World Bottling Company's assets were seized for nonpayment of taxes, and the drink disappeared from the market. In 1963, Wright Root Beer Company brought Dr. Nut back, but with a cherry flavoring, and it was discontinued after about five years. In 1977, Bayou Bottling, Inc., of Jennings, Louisiana, revived Dr. Nut, but fans of the original drink claimed the taste was different, and it was once again discontinued.

Early Times Whisky. Created in Early Times Station, Kentucky, in 1860. This bottled whiskey is remarkable because it was the one brand that prospered during Prohibition, when the company was acquired by Brown-Forman Distillers, a holder of a medicinal whiskey permit. Early Times was America's best-selling whiskey through the mid-1950s.

Fazzio's Bowling Alley. Through the years, the Fazzio family has owned several bowling alleys throughout the New Orleans area.

French Quarter. Also known as the "Vieux Carré," the old city, and the oldest part of the City of New Orleans.

French Quarter Police Station. At the time Mr. Robichaux and Burma Jones were hauled off to the "precinct," they would not have been taken to the now-familiar Eight District Station on Royal Street, but to the First District Police Station located at 501 North Rampart Street, where the First District is still located today. In 1985 the Vieux Carré Police District was formed, and that station moved to the heart of the French Quarter at 334 Royal Street in the Old Bank of Louisiana building, built in 1826. Then in the early 1990s the Vieux Carré District was made the Eighth District, and the old Eighth District, which had been at 715 North Broad Street, became part of the Third District.

"German" Bakery. Fictitious sweet shop widely believed to be modeled after Schwabe's Bakery in Uptown on Magazine Street, close to General Pershing.

Harmons and Hupmobiles. Detroit's Hupp Motor Company built the Hupmobile automobile to be in "the working man's price range," and it was manufactured from 1908 to 1940. The Harmon is really a Marmon (probably an alliteration on Ignatius's part), and this fast, upscale car was produced by Marmon Motor Car Company from 1902 to 1933. In 1911, a Marmon Wasp won the first Indianapolis 500.

Hibernia Bank. Founded by Irish immigrants in 1870 and acquired by Capital One Financial Corporation in November 2005.

Homestead. When considering taking out a loan, Mrs. Reilly was probably threatening to go to the Fidelity Homestead Savings Bank, then called Fidelity Homestead Association. "Homestead" is a term used only in Louisiana when referring to a savings and loan.

Infant of Prague. On her mantelpiece, Santa Battaglia keeps a replica of the statue of the child Jesus holding a *globus cruciger,* a gold ball topped with a cross. Housed in a Carmelite church in Prague, the original wax-coated wooden statue is said to have miraculous powers. The Infant of Prague is popular with New Orleans Catholics because it has a large crown and long cape, like most Mardi Gras kings. Home figurines are usually attired with taffeta or satin capes that often change with church liturgical seasons.

Lautenschlaeger Market. The market where Santa Battaglia's momma had her seafood stand was located at 1930 Burgundy Street at Touro.

Levy Pants. According to John Kennedy Toole's mother, Thelma, the fictitious clothing factory was a parody of the Haspel Company, inventor of the seersucker suit, and where her son had worked briefly.

Mandeville State Mental Hospital. Then officially called Southeast Louisiana Hospital and sitting on three hundred acres of park-like setting, the facility has been operating near the city of Mandeville since the early 1950s. Governor Earl Long was briefly committed there in 1959. In 2013, the hospital converted from a state-run facility to a private enterprise, and now operates on a smaller scale under the name Northlake Behavioral Health System.

Mattie's Ramble Inn. Although there were lots of corner groceries in New Orleans at the time, the store where Burma Jones and Mr. Watson solved all the world's problems did not exist. Also, the fictitious Mattie's was plagued by odors from an "alcohol distillery on the river." This is likely a take on an actual smelly molasses factory that operated more than seventy years at the corner of Leake Avenue and Broadway, not far from where Mattie's would have sat.

Night of Joy Club. There is no record of such a strip club on Bourbon Street, but it is a good example of many of the faded bars that lined the famous area in the 1960s.

Paradise Vendors. Not a real corporation, but modeled on Lucky Dogs, a company that has been selling hot dogs from mobile carts in New Orleans since 1947.

Penny Arcade. Actually called Pennyland, and formerly at 131 Royal Street. Home to more than a hundred luck-and-skill games and open twenty-four hours a day, the emporium opened in 1931 and closed in the early 2000s. The space is now a convenience store.

Prytania Theatre. Opened in 1914, the Prytania is the only single-screen movie theater in Louisiana, and it's housed in a red-brick building on Prytania Street, perpendicular to and not far from Constantinople Street.

Pyloric Valve. Yes, we all have one! Also known as the pyloric sphincter, it's a ring of muscle located between the juncture of the stomach and small intestine, and regulates movement of food and bile.

Shirley Temple Mug. The cup Ignatius used for coffee was produced by the Hazel Atlas Glass Company and U.S. Glass Company from 1934 to 1942. Sets featuring a cobalt blue bowl, pitcher, and mug with the child star's image and autograph were originally giveaways for Wheaties and Bisquick, and promoted as a "Sure-Fire Way to Get Your Child to Drink Milk."

St. Louis Cathedral. The church where George hid out and upon whose steps Ignatius uncomfortably rested is the oldest continually active Roman Catholic Cathedral in the United States. Originally built in 1727 and dedicated to King Louis IX of France, the original cathedral burned in 1794, but was rebuilt. The present structure was completed in the 1850s.

St. Odo of Cluny Parish. Although there is a Catholic saint named Odo of Cluny, there is no such church parish in New Orleans. At the time of Ignatius, in the early 1960s, Santa Battaglia presumably lived in the Ninth Ward, the easternmost downriver portion of the city, and a neighborhood home to a largely blue-collar population that mostly was Catholic. In real life, the Ninth Ward received dubious national attention when catastrophic flooding was caused by Hurricanes Betsy in 1965 and Katrina in 2005.

Venus Medalist Pencil. In 1905, the American Lead Pencil Company targeted architects and artists by introducing its high-end Venus brand of wood-cased and metal mechanical pencils. The company officially changed its name to Venus Pen and Pencil Corporation in 1956, then in 1967 to Venus-Esterbrook, which was bought out by Faber-Castell in 1973.

Werlein's. At 605 Canal Street, this venerable music store also manufactured and sold pianos, and was in business in the New Orleans area from 1853 through the early 2000s. In the 1990s, the historic Werlein building where Ignatius Reilly bought his sheet music became home to the Palace Café.

A Confederacy of Dunces
COOKBOOK

D. H. Holmes Department Store in the 1950s.

Charles L. Franck/Franck-Bertacci Photographers Collection
in The Historic New Orleans Collection

1

Under the Clock at D. H. Holmes

> "Sweetheart, you wanna gimme two dozen of them fancy mix?"
>
> —Irene Reilly to the clerk behind the glass case of the bakery at the D. H. Holmes Department Store.

Author John Kennedy Toole opens *A Confederacy of Dunces* with a scenario that instantly endears his novel to most New Orleanians: Irene Reilly is shopping downtown, while her son, Ignatius, waits for her "under the clock" outside the landmark D. H. Holmes Department Store. Before the advent of the shopping mall, "Meet me under the clock" was all anyone had to say to arrange any kind of rendezvous. And "Holm-zez," as many locals affectionately called the store, was considered the finest of the many that lined Canal Street, the grand boulevard that, during the 1960s, was arguably the most fashionable retail district in the South.

At the time, a day spent shopping downtown was considered an elegant outing. And Ignatius Reilly, attired in his hunting cap and plaid shirt, would have definitely been out of place among the sea of shoppers dressed in hats, gloves, suits, and ties.

The refined D. H. Holmes was founded by Daniel Henry Holmes in 1842 and was part of a myriad of grand shops that included Maison Blanche, Kreeger's, Godchaux's, Gus Mayer, Krauss, and Goldrings, along with massive "five and dime" stores, such as Woolworth's and S. H. Kress, and the drug stores Walgreens and K&B.

Ignatius bought sheet music and a new string for his lute at Werlein's Music, where most of New Orleans's real-life musicians and wannabes bought instruments and took music lessons. For those with time to kill, there was the Pennyland Arcade, the amusement parlor where Ignatius gets into a scuff over a mechanical baseball game, and it was a block off Canal at 131 Royal Street.

Inside the air-conditioned D. H. Holmes, customers could ride on elevators operated by real people who called out floors, or they could weigh themselves on the store's huge mechanical scale. When ready to shop, they could buy just about anything imaginable, including jewelry, clothing, fabrics, furs, books, shoes, appliances, hardware, televisions, toys, sporting goods, and house paint.

D. H. Holmes was locally owned and catered to New Orleans tastes, as did most of the district's larger department stores. Some windows were even brandished with the words "Ici on parle français" (French is spoken here), reminding shoppers that, not too long before, the city was decidedly French. Food at D. H. Holmes, too, had a local flavor. At the bakery, alongside doughnuts, brownies, and macaroons, sat specialties such as Ignatius's beloved wine cakes, and pecan pie and Russian

Former site of Werlein's Music Store on Canal Street, where Ignatius bought sheet music and a string for his lute. Now home to the Palace Café.

Pennyland Arcade on Royal Street, home to hundreds of games of chance, including Ignatius's favorite baseball game. Open from 1931 to the early 2000s. Now a convenience store.

Cake, a dense rum-soaked trifle made from compressed cake scraps. A gourmet shop did display exotic fare from around the world. And the candy shop tempted shoppers with the expected fudge, raspberry whips, and jellies shaped like fruit slices. But there were also signature local treats, such as chocolate-covered Louisiana strawberries, pecan eggs, and the Hulk, a decadent bar of pecans, marshmallow, and caramel covered in dark chocolate.

Then there was the elegant white-tablecloth cafeteria, decorated with original paintings by Alexander Drysdale, who was considered the national painter of Louisiana. Many a grand luncheon was served at D. H. Holmes, where diners could start out with beer, wine, and mixed drinks and move on to liver and onions or fried trout, or a chicken salad that is still the proverbial stuff of legend. Holmes also cooked time-honored southern standards, such as fried chicken. Creole specialties, too, were aplenty, with such offerings as Oysters Rockefeller, turtle soup, shrimp remoulade, and redfish courtbouillon. Desserts ranged from a tipsy bread pudding with whiskey sauce to child-friendly ice cream sundaes topped with frozen Elmer's Gold Brick Eggs, a commercial chocolate candy made locally.

One thing found all over New Orleans today, but which is glaringly missing from the D. H. Holmes 1960s menus is Cajun food, such as sausage-like boudin, greasy cracklins, heavily smoked pig parts, dark-rouxed gumbos, and anything with crawfish. When Toole began writing *Dunces* in 1963, Interstate 10 had not yet connected New Orleans with Louisiana's Acadian parishes to the city's west, and there wasn't much culinary interaction between the two cultures. Consequently, New Orleanians strictly ate relatively more refined Creole food as opposed to rustic Cajun.

The word "Creole" means "born to the New World." As it applies to food, Creole cuisine started when French chefs and African slave cooks used the produce and animals sold by Native Americans and Germans to recreate what the French had remembered as haute cuisine. Add to that the tomatoes from the Spanish and seasonings from Caribbean immigrants. The result was the creation of a slew of relatively fancy new dishes that barely resembled what was served back in France, but tasted great and, over time, have endured.

"Cajun" is a corruption of the word Acadian and identifies the French people the English kicked out of Nova Scotia in the mid-1700s. Thousands of those provincial Acadians ended up in sophisticated New Orleans, only to be banished yet again, this time to the unsettled parishes west of the city. But there they thrived. And with inspiration from Native Americans and African slaves, this resilient yet fun-loving lot created a new cuisine centered on robust, hearty foods that could be stretched to feed large families. This peasant style of eating didn't influence New Orleans restaurants until Cajun-born chef Paul Prudhomme took over the kitchen of Commander's Palace, and that wasn't until the mid-1970s. Cajun-style food received even more recognition during the World's Fair in New Orleans in 1984, when food vendors from southwest Louisiana sold specialties such as boudin and crawfish bisque.

Not only have food styles changed since the time Ignatius stood waiting under that clock, but the New Orleans shopping landscape, too, is dramatically different. After eighty-five years in business, Werlein's moved to the suburbs, but eventually closed. The venerable music shop's anchor building is now the site of the upscale Palace Café. After seventy years in business, the Pennyland arcade shut its doors, and its building is now home to a neighborhood convenience store. The long-closed Woolworth's has just been torn down to make room for a high-rise mixed-use development. Like most of the older upscale department stores, D. H. Holmes could not survive competition from suburban shopping malls and larger corporations. And, after growing to a chain of twenty-one, D. H. Holmes finally sold out to the Dillard's chain in 1989.

Statue of Ignatius J. Reilly waiting for his mother "under the clock" in front of the former D. H. Holmes Department Store building (now the Hyatt French Quarter Hotel), Canal Street.

Upon hearing the news of the sale, two local residents and *Confederacy of Dunces* fans, Tony Rihner and Frank Tripoli, began worrying Dillard's would lose the famous clock. So on May 17, 1989, at 10:30 p.m., the distraught friends pulled their car up to the front of D. H. Holmes and stole the timepiece. During the heist, the two were caught by Sally Reeves, a daughter-in-law of a one-time Holmes's president. After a few bumbling lies that led to a confession, the burglars ended up giving the sympathetic Reeves their phone numbers, and for the next six years they kept in touch, while the clock lay safely hidden under Rihner's bed.

The former D. H. Holmes Canal Street site opened as the Chateau Sonesta Hotel in 1995, and it was at that time Rihner returned the clock. Today, the building is the Hyatt French Quarter. But although the revered department store is long gone, its landmark clock still hangs above the building's front door. And under it stands a bronze statue of a relatively svelte Ignatius J. Reilly. Complete with a bag from Werlein's, a floppy-eared cap and baggy clothes, the statue was cast by the New Orleans–based sculptor William Ludwig in 1996, and New Orleans–based actor John "Spud" McConnell was its model. The tourist magnet is stored for safekeeping during the Mardi Gras season. But other than those crazy few weeks, Ignatius perpetually stands under the clock at 819 Canal Street. And, on the pillar where Officer Mancuso stood hiding and stalking the unfashionable Ignatius, there sits a plaque that reads, "In the shadow under the green visor of the cap Ignatius J. Reilly's supercilious blue and yellow eyes looked down upon the other people waiting under the clock at the D. H. Holmes department store, studying the crowd of people for signs of bad taste in dress. John Kennedy Toole."

> Full, pursed lips protruded beneath the bushy black moustache and, at their corners, sank into little folds filled with disapproval and potato chip crumbs.
>
> —Ignatius, waiting for his mother under the clock at D. H. Holmes.

. . . .

Crunchy Potato Chips

Makes 6 servings.

. . . .

In the summer of 1853, George Crum, the half–African American and half–Native American chef at a Saratoga Springs, New York, restaurant, received a complaint that the potatoes he had just served were too thick and soft. So Crum sliced a new batch as thinly as possible, fried them extra-crispy, and doused them in salt. The picky customer, who some believe was the tycoon Cornelius Vanderbilt, loved the new dish. And from that experiment at aiming to please, the potato chip was born.

> 4 large russet potatoes, unpeeled and scrubbed
> Vegetable oil for frying
> Seasonings (coarse salt, pepper, garlic salt, chili powder, etc.)

1. Slice potatoes as thin as possible using a mandolin or a very sharp knife. Immediately submerge potato slices into a bowl of ice water and soak 1 hour. Remove potatoes from water and blot as dry as possible.
2. Pour 2 inches oil into a deep fryer or large pot and heat to 365°F. Fry potatoes until crispy and light brown. Drain well on paper towels.
3. Sprinkle seasoning on warm potatoes and serve. Cooled chips can be stored in sealed plastic several weeks.

. . . .

Shrimp Remoulade and Avocado Salad

Makes 6–8 servings.

. . . .

In the 1960s, shrimp remoulade, a cold appetizer made with shrimp and a tangy sauce, appeared on the menu of just about every self-respecting Creole restaurant in the city, including that of D. H. Holmes. Remoulade originated in France, where a mustardy mayonnaise-based version of the condiment still shows up in *céleri-Rave rémoulade,* a classic bistro salad made with julienned celery root. The local and often sinus-clearing version of remoulade sauce is used to jazz up seafood, and its color can range from creamy white to reddish-pink or red. This recipe is a modern take on the old remoulade dishes, all of which rarely deviated from placing the sauced shrimp on top of shredded iceberg lettuce.

3 pounds medium, headless, unshelled shrimp

3 tablespoons salt

10 whole cloves

1 sprig fresh rosemary

1 tablespoon whole mustard seed

2 teaspoons ground black pepper

1 teaspoon cayenne pepper

4 lemon slices, plus lemon wedges for serving

Remoulade Sauce (recipe follows)

6–8 large romaine lettuce leaves

3 ripe, medium-sized avocados

1. Rinse shrimp and set aside. Bring 3 quarts water to a boil and add salt, cloves, rosemary, mustard seed, black pepper, cayenne, and lemon slices. Boil vigorously 5 minutes; then add shrimp. When water comes back to a boil, remove from heat and let sit 5 minutes for the seasoning to soak in. By now, shrimp should be curled and pink.

2. Drain shrimp and, when they are cool enough to handle, peel them and devein. Gently stir peeled shrimp into Remoulade Sauce and chill 1–24 hours.

3. To serve, line salad plates with lettuce. Peel and slice avocados and arrange on top of lettuce-lined plates. Top avocado with shrimp and sauce, and garnish with lemon wedges.

Remoulade Sauce

Makes 2½ cups

1 boiled egg

⅓ cup coarsely chopped celery

¼ cup coarsely chopped red onion

¼ cup coarsely chopped green onion

1 clove garlic, chopped

⅔ cup mayonnaise

⅓ cup Creole mustard

¼ cup ketchup

2 tablespoons extra-virgin olive oil

1 teaspoon Crystal brand hot sauce, or any Louisiana-style hot sauce

1 tablespoon prepared horseradish

1 teaspoon sweet paprika

1 tablespoon freshly squeezed lemon juice

1 teaspoon Creole seasoning (purchased, or use following recipe), or salt and pepper to taste

½ teaspoon powdered mustard

In a food processor, finely chop together egg, celery, red onion, green onion, and garlic. Transfer mixture to a bowl and stir in remaining ingredients. Store covered in the refrigerator. Best if made a day ahead.

Creole Seasoning

Makes ½ cup

When it came to 1960s-era seasoning, recipes in New Orleans cookbooks usually listed salt, pepper, spices, and herbs individually. Nowadays, many ingredient lists simplify things by calling for Creole seasoning, the workhorse of the Louisiana kitchen and a savory blend of spices that would have been familiar to the French, Spanish, African, and Caribbean immigrants who created Creole cooking in the first place. Numerous Creole seasoning mixes are certainly available commercially, but blending your own is easy, and also lets you control the salt and spices.

    2 tablespoons salt
    1 tablespoon ground black pepper
    1 tablespoon paprika
    1½ teaspoons dried oregano
    1½ teaspoons dried basil
    1½ teaspoons garlic powder
    1 teaspoon onion powder
    ½ teaspoon cayenne pepper
    ¼ teaspoon ground thyme

Combine all ingredients and store in an airtight container.

Chunky Curry Chicken Salad with Fruit and Poppy Seed Dressing
Makes 4 servings.

Mention lunch at the old D. H. Holmes, and many folks still swoon when describing the department store's chicken salad. In 1984, D. H. Holmes self-published a cookbook, *Bayou Banquet: Recipes from a Potpourri of Cultures.* Although this book does not claim to be a collection of the store's actual restaurant recipes, it does have a recipe for Lacombe Chicken Salad, which certainly sounds similar, and is the inspiration for this recipe.

    2 cups chicken broth
    4 cups water
    ½ cup chopped onion
    1 cup chopped celery, divided
    ½ teaspoon Creole seasoning (purchased, or use recipe
        on pages 6–7)
    4 chicken breast halves, with skin and bones

1 tablespoon minced fresh parsley

½ cup mayonnaise

½ teaspoon curry powder

1 tablespoon fresh-squeezed lime juice

Salt and black pepper to taste

1 small unpeeled apple, cored and chopped

Raw baby spinach for lining plates

½ cup pecans or walnuts

¼ cup sliced green onion

Strawberries, grapes, and fresh pineapple chunks
for garnish

Poppy Seed Dressing (recipe follows)

1. In a large saucepan, bring broth, water, onion, ¼ cup celery, and Creole seasoning to a boil. Add chicken, bring back to a boil, lower to a simmer, and cook uncovered until done, about 15 minutes. Remove chicken from liquid and separate meat from skin and bones. Chop meat into bite-sized portions. Discard broth, or use for another purpose.

Poppy Seed Dressing   Makes 1½ cups

1 cup canola oil

2 tablespoons grated onion

¼ cup honey

⅓ cup apple cider vinegar

1 tablespoon freshly squeezed lemon juice

1 teaspoon dry mustard

½ teaspoon salt

4 teaspoons poppy seed

Shake all ingredients together in a covered glass jar. Keeps in the refrigerator up to 1 month.

2. In a large bowl, combine remaining ¾ cup celery, parsley, mayonnaise, curry powder, lime juice, and salt and pepper to taste. Gently stir in apple and chicken.

3. Line 4 plates with spinach, and mound chicken on top. Sprinkle with pecans and green onion, and surround chicken salad with strawberries, grapes, and pineapple. Drizzle Poppy Seed Dressing over fruit and serve.

Newfangled Crispy Buttermilk Fried Chicken
Makes 8 pieces.

Home cooks have been frying chicken ever since the Scottish introduced the technique to the American South. And D. H. Holmes was serving crispy fried chicken long before 1972, when entrepreneur Al Copeland first opened the New Orleans area's most famous chicken joint, Popeye's. This recipe deviates from tradition by adding a dash of cornstarch to the coating for crunch. And to eliminate the age-old problem of under-cooked insides, the chicken is finished in the oven.

1 frying chicken (3½ pounds),
   cut into 8 pieces
1 large egg
1 cup buttermilk
2½ teaspoons salt, divided
1 teaspoon liquid hot sauce
1¼ cups all-purpose flour
¼ cup cornstarch
1 teaspoon ground black pepper
1 teaspoon paprika
1 teaspoon garlic powder
¼ teaspoon cayenne pepper
Vegetable oil for frying

1. Preheat oven to 350°F. Set a rack inside a large baking sheet or pan lined with foil or parchment paper and set aside. Wash chicken and pat dry.
2. In a large bowl or pan, mix together egg, buttermilk, 1 teaspoon salt, and hot sauce. Place chicken pieces in buttermilk, and coat all sides. Let sit 15 minutes.
3. In a large shallow bowl, combine flour, cornstarch, remaining 1½ teaspoons salt, black pepper, paprika, garlic powder, and cayenne. Shake excess buttermilk off chicken pieces, and dredge chicken well in flour mixture. Transfer chicken to a wire rack, and let sit while oil heats.
4. Fill a large, heavy pot with ¾ inch oil, and heat to 350°F. Dredge chicken in seasoned flour again, packing it on in the bare spots, and fry until golden, about 4 minutes each side. Lay browned chicken pieces on rack in prepared pan and bake until an instant-read thermometer reads 165°F for thighs and 160°F for breasts, about 30–40 minutes. Serve warm or cold.

Redfish Courtbouillon
Makes 4–6 servings.

D. H. Holmes excelled at making Creole specialties, such as courtbouillon (coo-bee-yohn), literally meaning "short broth." In France, a courtbouillon is an assortment of vegetables and meats, fish, and shellfish poached in a wine and vegetable stock, and everything is served in a soup bowl. For as long as anyone can remember, Creoles have been making the dish with redfish in a thick gravy brightened with tomatoes, and everything is served over rice.

Caught year-round in Louisiana's marsh and coastal waters, redfish are actually bronze, and sport a characteristic black dot on their tails. In the 1980s, the popularity of chef Paul Prudhomme's Blackened Redfish threatened the redfish supply, and made it hard to find commercially. Fortunately, conservation methods have once again made this member of the drum family available in markets.

4 tablespoons (½ stick) unsalted butter
3 tablespoons all-purpose flour
1 cup finely chopped onion
½ cup finely chopped celery
½ cup finely chopped green or red bell pepper
2 cloves garlic, minced
1½ cups fish stock
1½ cups diced or crushed tomatoes
½ teaspoon dried thyme
2 bay leaves
1½ teaspoons Creole seasoning (purchased, or use recipe on pages 6–7)

2½–3 pounds redfish fillets (or substitute catfish
or any firm fish)
Salt and black pepper
½ lemon, sliced
¼ cup chopped parsley
Hot cooked rice for serving
2 tablespoons minced green onion for garnish

1. In a large, heavy pot big enough to hold the fish, melt butter and add flour. Stir over medium heat until the color of light peanut butter. Add onion, celery, and bell pepper, and cook until onion is translucent. Add garlic, and cook, stirring constantly, 30 seconds.
2. Add fish stock, tomatoes, thyme, bay leaves, and Creole seasoning. Bring mixture to a boil, cover, reduce to a simmer, and cook 30 minutes, stirring occasionally. Remove cover and, if necessary, thicken by boiling a few minutes.
3. Cut fish into serving-sized portions, and season lightly with salt and black pepper. Place fish pieces on top of sauce. Scatter lemon slices on top of fish. Spoon on enough sauce just to cover fish, and sprinkle with parsley.
4. Cover and simmer over low heat until fish is just cooked through, about 10–15 minutes.
5. To serve, place fish and sauce over rice, and garnish with green onion.

> Inside D. H. Holmes, Mrs. Reilly was in the bakery department pressing her maternal breast against a glass case of macaroons. With one of her fingers, chafed from many years of scrubbing her son's mammoth, yellowed drawers, she tapped on the glass case to attract the saleslady.

Effortless Heavenly Hash Candy

Makes an 8 × 8-inch square of candy.

Here's a simple recipe for a candy everyone associates with D. H. Holmes. Officially, heavenly hash is a layered fruit, marshmallow, wine, whipped cream, nut, and cherry dessert. Around the year 1900, however, the name was tacked on to a newly invented marshmallow, almond, and chocolate candy made by one of New Orleans's downtown department stores (and it may have been D. H. Holmes, but no one knows for sure).

In 1923, the city's own Elmer Candy Company popularized the chocolate confection by manufacturing it and packaging it in a now-familiar shiny blue wrapper. Begun in 1855 as the Miller Candy Corporation, Elmer's received its current name around the turn of the twentieth century. In the 1960s Elmer's moved its operations north of New Orleans to Ponchatoula, where the confectioner focuses on Easter candies, such as Heavenly Hash, along with its also popular Pecan Egg and Gold Brick Egg.

1 can (14 ounces) sweetened condensed milk
12 ounces semisweet or milk chocolate chips
Pinch salt
1 cup toasted, salted almonds or pecans
1½ cups miniature marshmallows

1. Line the bottom and sides of an 8×8-inch baking pan with parchment paper or aluminum foil, and let a few inches of paper hang over sides. In a medium, heavy-bottomed saucepan, combine condensed milk, chocolate chips, and salt. Over low heat, stir mixture just until chips are melted. (Do not let boil.)
2. Remove from heat and spread one-third of chocolate mixture evenly onto bottom of parchment-lined pan. Sprinkle on almonds and marshmallows, and top with remainder of chocolate. Refrigerate until just firm, about 2 hours. Grasping paper overhang, lift candy out of pan. Slice into pieces, and store tightly covered at room temperature.

Chocolate-Covered Strawberries

Makes 15 strawberries.

Another beloved confection at D. H. Holmes's was eye-catching chocolate-covered strawberries, a treat that looks exotic but, like heavenly hash, is simple to make.

Louisiana's commercial strawberries grow mostly in the Pontchatoula/Hammond area north of New Orleans and are available in markets from November to April. The strawberry reigned as Louisiana's official fruit for the year 1983, having shared the honor during that decade with the peach in 1980 and 1984, the watermelon in 1981, the fig in 1982, the orange in 1985, the tomato in 1986, and the cantaloupe in 1987. The strawberry came into its own in 2001, when Governor Mike Foster signed legislation declaring this tasty member of the rose family the one and only official state fruit.

12 large, unblemished strawberries with fresh
    green caps
6 ounces chocolate, chopped (any kind but
    unsweetened)
1 tablespoon solid vegetable shortening

1. Wash strawberries and blot as dry as possible. Refrigerate until ready to use.
2. Melt chocolate and shortening in top of a double boiler and stir until mixture is smooth. Remove top of double boiler from bottom.
3. Stick a toothpick down through the green top of a strawberry and dip red part of strawberry into chocolate. Place finished strawberries on a parchment-lined plate. Refrigerate at least 30 minutes and up to 8 hours.

Orange and Pecan Muffins

Makes 18 regular-sized muffins. Adapted from Bayou Banquet: Recipes from a Potpourri of Cultures *(D. H. Holmes, 1984).*

This recipe is inspired by another D. H. Holmes bakery item lots of folks remember as being best of the best.

2½ cups all-purpose flour
2½ teaspoons baking powder
½ teaspoon baking soda
¾ teaspoon iodized salt

1 teaspoon ground ginger

1 cup buttermilk, at room temperature

Finely minced orange rind from 1 large orange

¼ cup orange juice

1 teaspoon orange extract

1 teaspoon vanilla extract

1 cup sugar

4 tablespoons (½ stick) unsalted butter, at room
  temperature

¼ cup vegetable oil

2 eggs, room temperature and beaten

1½ cups chopped pecans

1. Preheat oven to 375°F. Line muffin tins with 18 paper
   liners, or coat insides well with cooking oil. In a bowl, sift
   together flour, baking powder, baking soda, salt and
   ginger. In another bowl mix together buttermilk, orange
   rind, orange juice, orange extract, and vanilla.

2. In a large bowl, use a wooden spoon to cream together
   sugar, butter, and vegetable oil until smooth. Add eggs
   one at a time, beating well after each addition.

3. Alternate adding the flour mixture and wet ingredients
   into the butter, beginning and ending with flour, and mixing just until barely blended. Batter should be thick and
   slightly lumpy. Gently fold in pecans.

4. Fill muffin tins ⅔ full and bake until a toothpick in centers comes out clean, about 18–20 minutes. Cool in pans
   at least 5 minutes. Serve warm.

> "I think that I shall have a macaroon or two. I have
> always found coconut to be good roughage."
>
> —Ignatius, purposefully picking around in a cake box
>   from D. H. Holmes.

Coconut and Macadamia Macaroons Dipped in White Chocolate

Makes 3 dozen.

The name "macaroon" derives from the Italian *macca-
rone,* meaning to crush or beat, referring to the crushed
almonds Italian monks used to make their meringues.
The recipe followed the Florentine noblewoman Catherine de Medici to France in 1533, when she married
King Henry II. At the beginning of the twentieth century, Parisian pâtissier Pierre Desfontaines joined two
almond meringues and filled them with ganache, invent-
ing the French-style macaroons that today are sold in
limitless colors and flavors.

In the United States, the most popular macaroon variety is coconut. A taste for this humble sweet started
with Italian Jews, who took to the cookie because most
versions of the time had no flour or leavening, and could
be enjoyed during the eight-day observation of Passover.

The coconut itself holds a prominent place in New
Orleans Mardi Gras festivities. In the 1940s, the Zulu
Social Aid and Pleasure Club started throwing deco-

rated coconuts to revelers during the group's annual Fat Tuesday parade. Unfortunately, injuries from tossed coconuts prompted lawsuits. So, in 1988, Governor Edwin Edwards signed #SB188, the "Coconut Bill," that removes liability from any coconut handed from a Zulu float.

4 egg whites

¼ teaspoon iodized salt

¾ cup sugar

¼ cup all-purpose flour

¼ teaspoon baking powder

1 teaspoon vanilla extract

½ teaspoon almond extract

14 ounces shredded, sweetened coconut

1 cup coarsely chopped macadamia nuts

1 package (12 ounces) high-quality white chocolate chips

1 tablespoon unsalted butter

1. Place rack in middle of oven, and preheat oven to 325°F. Line a cookie sheet with parchment paper.

2. In a medium glass bowl, use a whisk or electric mixer to beat together egg whites and salt until thick and foamy, but not stiff. Stir in sugar, flour, baking powder, vanilla, and almond extract.

3. Fold in coconut and macadamia nuts. Drop by tablespoons onto prepared cookie sheet. Bake until golden brown, 18–20 minutes. Cool completely on a rack.

4. Stirring constantly, melt white chocolate and butter in the top of a double boiler over barely boiling water. Remove chocolate from heat. Dip one end of each cooled macaroon in warm chocolate, shaking off excess. Dry on parchment or wax paper until chocolate is firm, about 30 minutes. Store in an airtight container up to 1 week.

Grasshopper Cocktail Malts
Makes 2 large drinks.

This recipe combines two beverages popular in the 1960s, malts and the grasshopper cocktail. Malted milk powder was invented in 1897 by William Horlick, a Racine, Wisconsin, food manufacturer who was trying to make an easily digestible food for children and invalids. In 1922, Walgreens employee Ivar "Pop" Coulson added a couple of scoops of ice cream to a regular malted milk (milk, chocolate, and malt) and created the malted milkshake. Ironically, the ice cream drink's popularity started dwindling in 1950, the year the Walgreens pharmacy chain introduced self-service. Even so, it was still easy to buy a malt in the 1960s, especially at drive-in burger joints.

The grasshopper cocktail was considered chic in the sixties. The creamy drink's leaf-green color comes from crème de menthe, a liqueur that often popped up as an ingredient in then-trendy desserts, such as grasshopper pie.

To turn this recipe into a child-friendly vanilla malt, eliminate the alcohol and add a teaspoon of vanilla extract.

1½ pints (3 cups) vanilla ice cream (purchased, or Vanilla Bean Ice Cream recipe on pages 192–93)

¼ cup plain (original) malted milk powder

2 tablespoons crème de menthe liqueur

2 tablespoons white crème de cacao liqueur

¼ cup whole milk

Combine all ingredients in a blender, and blend just until smooth, adding more milk as necessary to make a thick drink. Serve each malt in a tall glass with a straw.

Nectar Ice Cream Soda

Makes 1 drink.

Nectar soda was a soda fountain flavor favorite exclusive to New Orleans. The pink, almond-cherry syrup was created in the late 1800s by pharmacist I. L. Lyons, who was a primary supplier to the K&B pharmacy chain, which was a New Orleans institution until it was bought out by the Rite Aid chain in 1997. Nectar soda syrup disappeared when pharmacy soda fountains vanished, but the flavor was resurrected locally as a bottled soft drink in 1999, and it also lives on as a snoball topping.

¼ cup nectar syrup (recipe follows)
2 scoops Vanilla Bean Ice Cream (purchased, or use recipe on pages 192–93)
Club soda or sparkling water
Whipped cream, the squirt kind from a can
Maraschino cherries

In a tall glass, add nectar syrup. Top with ice cream; then fill glass almost full with club soda. Stir gently; then top with whipped cream and a cherry. Serve immediately.

Nectar Syrup   Makes 1 pint

This is an adaptation of a recipe found in the Ursuline Academy's classic cookbook *Recipes and Remembrances of New Orleans* (1971).

2 cups sugar
1 cup water
2 tablespoons vanilla extract
2 tablespoons almond extract
½ teaspoon red food coloring

1. In a medium, heavy-bottomed saucepan, bring sugar and water to a rolling boil and cook 15 seconds. Remove from heat, and cool to room temperature.
2. Stir in extracts and food coloring; then cover and refrigerate until cold.

2

·········

Refreshments at the Night of Joy

> Mrs. Reilly pulled [Ignatius] around the corner onto Bourbon Street, and they started walking down into the French Quarter....
>
> She pushed him through the door of the Night of Joy bar with one of the cake boxes. In the darkness that smelled of bourbon and cigarette butts they climbed onto two stools....
>
> A few other customers were in the Night of Joy, a man who ran his finger along a racing form, a depressed blonde who seemed connected with the bar in some capacity, and an elegantly dressed young man who chain-smoked Salems and drank frozen daiquiris in gulps.
>
> —Ignatius and his mother dodging Officer Mancuso, who suspects Ignatius is a pervert and is attempting to arrest him.

On this late afternoon, Ignatius and his mother have just stumbled into a fictitious strip club representative of a steady decline that, at the time, really was afflicting much of Bourbon Street.

"The street," as locals call Bourbon, was named in the early 1700s for France's dukes and kings of the Royal House of Bourbon. And there's also strong evidence that in the early 1800s the South's favorite liquor, bourbon, was actually named for New Orleans's Bourbon Street and not the region of Kentucky where the spirit was first distilled. So, even though the famous strip started out mostly residential, for a long time it has been associated with fast living.

In antebellum days, the love of drinking, gambling, dancing, and dueling was a hallmark of this Catholic port city, and even took place on Sundays—after Mass, of course. The concentration of debauchery began in the late 1800s, when the Storyville Brothel District cropped up near the French Quarter and some of the carnal pleasure business crept in. Storyville was shut down in 1917, and feeling the city's well-earned heathen reputation had to be upheld, entrepreneurs opened up strip clubs and bars on Bourbon Street.

During World War II, New Orleans was filled with war workers and troops passing through, and most of them were looking for fun. Consequently, through the 1940s and 1950s, Bourbon Street enjoyed a burlesque heyday. During that time, hoards of well-dressed thrill-seekers strolled the neon fantasyland in search of entertainment from comics and magicians. Live bands played jazz, bawdy singers crooned and, of course, there were "exotic" dancers. But with the end of the war, the advent

The Night of Joy bar did not exist, but there were plenty of shabby real-life
nightclubs on Bourbon Street in the 1960s. This one is Madame Francine's
(1962). Three posters of dancing ladies in various stages of undress are
displayed on the club's exterior.

of television, and the 1960s' changing societal norms, Bourbon Street began losing its luster. Even so, gambling, scantily clad showgirls, and prostitutes were still easy to find. And B-drinking, the illegal act of accepting drinks from customers for compensation, was also common.

In *A Confederacy of Dunces,* the Night of Joy's Darlene is a B-drinker, or B-girl, as Ignatius calls her. And we soon learn the "depressed blonde" desperately wants the nightclub's tightwad owner Lana Lee to let her do a strip show that includes her pet cockatoo.

The real strippers of Bourbon Street had lured in big dollars by cat-walking across stages in pasties and G-strings, and by using eye-catching props, such as pistols, life-sized oyster shells, oversized fans, and combustible sofas. Strutting to live jazz, these strikingly attractive women performed under names like Stormy, Wild Cherry, Evangeline the Oyster Girl, Alouette the Tassel Twirler, and Rita Alexander the Champagne Girl. Teacher-turned-stripper Patti White was called "The Schoolboys' Delight," and it's not hard to imagine why Evelyn West was called "The Treasure Chest." Then there was Blaze Starr, the buxom redhead who famously had a long-term affair with Louisiana Governor Earl Long.

To heighten their celebrity, dancers sometimes staged catfights. And vice charges were considered good publicity. So, compared to what really transpired, *Dunces*'s Darlene and her bird sorta look tame.

In 1962, real-life District Attorney Jim Garrison took office and went on a crusade to clean up the vice. Eventually, a dozen or so Bourbon Street nightclubs were closed. But the party in this heart of the French Quarter really never did stop—it just changed a little with the times.

Through the years, many bars have modernized. But just as many look like the downbeat Night of Joy, and some haven't upgraded much since they opened in the 1800s. One big change happened in the 1970s, when Bourbon Street was turned into a pedestrian mall at night. And lately T-shirt and institutional-batch daiquiri shops have given the place a hint of commercialism. But Bourbon Street is still unique, and has plenty of flashy neon, blaring music, and mostly naked bodies. And, of course, as with Ignatius and his mother, it's still a good place to hide from whatever's dogging you.

> The elegant young man spilled his daiquiri on his bottle-green velvet jacket. . . .
> "What's that you drinking? It looks like a pineapple snowball."
> "Even if I described it to you, I doubt whether you'd understand what it is."
>
> —Irene Reilly acquaints herself with Dorian Greene.

Pineapple-Ginger Snoball.

Organic Banana's Frozen Tropical Daiquiri.

Pineapple, Ginger, and Mint Snoballs

Makes 2 ½ cups syrup.

In New Orleans, slurping on a snoball (snow cone, and spelled without a "w") doused with one or many of a mind-boggling number of flavors is one of those summer rituals one never outgrows. Snoballs made from hand-shaved block ice were first sold by street vendors. Then in the 1930s, a machinist named Ernest Hansen mechanized the industry when he tinkered with an ice-crushing device and created the patented "Sno-bliz" machine, which produces finely shaved, fluffy ice. Grocer George Ortolano later invented the Sno-Wizard, an ice-shaving machine similar to Hansen's, and the machine that today is used commercially throughout the South.

1½ cups unsweetened pineapple juice

2 slices fresh ginger, ¼-inch each

1 tablespoon minced fresh mint

2 cups chopped fresh or unsweetened canned
  pineapple

2 cups sugar

Shaved ice for making snoballs

1. In a medium saucepan, bring pineapple juice, ginger, mint, and chopped pineapple to a boil over medium heat and simmer 2 minutes. Remove from heat, add sugar, and stir until sugar is dissolved. Let mixture steep until it cools to room temperature.
2. Strain syrup through a fine sieve. (The leftover pineapple bits are great on ice cream.)
3. To make snoballs, follow manufacturer's directions for chopping ice using the ice-shaving attachment of a blender or food processor. (Or you can do what lots of folks do: go to a snoball stand and buy professionally shaved ice.) Pour shaved ice into a paper cup or cone halfway up, and pour on syrup. Add more ice until cup is full, and top with more syrup.
4. Store unused syrup in a covered glass jar in the refrigerator. Keeps 1 month.

Organic Banana's Frozen Tropical Daiquiri

Makes 1 drink. Recipe is from Organic Banana Daiquiri Shop in the French Market.

Someone should explain to Mrs. Reilly that the frozen daiquiri has been around since the 1930s, when a Havana bartender nicknamed "The Daiquiri Constant" gave the world this famous cocktail. Nowadays, the sweet icy drink is common in the popular "to-go" cups revelers carry around the French Quarter. And the frozen daiquiri is so esteemed by locals that in 2011 the city of New Orleans started an annual Daiquiri Festival.

8 ounces ice

1 ounce coconut cream

½ ounce pineapple juice

1 ounce white rum

Pineapple slice and cherry for garnish

1. Combine ice, coconut cream, pineapple juice, and rum in a blender, and blend at low speed 10 seconds. Raise speed to high, and blend until mixture is smooth.
2. Pour into a chilled glass, and garnish with pineapple and cherry. Serve immediately.

The Columns Classic Daiquiri

Makes 1 drink. Recipe is from bartender Justin Stern of the Columns Hotel Bar.

The frozen daiquiri is actually a spinoff of the sour classic daiquiri, born in the late 1800s near the Daiquiri Beach region of Santiago, Cuba, where there was an iron mine full of thirsty workers, as well as plentiful sugar, limes, and rum. This, the original daiquiri, gained popularity in the United States in the 1940s, when President Franklin Roosevelt initiated the "Good Neighbor Policy," which opened trade relations with the Caribbean, thus making rum readily available. President John Kennedy and Jacqueline Kennedy famously enjoyed daiquiris, as did Ernest Hemingway, a favorite author of the character Mrs. Levy from *A Confederacy of Dunces*.

Enough ice to barely fill a rocks glass
½ lime
½ ounce simple syrup (recipe this page)
2 ounces light rum

1. Put ice in a shaker and crack with a muddler until finely crushed.
2. Squeeze in juice from lime. Add simple syrup and rum. Cover and shake vigorously 20 seconds. Pour into a chilled rocks glass, and serve immediately.

Simple Syrup
Makes 1 cup

⅔ cup sugar
⅓ cup water

Combine sugar and water in a small saucepan. Stirring constantly, bring to a boil and cook until sugar is dissolved, about 2 minutes. Cool completely. Can be refrigerated up to 1 month.

"I'll take a Dixie 45," Mrs. Reilly said to the bartender.

"And the gentleman?" the bartender asked in a rich, assumed voice. "What is his pleasure?"

"Give him a Dixie, too."

"I may not drink it," Ignatius said as the bartender went off to open the beers.

One of Mrs. Reilly's favorite adult beverages, Dixie 45 Beer, brewed by the Dixie Brewing Company until 1963.

Lemon and Double Orange Jell-O Shots
Makes 16.

Since Ignatius isn't enthusiastic about drinking beer, maybe he'd be more excited about a Jell-O shot, the alcoholic drink that looks like dessert. A recipe for a boozy molded drink called Punch Jelly goes back to 1862. But the modern Jell-O shot is usually attributed to Tom Lehrer, the Manhattan-born musical satirist who, while in the army in the 1950s, sneaked alcohol into a Christmas party by mixing vodka with orange Jell-O.

Dixie 45, the beer Mrs. Reilly is ordering, was brewed by the Dixie Bottling Company of New Orleans. Urban legend has it the name Dixie 45 originated when brewery workers were sipping suds at Nick's Original Big Train Bar across the street and asked bar owner Nick Castrogiovanni why his establishment had never been robbed. Castrogiovanni supposedly pulled a .45 caliber revolver out from under the bar and exclaimed, "Nobody messes with a .45." The story then goes three ways: either Dixie 45 was named after said owner's single but significant action, it was named when customers asked for a Dixie from "45," as the bar owner came to be known, that is, "I'll have a Dixie, 45," or the beer was bestowed the honor because Dixie was said to have the kick of a .45. Regardless, Dixie Brewing, which had not patented its Dixie 45 name, had to stop using the "45" when Colt 45 malt liquor received its patent in 1963.

Nick's had been left leaning after Hurricane Betsy in 1965 and was totally demolished by Hurricane Katrina, and all that remains is a vacant lot. The Dixie Brewery building is being renovated and incorporated into a research facility for a new hospital complex.

1 (3-ounce) package orange Jell-O
1 cup boiling water
⅓ cup cold, pulp-free orange juice
¼ cup cold, pulp-free lemon juice
½ cup chilled vodka (more or less)

1. Add Jell-O to a medium bowl and stir in boiling water until gelatin is completely dissolved.
2. Stir in cold orange juice and lemon juice. Stir in chilled vodka.
3. Pour into shot glasses lightly sprayed with cooking spray. (Plastic shot cups are best because the shot can be squeezed out.)
4. Refrigerate at least 2 hours, and preferably overnight. Serve cold.

"I smell wine cakes," Darlene cried, looking past Ignatius. . . .

"Where you bought these nice wine cakes, lady?" Darlene asked Mrs. Reilly. "They're nice and juicy."

"Over by Holmes, sugar. They got a good selection. Plenty variety."

—Darlene and Mrs. Reilly, sitting at the Night of Joy's bar.

Juicy Wine Cakes

Makes six 4-inch cakes, or 12 baked in muffin tins.
(Make 1 day ahead.)

An affection for cakes soaked in wine or rum and topped with whipped cream and cherries goes all the way back to Creole Louisiana's antebellum days, when desserts such as savarin, a French cake doused with alcohol, were a must at holiday dinner tables. In New Orleans you can still buy wine cakes at Dorignac's Grocery Store, and Brocato's Bakery sells its close cousin, Baba Rhum.

2 cups cake flour

1 teaspoon iodized salt

1 teaspoon baking powder

12 tablespoons (1½ sticks) unsalted butter, room temperature

2 cups sugar, divided

4 large eggs, room temperature

¼ teaspoon ground cloves, optional

1 teaspoon vanilla extract

1½ cups dark rum, divided (or port, sherry, marsala, or even wine!)

½ cup chilled whipping cream

6 cherries

1. *Make cakes:* Preheat oven to 325°F. Generously grease and flour six 4-inch baking molds or 12 muffin tins, and set aside. Sift flour, salt, and baking powder together, and set aside.

2. In a large bowl, cream together butter and 1 cup sugar on medium-high mixer speed until light and fluffy, about 3 minutes. (Scrape down sides occasionally.) Beat in eggs, one at a time. Add cloves and vanilla.

3. Using low mixer speed, add flour mixture and ½ cup rum to butter mixture, beginning and ending with flour. Beat until just combined.

4. Pour batter into prepared pans until they're ⅔ full, and level off tops. Bake on center rack of oven until brown, and center springs back when lightly touched, about 40 minutes (30 minutes for muffins).

5. Remove from oven, and cool 5 minutes in pans. Remove cakes from pans, and place on a rack to cool.

6. *Make Wine Syrup:* Boil together ⅔ cup water and remaining 1 cup sugar until sugar is dissolved. Remove from heat, pour into a 4-cup measuring cup or equivalent shaped bowl, and cool 2 minutes. Stir in remaining 1 cup rum.

7. Completely submerge each cake into syrup, and hold down in the liquid a few seconds. Place saturated cakes

in a rimmed baking pan. Pour remaining wine syrup over cakes. Wrap pan tightly with plastic wrap, and refrigerate overnight.

8. When ready to serve, place cream in a medium bowl and beat with an electric mixer at medium-high speed until stiff peaks form. Place cakes on a rimmed serving dish, and pour remaining wine syrup over each. Top each with a spoonful of whipped cream and a cherry.

Darlene's Spanish Rice
Makes 6–8 side servings.

This tomato and rice side dish, also known as Mexican Rice, is common in northern Mexico. The name probably started as a nod to the Spanish, who introduced rice to Mexico in the 1500s.

3 tablespoons olive oil

1 tablespoon butter

1½ cups raw, long-grain white rice

1 cup minced onion

½ cup minced bell pepper

2 cloves garlic, minced

2 cups chicken broth

1 can (8 ounces) tomato sauce

2 teaspoons chili powder

¾ teaspoon salt

½ teaspoon cumin

¼ teaspoon ground black pepper

¼ cup chopped fresh cilantro

1. Heat olive oil and butter in a large, heavy-bottomed saucepan over medium-high heat and sauté rice, onion, and bell pepper until rice is browned and onion is tender, about 6–7 minutes.

2. Stir in garlic. Add broth, tomato sauce, chili powder, salt, cumin, and black pepper. Bring to a boil; then turn heat down to very low. Cover pot tightly, and simmer until rice is cooked and liquid is absorbed, about 30 minutes.

3. Remove pot from heat, and allow to sit, covered, 15 minutes. Fluff up rice, stir in cilantro, and serve.

"I use to cook too when I was married," Darlene told them. "I sort of used a lot of that canned stuff, though. I like that Spanish rice they got and that spaghetti with the tomato gravy."

—Darlene, to Ignatius and his mother.

Elizabeth's Spinach Salad with Crispy Hog Jowls

Makes 4 entrée salads. Recipe is by executive chef Byron Peck of Elizabeth's Restaurant.

Pork jowl is the actual cheek of a hog and is similar to thick-cut bacon. Typically cured or smoked, pork jowl can be fried and served like bacon or used as a seasoning meat in beans or greens. Chef Peck seasons and smokes his own hog jowls using the technique Cajuns use to smoke tasso, the heavily smoked strips of pork and beef.

2 cups diced smoked hog jowls (or substitute 8 slices thick-cut bacon)

⅓ cup crumbled Maytag blue cheese

¼ cup golden raisins

2 tablespoons chopped shallots

¼ cup sherry vinegar

½ teaspoon freshly ground black pepper

10 ounces fresh baby spinach

1. In a skillet, render smoked jowls over medium-high heat until dark brown and crispy. Remove skillet from heat. Leave jowls in skillet, and discard all but ¼ cup rendered fat.
2. In a stainless steel bowl, combine blue cheese, raisins, shallots, vinegar, and black pepper. Stir mixture into jowls and fat in skillet.
3. Add spinach to skillet, and toss to coat. Divide among 4 large salad bowls, and serve immediately.

Ignatius likes to drink his café au lait from a Shirley Temple mug.

"You're just coming in from a big ball where a lot of southern gentlemen were trying to feel you up over the fried chicken and hog jowls. But you cooled them all. Why? Because you're a lady, dammit."

—Lana Lee, coaching Darlene on how to perform a virginal southern belle act with her bird.

Café au Lait (Coffee with Milk)

Makes 10 servings.

As in the Reilly household, café au lait, hot milk and coffee, is a favorite drink in New Orleans. Here it's being made at the 1930s Morning Call coffee and beignet shop in the French Quarter. Photo courtesy State Library of Louisiana, from the WPA files

Ignatius just ordered café au lait, a hot drink made from half strong, bitter chicory coffee and half warm milk. Made famous by the Café du Monde and Morning Call restaurants, café au lait is still very much enjoyed in New Orleans, as is café noir, black coffee.

In the early 1800s, New Orleans's strategic location at the mouth of the Mississippi River earned the city the nickname of "Logical Port" for coffee imports from Latin America and the Caribbean. Obviously, locals back then really loved their coffee because, right before the Civil War, New Orleans had more than five hundred coffeehouses (although it's been rumored something stronger than coffee was occasionally sold). Today, approximately 25 percent of the coffee imported annually by the United States comes through New Orleans, with 40 percent of those beans staying in the area for roasting.

Chicory is a coffee extender made from the caffeine-free, dried, roasted, and ground root of the perennial chicory, a plant native to the Mediterranean. The use of chicory as a coffee substitute started in France, when a blockade during the Napoleonic wars deprived that country of coffee. During the American Civil War, coffee shipments to New Orleans were cut drastically and, throughout the South, substitutes for the popular beverage included ground acorns, beets, corn, groundnuts, parsnips, and burnt sugar, with New Orleans's French residents also turning to wild chicory root.

The use of chicory became extremely popular during the Depression and World War II, when the filler again stretched precious supplies of expensive coffee. Over time and for many, the sharp tinge of chicory naturally became the preferred coffee taste. So in New Orleans it's easy to find coffee and chicory blends, which are produced by companies such as Community, Luzianne, French Market, Mello Joy, and CDM, which is produced by Café du Monde. And, if you look hard enough, you can even find ground pure chicory and blend it into your own coffee.

As for brewing, we learn that at home Mrs. Reilly uses the drip method, as did many South Louisianians of the time, when it was common to replenish dented aluminum coffeepots and enamel French biggins all day long. In between service, the half-filled pots often waited on the stove in pie pans of warm water. And, although it's nostalgic to brew coffee the old way, using an electric drip pot also produces an excellent cup. Regardless of how you brew it, if you're making café au lait, be sure to brew the coffee extra strong.

8 tablespoons ground coffee with chicory

8 cups water

7 cups whole milk

Sugar to taste, optional

Brew coffee in a drip or electric drip coffeemaker. In a medium saucepan, heat milk just until scalding, but not boiling. Fill large coffee cups halfway with hot coffee, then fill with hot milk and stir in sugar. Or fill the cups the way they did in the old days: simultaneously pour in equal amounts of coffee and hot milk. Serve hot.

. . . .

Creamy Mocha Cheese Cake Topped with Fresh Strawberries

Makes a 10-inch cheese cake. Recipe is by Ellen Sistrunk.

. . . .

Although instant coffee certainly isn't as tasty as fresh-brewed, it is not at all an "abomination" when used to intensify the flavor of chocolate, as in this cheese cake.

Crust

1 (8½-ounce) package chocolate graham crackers, crushed

5 tablespoons butter, melted

¼ cup ground pecans, toasted

2 tablespoons sugar

1 teaspoon instant coffee granules

Filling

4 (8-ounce) packages cream cheese, at room temperature

1⅔ cups sugar, divided

¼ cup cornstarch

1 tablespoon vanilla extract

2 extra-large eggs

¾ cup heavy whipping cream

4 ounces semisweet chocolate

1 ounce unsweetened chocolate

1 teaspoon instant coffee granules

2 teaspoons hot water

Topping

1½ cups sour cream

3 tablespoons sugar

2 teaspoons instant coffee granules

Fresh strawberries for garnish, optional

1. Make crust by first wrapping the outside of a 10-inch springform pan with aluminum foil, covering the bottom and extending all the way up the sides. Combine all crust ingredients, and press in bottom and 1 inch up sides of foil-covered pan. Set aside.

2. Preheat oven to 350°F. To make filling, put one package of cream cheese, ⅓ cup sugar, and cornstarch in a large bowl. Beat with an electric mixer on low speed until creamy, about 3 minutes, scraping down the bowl several times. Blend in remaining cream cheese, one package at a time, scraping down the bowl after each one.

3. Increase the mixer speed to medium, and beat in the remaining 1⅓ cups sugar and vanilla. Blend in eggs, one at a time, beating well after each addition. Beat in the cream just until completely blended.

4. In a double-boiler, melt semisweet and unsweetened chocolate. Cool slightly and add to cheese cake mixture. Dissolve instant coffee in hot water, and add to cheese cake mixture. Gently spoon batter over the crust.

5. Place cake in a large shallow pan containing hot water that comes about 1 inch up the sides of the springform pan. Bake until edges are firm and center is just slightly firm, with no sheen on top, about 1¼ hours. (Do not over-bake.)

6. Make topping by combining sour cream, sugar, and coffee granules in a small bowl. Spread over cheese cake. Bake at 500°F for 5 minutes. Let cool to room temperature on a wire rack. Chill 8 hours. Decorate with strawberries just before serving.

3

. . . .

Hangin' Out with Burma Jones

"Me, they probly gimma a little talk think it scare me, even though they know I ain got them cashews. They probly try to prove I got them nuts. They probly buy a bag, slip it in my pocket. Woolsworth probly try to send me up for life."

—Burma Jones to Mr. Robichaux, waiting at the jail after their respective arrests.

Here we have Burma Jones, who is black, and the retired white grandfather, Claude Robichaux, who has just been arrested for calling Patrolman Mancuso a "communiss." Robichaux obviously represents America's zealous communist-hunting of the 1950s. But it's the farsighted Burma Jones who connects with a wider local audience. That's because New Orleans's population in the early 1960s was 40 percent African American, and everyone at the time was going through the pains of desegregation.

Toole touches local nerves by having Jones accused of stealing cashews at the Woolworth's Department Store at Canal and Rampart streets. The scenario is historically significant because on September 9, 1960, "Woolsworth," as locals often called the chain, had been the actual site of a student-led sit-in.

During segregation, the ritzy Canal Street stores encouraged African Americans to shop, but they were rarely employed or allowed to use restrooms and restaurants open to whites. Then the nationwide civil rights movement began gaining steam, and much of that strategy was planned right in New Orleans.

Locally, picketing had started on Dryades Street, the black-designated shopping district that had been owned mostly by Jews. It was about a year later when members of CORE, the Congress of Racial Equality, sat at the segregated Woolworth's lunch counter, resulting in the integrated group of blacks and whites being arrested and charged with "criminal mischief." A week after the Woolworth's sit-in, picketers were arrested for targeting stores on Claiborne Avenue and, later, for sitting-in at the McCrory's five-and-dime whites-only lunch counter. The McCrory's protest resulted in the legal case *Lombard v. Louisiana,* which went all the way to the U.S. Supreme Court.

In 1963, the high court threw out the arrests. And, after two years of sit-ins, protests, political roadblocks, bomb threats, name calling, and rock throwing, New Orleans schools, trade unions, professional organizations, and streetcars were desegregated, and even City Hall's cafeteria was serving to African Americans. (Mardi Gras krewes stayed segregated until 1991. Many of these social organizations are still based on race and gender, but's that's mostly because all-female krewes want to preserve their exclusive membership.)

Despite all the uproar, the integration process in New Orleans was vastly less violent than it had been in many large cities. Even so, it did leave most residents in some sort of pain, as it does with *Dunces*'s Burma Jones, who has to walk on eggshells because of a bag of cashews.

. . . .

Cashew Chicken with Pineapple

Makes 4 servings.

. . . .

Had Jones actually committed the cashew crime, he could have used his spoils in this easy recipe. Cashews have toxic shells, which is why they're always sold ready-to-eat. The cashew plant originated in Brazil. Sixteenth-century Portuguese explorers took it to India, and from there it spread to Asia and Africa.

2 teaspoons ground cinnamon, divided

¼ teaspoon ground black pepper

3 tablespoons olive oil, divided

4 boneless, skinless chicken breast halves, cut into 1-inch pieces

1 medium bell pepper, coarsely chopped

2 cloves garlic, chopped

½ cup chicken stock

1 can (14 ounces) pineapple chunks, drained, juice reserved

1 tablespoon butter

2 tablespoons chopped fresh cilantro

½ cup roasted cashews

1. Preheat oven to 300°F. In a small bowl, combine 1 teaspoon cinnamon, black pepper, and 1 tablespoon oil. Rub seasoning mixture into chicken pieces.

2. Heat remaining 2 tablespoons olive oil in a large skillet over medium-high heat. When oil is hot, add chicken and sauté until done, flipping over every 3 minutes, for a total of about 10 minutes. Remove chicken to a rimmed baking pan, and place in oven.

3. In same skillet, sauté bell pepper 1 minute. Add garlic, stock, reserved pineapple juice, and remaining teaspoon cinnamon, and reduce by half. Stir in pineapple and butter, raise heat to high, and stir until slightly thick.

4. Remove chicken from oven, and place on a platter. Add any accumulated juices to sauce, and simmer 1 minute. Pour sauce over chicken, sprinkle with cilantro and cashews, and serve.

> "You try you a little sabotage. That's the only way you fight that kinda trap."
>
> "Wha you mean 'sabotage'?"
>
> "You know, man," Mr. Watson whispered. "Like the maid ain bein paid enough to throw too much pepper in the soup by accident."
>
> —Mr. Watson advising Burma Jones on how to undermine Lana Lee and his low-wage job at the Night of Joy.

New Orleans–style Vegetable Beef Soup (minus too much pepper)

Makes 8–10 servings. This recipe is by Maureen Detweiler, who serves the fall-apart tender brisket on separate plates. Sides include a traditional sauce made of equal parts ketchup and horseradish, along with French bread and butter.

This hearty vegetable-and-beef soup has always been a winter staple in New Orleans. Back in the late 1700s and through 1881, New Orleans was a major final destination for cattle drives that followed what was known as the Opelousas Trail, snaking its way from East Texas and through the Acadian parishes of southwest Louisiana. Cattle reaching New Orleans walked these hundreds of miles eating nothing but whatever grew along the way. Consequently, their meat was usually stringy and tough. But, because of these rangy cows from long ago, today's local cooks have a knack for turning chewy cuts of beef into something sublime.

Amazingly, a hundred years or so ago, after broth was finished cooking, it was common to throw away the bouilli, the cooked soup meat, usually beef brisket. Several restaurants of the time took the bold step of serving up those supposedly tasteless cuts, usually with a horseradish sauce, the same way Detweiler still serves it.

2 pounds whole beef brisket, trimmed of most of
   its fat
2 bay leaves
Salt
1 cup peeled and diced potato
1 cup chopped onion
1 cup chopped celery
1 cup chopped bell pepper
1 cup sliced carrot
1 cup chopped cabbage
2 cups diced, canned tomatoes, with liquid
1 cup frozen green peas
¾ cup chopped parsley
Pepper to taste, or use Creole seasoning (purchased,
   or use recipe on pages 6–7)

1. Place whole brisket, bay leaves, and 2 teaspoons salt in a soup pot with 3 quarts water. Bring to a boil; then simmer on low until meat is fork tender, about 2 hours. Replenish water as necessary.
2. Remove bouilli (cooked soup meat), and discard bay leaves. Slice meat against the grain into ½-inch slices, and return to pot.
3. Add remaining ingredients and simmer 1 hour. Taste for salt and add pepper (but not too much!). To serve, either dice meat and return to soup or serve meat separately on small plates.

· ·

Creole Okra–Filé Gumbo

Makes 1 gallon, or 8–10 entrée servings. Adapted from a recipe from the files of the late Victoria B. Prudeaux, and courtesy of her niece Ione Bertrand.

· ·

Sausage adds smoky flavor to this family recipe for a style of hearty, down-home gumbo that's been cooked by generations of New Orleanians, and is especially favored by African American Creoles in and around the neighborhoods known as the Sixth and Seventh wards. Differing from the more delicate okra and seafood ver-

sion connected with French Creoles, this gumbo calls for three kinds of meat, in addition to shrimp and crab, and it leaves out tomato. As opposed to Cajun-style gumbo, this recipe calls for a minimum of roux.

Earthy-flavored filé is the ground leaf of the sassafras tree, and was introduced to Creoles by the Choctaw. There is much debate about whether gumbo should be thickened with okra, roux, or filé, or if any can be properly used in combination. This recipe settles the matter by including okra, roux, and optional filé.

10 chicken drumettes

Salt, ground black pepper, and cayenne pepper

2 pounds sliced fresh or frozen okra

5 tablespoons vegetable oil, divided

1 pound smoked sausage, cut into bite-sized pieces

1 pound smoked ham, cut into bite-sized pieces

2½ cups chopped onion

2 tablespoons all-purpose flour

½ teaspoon paprika

1½ quarts water

4 fresh crabs, cleaned, with legs and claws removed and discarded

1 pound fresh medium shrimp, peeled and deveined

1½ teaspoons filé powder, optional

Cooked white rice for serving

1. Preheat oven to 375°F. Sprinkle chicken with seasoning to taste. Place chicken in one layer in a baking pan, and brown in oven 1 hour. At the same time, coat a large baking pan with cooking spray, and add okra. Drizzle with 3 tablespoons oil, and bake until soft and turning brown, stirring occasionally, about 1 hour.

2. In a large Dutch oven, sauté sausage over medium-high heat until it releases some of its fat, about 2 minutes.

Add ham and sauté an additional minute. (Or microwave sausage and ham 3 minutes.) Remove ham and sausage, and set aside.

3. In same pot, add remaining 2 tablespoons oil, and sauté onions over medium-high heat until translucent. Add baked okra and cook, stirring often, until slime is almost gone. Stir in sausage and ham, and cook, stirring constantly, until slime is completely gone.

4. Remove ¾ of okra and meats from pot, and cook remainder over medium-high heat, stirring constantly, until it begins to stick. Lower heat to medium, and sprinkle in flour and paprika. Cook, stirring constantly, 1 minute.

5. Slowly stir in water. When mixture begins to boil, add the set-aside okra/meat mixture and crabs. Bring back to a boil, and simmer 15 minutes. Add shrimp and cooked chicken, bring to a boil, and cook an additional 10 minutes. Check for seasoning and, if gumbo gets too thick, add more water.

6. When ready to serve, lower gumbo to a bare simmer and sprinkle on filé powder (or allow guests to sprinkle filé into their own bowls). To serve, ladle gumbo into bowls over rice.

Purple Hull Peas with Pickle Meat

Makes 6 servings as a side dish, or 4 as an entrée over rice.

The purple hull pea is a member of a broad category of "southern peas" and also includes black-eyed peas, crowder peas, field peas, and cream peas. Purple hulls are extremely meaty and flavorful and, therefore, don't

> "You tryina sell me another beer, a poor color boy bustin his ass for twenny dollar a week? I think it about time you gimme a free beer with all the money you make sellin pickle meat and sof drink to po color peoples."
>
> —Burma Jones to Mr. Watson.

Pickled meat, locally known as "pickle meat," is salted, spiced pork butt or rib ends, and before the days of refrigeration it was a staple in Creole kitchens. Historic pickled meat recipes call for layering fresh pork in barrels with saltpeter, salt, allspice, onions, and bay leaves, and letting everything cure a couple of weeks. Commercially sold pickled meat is still easy to find in New Orleans. And since it takes a few hours to tenderize, it's commonly used for seasoning red beans. But pickle meat is good with just about any bean, and is often used in one-pot meals such as string beans and potatoes. When seasoning fast-cooking beans with pickled meat, always cook the meat until tender before adding the beans.

require much fuss. Like most southern peas, purple hulls came to the United States through the African slave trade, and records indicate that it, with its trademark deep purple hull, was commonly sold in old New Orleans open-air markets. During the time Ignatius Reilly would have lived in New Orleans, unshelled southern peas were still sold in bulk in local supermarkets.

8 ounces pickle meat (pickled pork)

2 cups chicken stock

1 cup water

Ground black pepper and cayenne to taste

1 pound fresh or frozen purple hull peas

¼ teaspoon salt

1. Combine pickle meat, stock, water, black pepper, and cayenne in a large saucepan. Bring to a boil. Cover tightly, lower heat to a simmer, and cook until tender, about 1 hour.
2. To same pot, add peas and enough water to cover peas by 1 inch. Bring to a boil, lower heat and simmer 45 minutes to an hour, stirring occasionally and maintaining water level.
3. Beans are ready when they're tender but not falling apart, and liquid is creamy. Stir in salt and serve warm.

"You got you a little business, got you a son teachin school probly got him a bobby-cue set, Buick, air-condition, TV. Whoa! I ain even got me a transmitter radio. Night of Joy salary keepin peoples below the air-condition level."

—Burma Jones sounding envious of Mr. Watson's success.

Cochon de Lait (barbecued whole suckling pig)

Serves 70–80 (and makes excellent pulled-pork sandwiches). Recipe is by Trey Nobles and Ben Sarrat, members of the New Orleans–based "Hog Dat Nation" barbecue team.

Air-conditioning, big cars, and barbecue pits were all 1960s status symbols. The first portable grill as we know it was invented in the 1930s. The 1950s saw the debut of Weber's round kettle grill, and the outdoor gas grill was invented in the 1960s. And, if Burma Jones were around today and he hit it big, he could even buy an oversized custom trailer pit like the kind used in competitions.

Mammoth-sized pits are aplenty at the New Orleans annual charity event "Hogs for the Cause," which raises money for families of children with brain cancers. Begun in 2008, this wildly popular cookoff is named for Ben Sarrat Jr., a six-year-old who lost his battle with brain cancer in 2010. The event takes place every March in New Orleans's City Park, with top chefs, professional barbecue teams, and backyard cooking fanatics vying in the categories of Whole Hog, Ribs, Pork Butt/Shoulder, and Porkpourri (anything pork).

"Cochon de lait" literally means "suckling pig." The word "pig" usually refers to a young domestic swine weighing under 120 pounds, while a "hog" is anything heavier. The original way of cooking a whole pig involved digging a pit in the ground, filling it with burning logs, and dangling the pig from a brace over the fire or laying it on a large metal rack. Many folks still cook pigs the old way, or they build pig-roasting pits on top of the ground with cinder blocks, or even construct smoke sheds with hanging rotisseries. The job gets done nicely, too, on a real smoker/barbecue pit, one that's at least six feet long.

Pork Marinade

2 cups chicken broth

8 tablespoons (1 stick) unsalted butter

¼ cup fresh lemon juice

2 teaspoons onion powder

1 tablespoon garlic powder

2 teaspoons finely ground black pepper

1 teaspoon Tabasco brand hot sauce

1 tablespoon Worcestershire sauce

1 teaspoon salt

Cuban Mojo Sauce (for serving)

2 cans (12 ounces each) orange juice concentrate

3¾ cups water

1 medium red onion, finely chopped

1 tablespoon finely minced garlic

1 teaspoon cumin

½ teaspoon ground black pepper

¼ teaspoon cayenne pepper

2 tablespoons honey

6 tablespoons freshly squeezed lime juice

2 tablespoons freshly squeezed lemon juice

To Cook Pig

40 pounds charcoal

10–15 (5-foot-long) pecan or hickory logs

1 (75–100-pound) dressed hog, cleaned, gutted, and hair removed from the skin

1. Combine marinade ingredients in a medium saucepan, and simmer until everything is dissolved. Allow to come to room temperature.

2. Make Cuban Mojo Sauce by combining all sauce ingredients and letting sit at room temperature until serving time.

3. On one side of a very large barbecue pit, start a fire with charcoal, and let it burn until white. Should take 30 minutes to an hour.

4. While charcoal is burning, make the pig lie flat by using a hatchet to hack along both sides of the inside of the spine and through the center of the head and snout, being careful not to cut so deep the skin breaks or the pig breaks in half.

5. Using a marinade injector, pierce flesh at intervals with injector needle and squeeze marinade into flesh.

6. After charcoal turns white, add 5 logs. After logs have caught fire and start to smoke, lay hog, rib cage side down, on the opposite end of pit from the fire. Close cover, open baffles to let air flow through, and maintain pit temperature at 250°F. Keep logs burning by adding wood as necessary. Pig is done when meat reaches 185–200°F, about 12 hours. (A 50 to 75-pound pig will take about 8–9 hours. Also, a higher final cooked temperature makes pulling the meat easier.)

7. When removing pig from the pit, solicit some help and, using pizza boards or any other large, flat spatula-type device, remove meat to a flat table. (Be careful moving cooked pig; dripping fat is extremely hot.)

8. Use a cleaver to chop into serving pieces, and serve with Cuban Mojo Sauce.

"A po-lice gimme a reference. He tell me I better get my ass gainfully employ," Jones said and shot a jet of smoke out into the empty bar.

—Burma Jones to Lana Lee, as he interviews for the porter job at the Night of Joy nightclub.

Barbecued Pork Spareribs with Pineapple Bourbon Sauce

Makes 6 servings.

If Jones doesn't want to cook a whole hog, he can just barbecue relatively small and inexpensive spareribs. The sparerib is the cut from the belly side of the rib cage below the back ribs. Compared to smaller baby backs, spareribs are a little tougher, but they have more meat and much more meaty flavor. St. Louis ribs are spareribs that have been trimmed to make a more uniform rectangular rack.

2 racks St. Louis-style spareribs (6–8 pounds total)
½ cup Second Line Dry Rub Seasoning Mix, plus 2 teaspoons (recipe follows)
1 cup pineapple juice
8 tablespoons (1 stick) unsalted butter
½ cup tomato sauce
½ cup white vinegar
¼ cup dark brown sugar
¼ cup Creole mustard, or any coarse-grained mustard
½ teaspoon salt
½ teaspoon ground black pepper
½ cup bourbon
2 cups hickory or mesquite wood chips

1. Work a long, slim screwdriver under the papery skin on the back of ribs, and move it along to loosen the skin. With your fingers, pull skin off. Pat ribs dry.
2. Season each side of rib racks with 2 tablespoons dry rub. Wrap ribs in plastic wrap and refrigerate 4–24 hours.
3. While ribs are marinating, make basting sauce. In a medium saucepan, combine pineapple juice, butter, tomato sauce, vinegar, brown sugar, mustard, salt, and ground black pepper. Bring to a boil, lower heat to medium and cook, uncovered, 10 minutes. Remove from heat. Cool to room temperature and stir in bourbon. If not using immediately, refrigerate up to 1 week.
4. One hour before ready to cook, remove ribs from refrigerator and soak wood chips in water.
5. Prepare a barbecue for indirect cooking by placing lit coals against the two sides of a barbecue pit and leaving center clear (or lighting the two outside burners of a gas grill). Toss drained wood chips onto coals (or put into a gas grill's smoker box), and put a drip pan in between the coals. Pour a cup water in drip pan. Arrange ribs, bone side down, on the grill over the cool middle. Cover the grill and cook 1 hour.
6. Brush ribs on both sides with basting sauce. Cover grill and cook until meat shrinks back from the bone, 30–45 minutes longer, basting every 15 minutes. At the beginning of the last 15 minutes, sprinkle 1 teaspoon seasoning mix on top of rib racks, baste, and leave cover open. When done, remove to a platter and allow to sit 15 minutes before serving.

Jones had seen the bird flap around on the stage while Darlene tried to dance. He had never seen a worse performance; Darlene and the bird qualified as legitimate sabotage.

—What Burma Jones thinks of Darlene's dance act.

Second Line Dry Rub Seasoning Mix

Makes ¾ cup

Since Darlene doesn't have rhythm, maybe she can lead the Night of Joy's customers in a second line dance, which requires very little talent. Originally, a second line was the group of parade-goers that followed the main line, the main section of a parade. Today, second lining usually involves twirling handkerchiefs or umbrellas while strutting behind a small brass band, and is increasingly becoming a component of private party and wedding entertainment.

2 tablespoons dried parsley

2 tablespoons sweet paprika

1 tablespoon dark brown sugar

¾ teaspoon salt

1 tablespoon garlic powder

1 tablespoon onion powder

1 tablespoon ground black pepper

1 teaspoon dry mustard

1 teaspoon dried thyme

1 teaspoon dried oregano

½ teaspoon cayenne pepper

Combine all ingredients in a screw-top glass jar, and shake well. Keeps stored away from light up to 6 months.

Bacon-Wrapped Grilled Quail

Makes 4 servings.

No one is suggesting that Jones solve his cockatoo-in-the-bar problem by grilling that yappy bird. But, if the downtrodden bar-sweep ever does get a barbeque pit, he should consider an entrée of quail, one of the best-tasting birds ever cooked over coals.

Northern bobwhite quail haven't been spotted scampering in downtown New Orleans in anyone's memory. But not so long ago the squeaky whistling sound of quail coveys was commonly heard in South Louisiana's rural parishes. Agricultural development has changed that relative abundance to virtual scarcity, with the North American Breeding Bird Survey showing wild populations in South Louisiana are 75 percent lower than in 1966. Fortunately, several local farmers raise and process domestic quail, and these smaller, quick-cooking birds are pretty easy to find in grocery stores and at farmers markets.

8 cleaned farm-raised quail

3 tablespoons olive oil

2 tablespoons red wine vinegar

2 garlic cloves, chopped

1 tablespoon fresh oregano

½ teaspoon salt

¼ teaspoon ground black pepper

8 toothpicks

8 slices bacon

1. Wash quail well and pat dry. Split each down the middle along the breast, and open quail flat.

2. In a gallon-sized food-storage bag, combine olive oil, vinegar, garlic, oregano, salt, and black pepper. Add quail to bag, making sure all surfaces are coated with marinade. Marinate 4 to 24 hours in the refrigerator. Soak toothpicks in water 15 minutes before removing quail from refrigerator.

3. Remove quail from bag, and wipe off excess marinade. Using a soaked toothpick, secure a slice of bacon around each quail. Leave out at room temperature while preparing barbeque pit.

4. With coals to one side, light a barbeque pit to medium-high heat. Cook quail over direct heat 5–6 minutes per side. Move to cool side of grill, cover, and let sit 5 minutes. Serve quail warm.

. . . .

Ginger-Scented Barbecued Shrimp
Makes 2 servings.

. . . .

Barbecued shrimp is not barbecued at all, and is, therefore, definitely a dish Jones can cook on his home stove. This masterpiece of shrimp sautéed in butter and black pepper was invented at Pascal's Manale Restaurant on Napoleon Avenue in the 1950s. One day a diner supposedly asked the restaurant's chef to replicate a dish served in Chicago at the time. The result didn't turn out quite the same, but the spicy new creation ended up on Manale's menu and has become one of New Orleans's most recognized dishes. As for the word "barbecue" in the recipe's title—who knows?

1½ pounds fresh jumbo shrimp, unshelled and
   heads left on

16 tablespoons (2 sticks) unsalted butter, cut into
   ½-inch cubes, divided
¼ cup Worcestershire sauce
1 tablespoon minced fresh garlic
1 tablespoon peeled and grated fresh ginger
2 teaspoons Creole seasoning (purchased, or use recipe
   on pages 6–7)
1½ teaspoons freshly cracked black pepper
1½ teaspoons ground black pepper
¼ teaspoon ground white pepper
Few dashes Tabasco brand hot sauce
¼ cup dry white wine
Juice from 1 fresh lemon
French bread for serving

1. Rinse shrimp well and set aside. In a very large skillet over medium-high heat, combine 1½ sticks butter, Worcestershire sauce, garlic, ginger, Creole seasoning, peppers, and hot sauce. When butter is melted, stir in wine and shrimp. Cook until shrimp are pink and tails curl, about 4 minutes, the whole while turning shrimp over and rearranging so they cook evenly.

2. Stir in remaining ½ stick butter and lemon juice, and heat until butter melts. Remove from heat.

3. Divide shrimp and sauce between 2 shallow soup bowls. To eat, wear a bib, and peel shrimp (and don't be afraid to suck the juice out of the heads). Use French bread for mopping up the sauce.

> "Hey, watch out," Jones called, violating the sanctity of the rite. "You droppin your profit from the orphans, butterfinger."
>
> —Burma Jones to Lana Lee, who physically worships and then drops a coin she's just received from George. Lana and George sell pornography to school children that the two code-word as "orphans."

But did someone say butterfinger?

Butterfinger Ice Cream

Makes 1½ quarts.

The Butterfinger candy bar was created in 1923 by Otto Schnering, owner of Curtiss Candy Company of Chicago, and was named in a public contest. A couple of years earlier, Schnering had also invented the Baby Ruth. As an early publicity stunt, the Curtiss Company flew an airplane across the United States and showered cities with Butterfingers and Baby Ruths attached to tiny parachutes.

4 Butterfinger candy bars
(2.1 ounces each)
1 can (14 ounces) sweetened condensed milk
1½ cups whole milk
1 cup chilled whipping cream
Pinch salt
¾ cup smooth peanut butter, at room temperature
2 teaspoons vanilla extract

1. Freeze Butterfinger bars at least 1 hour. In a large bowl, whisk together condensed milk, whole milk, whipping cream, salt, peanut butter, and vanilla until well combined and smooth. Chill 1 hour, whisk again to combine, then pour into ice cream maker and freeze according to manufacturer's directions.

2. While ice cream is churning, unwrap frozen Butterfinger bars and place in a gallon-sized resealable plastic food storage bag. Crush candy into small pieces with a meat pounder or rolling pin and return in the bag to the freezer. Five minutes before ice cream is ready, add broken Butterfingers to ice cream. Finish churning for the last 5 minutes.

3. Spoon ice cream into a storage container, cover, and freeze completely. Remove from freezer 15 minutes before serving.

Ignatius writes much of his journal on Big Chief writing tablets.

Ignatius's favorite drink, Dr. Nut, an almond-flavored soft drink that came in a seven-ounce bottle featuring a squirrel and nut logo, and originally manufactured in New Orleans

4

....

The Avenging Sword of Taste and Decency

> "What I want is a good, strong monarchy with a tasteful and decent king who has some knowledge of theology and geometry and to cultivate a Rich Inner Life."
> "A king? You want a king?"
> ... "Let me alone! I am in a very bad cycle."
> "What you mean, 'cycle'?"
>
> —Conversation between Ignatius and his mother, who worries about her son's mental health.

Ignatius's comments would make more sense to Mrs. Reilly if she would actually read some of the words her erudite, ejaculatory (literally) Ignatius writes, namely, the ramblings on his Big Chief tablets that state that he merely despises the modern world.

Ignatius has a medieval outlook grounded in the book *The Consolation of Philosophy,* a work intended to preserve ancient classical knowledge. While in prison for treason, the sixth-century Roman senator and philosopher Boethius wrote this popular text, a book which, other than the Bible, is often considered the most influential in the Middle Ages. Ignatius interprets Boethius to mean that humans are ruled by a destiny directed through the whims of nature and the cyclical wheel of the callous Fortuna, the Roman goddess of fate. This worldview is based on human powerlessness, and it's all the reason Ignatius needs to avoid work.

Another influence on his behavior is the austere, tranquil medieval lifestyle he thinks he wants, just like that of Hroswitha, the celebrated tenth-century nun-poetess. Hailed as the most remarkable woman of her time, the pious writer was celebrated for melodiously demonstrating the principle that, the greater the force of temptation, the more admirable is the final triumph of virtue.

Let's see—Ignatius abhors canned food and instant coffee, yet obviously thinks it's okay to devour cakes, doughnuts, hot dogs, and his favorite soft drink, Dr. Nut. And, for all his thunderous railings against modern conveniences, he sure does like buying unnecessary doodads. Also, when it comes to indecency, the judgmental Ignatius certainly doesn't shy away from steamy movies.

Then there's the dance shows. Although he plays the oh-so-civilized lute, Ignatius gets entertainment kicks from watching television and "lasciviously gyrating children." In real life, from 1961 until 1972, John Pela, WWL-

TV's version of Dick Clark, hosted *Saturday Hop,* with the name changing in 1963 to *The John Pela Show.* Local teenagers eager to get in front of the camera lined up for blocks. Once on the set, they let loose and showed New Orleans metro area viewers the latest dance moves. In *Dunces,* Ignatius acknowledges that his much-admired holy nun would not approve of such "horrors." But, face it, he's addicted, and just can't help but watch. Hroswitha would be appalled.

All right—the lazy, pathetically fat Ignatius is the ultimate contradiction. Maybe it's best that Mrs. Reilly not try to understand Boethius. The paradoxical truth might make her even more determined to take the advice she keeps getting from Santa Battaglia, that she should lock her son up in Charity Hospital's psych wing.

> That business in the note about "misleading and perverting the young" had been badly misunderstood. . . . And that phrase "underdeveloped testicles." Dr. Talc cringed. . . .
>
> Dr. Talc sipped the vodka and V8 juice that he always had after a night of heavy social drinking.
>
> —Tulane University history professor Dr. Talc, who has become the "butt of the campus" because an old threatening note written by his former "psychotic graduate student," Ignatius, has surfaced and is making the rounds.

Dr. Talc's Bloody Mary
Makes 1 large drink.

This ever-popular eye-opener may have started simply as the tomato juice and vodka cocktail downed by Vaudeville actor George Jessel at New York's 21 Club. A name was supposedly attached to the drink in 1921, when Fernand Petiot, a bartender at Harry's New York Bar in Paris, purportedly mixed one up for a customer, who some say was Vladimir Smirnov of vodka fame, and who chided that the drink reminded him of the Bucket of Blood Club in Chicago and a waitress there named Mary. Another story says the drink was named for the real-life Bloody Mary, Queen Mary Tudor, who is remembered for burning about three hundred heretical Protestants. Regardless, after Prohibition ended, bartender Petiot ended up working at the King Cole Bar at the St. Regis

Hotel in Manhattan, where he started adding the spices that give this cocktail its customary kick.

6 ounces V8 juice

2 ounces vodka

2 teaspoons Worcestershire sauce

¼ teaspoon Tabasco brand sauce

¼ teaspoon prepared horseradish

1 tablespoon freshly squeezed lemon juice

¼ teaspoon celery salt

Pickled okra (purchased, or recipe on page 76),
    lemon wedges and celery sticks for garnish

Pour all drink ingredients into an ice-filled cocktail shaker, and shake until thoroughly mixed. Pour into a large ice-filled glass, and garnish with okra, lemon wedges, and celery sticks.

A Promising Watermelon Salad

Makes 6 servings.

> "My nerves!" Ignatius said. He was slumped down in the seat so that just the top of his green hunting cap appeared in the window, looking like the tip of a promising watermelon.
>
> —Ignatius, after his mother slams the hood of a Volkswagen with the bumper of her 1946 Plymouth.

Watermelon is native to Africa, and Egyptians recorded cultivating them at least five thousand years ago. More than 90 percent water, this succulent, transportable fruit was valuable in deserts and where natural water supplies were contaminated. The watermelon made its way to North America with colonists and the slave trade. Today's average American eats more than fifteen pounds of watermelon a year.

2 tablespoons lime juice

3 tablespoons chopped fresh mint

¼ teaspoon salt

⅛ teaspoon cayenne pepper

¼ cup olive oil

6 cups seeded watermelon, cut in 1-inch pieces

1 cup crumbled feta cheese

4 thin red onion slices, chopped

1. Make a dressing by whisking together in a bowl the lime juice, mint, salt, cayenne, and olive oil. Set aside.
2. On a rimmed serving platter or shallow casserole dish, arrange watermelon pieces and top with feta and chopped onion. Drizzle dressing over everything, and serve immediately.

> "I made the mistake of heating the oven the other day before inspecting it properly. When I opened it to put in my frozen pizza, I was almost blinded by a bottle of broiled wine that was preparing to explode. I suggest that you divert some of the monies that you are pouring into the liquor industry."
>
> "For shame, Ignatius. A few bottles of Gallo muscatel, and you with all them trinkets."
>
> —Ignatius trying to convince his mother that, with a little economizing on her part, he won't have to get a job.

Saddled with the reputation as the preferred drink of winos, muscatel is a rich, sweet wine made from the Muscat family of grapes grown around the world. Mrs. Reilly would be dismayed to learn Gallo no longer makes its low-rent, screw-top muscatel. But there are other muscatels on the market, many of them high-end brandies and liqueurs. And with their characteristic floral, musty taste, these relatively sophisticated wines are great for making desserts and complementing meats such as duck, pork and lamb.

Muscatel Braised Lamb Shanks with Sour Cream Mashed Potatoes

Makes 4 servings.

4 lamb shanks, 1–1¼ pounds each

Salt and ground black pepper, or Creole seasoning
   (purchased, or use recipe on pages 6–7)

¼ cup all-purpose flour

2 tablespoons olive oil

1½ cups chopped onion

1 stalk celery, chopped

1 cup chopped carrot

½ cup chopped bell pepper

2 cloves garlic, minced

½ cup tomato sauce

1 tablespoon white vinegar

¼ teaspoon Tabasco hot sauce

1 cup beef broth

1 cup muscatel or muscat dessert wine

1 teaspoon finely chopped fresh rosemary

Sour Cream Mashed Potatoes
   (recipe follows)

Chopped green onion for garnish

1. Preheat oven to 325°F. Season lamb shanks well with salt and pepper, and dredge in flour. In a large, ovenproof pot, heat olive oil over medium-high heat and sear

lamb well. Remove lamb and set aside. To the same pot, add onion, celery, carrot, and bell pepper, and sauté until vegetables are soft.

2. Stir in garlic. Add 1 teaspoon salt, ½ teaspoon ground black pepper, tomato sauce, vinegar, hot sauce, broth, muscatel, and rosemary. Simmer on high heat 2 minutes.

3. Add lamb to sauce, cover pot, and bake until extremely tender, about 2 hours.

4. Remove lamb from pot, and puree sauce with an immersion blender or in a regular blender. Reheat sauce and lamb. Serve over Sour Cream Mashed Potatoes, and garnish with green onion.

Sour Cream Mashed Potatoes

Makes 4 servings

2 pounds Yukon Gold potatoes, peeled and quartered

4 tablespoons (½ stick) unsalted butter, softened

½ cup sour cream, at room temperature

¼ cup half-and-half, at room temperature

Salt and freshly ground black pepper

1. Place potatoes in a large pot of salted water that covers potatoes by 2 inches. Bring to a boil, then lower to a simmer and cook until potatoes are tender, about 15 minutes. Drain extremely well.

2. Add butter, and mash potatoes well with a potato masher. Add sour cream and half-and-half, and beat with a spoon. Season with salt and pepper.

From-Scratch Pizza

Makes a 12-inch pizza.

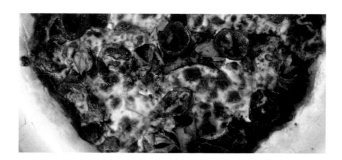

Ignatius Reilly was buying frozen pizza when the concept was still in its infancy. Frozen pizza produced by New Jersey's Celentano Brothers did reach supermarkets in 1958. But the first name to make it big was Totino's, named for Minneapolis residents Rose and Jim Totino, who didn't start selling their pizzeria's product frozen until the early 1960s.

Of course, flatbreads with toppings have been consumed in Greece, Egypt, and Italy since at least the time of Plato. The modern pizza began as the famous Neopolitan Pizza Margherita in 1889 and, in 1905, Lombardi's in New York City's Little Italy became the first licensed pizzeria in the United States. Back then, however, pizza was mostly shunned by everyone who wasn't Italian. Pizza didn't become Americanized—that is, made with hardly detectable garlic and oregano—until 1943, when restaurateur Ike Sewell of Chicago created a lightly seasoned deep-dish pizza.

Pizza really took off with returning World War II servicemen who were craving the "pizza pies" they'd been wolfing down in Italy. Across America, the number of pizza parlors skyrocketed from five hundred in 1934 to twenty thousand in 1956. The first New Orleans restaurant to focus on pizza was Domino's (no relation to the chain), and this establishment was on the corner of St. Charles Avenue and Girod. By the 1960s, several chains had opened locally and many existing Italian restaurants had added pizza to their menus.

Today, Americans eat a whopping 3 billion pizzas a year, with pepperoni the favorite topping. Super Bowl Sunday always wins the contest for most pizzas purchased in a twenty-four-hour period. On that day, insurance companies also receive the highest number of accident reports from pizza delivery drivers.

Pizza Dough

1½ teaspoons active dry yeast

¾ cup lukewarm water

¼ teaspoon sugar

1¼ cups cake flour

¾ cup all-purpose flour

½ teaspoon iodized salt

2 tablespoons olive oil, plus additional for brushing pan

Suggested toppings

½ cup Pizza Sauce (recipe follows)

Sliced meats, such as ham; Italian sausage or proscuitto, pepperoni, pancetta, or capicolla; sliced Creole smoked sausage; Canadian bacon; browned ground beef or turkey, grilled chicken, and cooked ground lamb, as well as cooked shrimp and anchovies

Raw or sautéed vegetables, such as onions, black olives, garlic, roasted peppers, mushrooms, eggplant, arugula, spinach, tomatoes, and herbs

Cheese (just about any kind)

1. Position a rack in lower third of oven and preheat oven to 450°F. In a small bowl, mix together yeast, water, and sugar. Let sit 5 minutes.

Pizza Sauce

Makes 1½ cups, enough for three 12-inch pizzas

2 tablespoons olive oil

1 medium onion, chopped

1 small carrot, chopped

1 tablespoon chopped garlic

1 (28-ounce) can crushed tomatoes or 2½ pounds fresh tomatoes, peeled and seeded

1 tablespoon tomato paste

¼ cup fresh chopped basil, or 2 tablespoons dried

2 tablespoons fresh oregano, or 1 tablespoon dried

1 teaspoon salt

½ teaspoon red pepper flakes

1. In a large saucepan over medium-high heat, add olive oil, and sauté onion and carrot until soft but not browned, about 5 minutes. Stir in garlic and sauté 30 seconds.

2. Add tomatoes, tomato paste, basil, oregano, salt, and pepper, and simmer 10 minutes, stirring occasionally. Remove from heat. Cool a few minutes; then puree in a blender or food processor. Can be made up to 3 days ahead and refrigerated.

2. In a large bowl, combine yeast mixture with cake flour, all-purpose flour, salt, and 2 tablespoons olive oil. Beat vigorously until well combined. Cover dough with plastic wrap, and let rest 15 minutes.

3. Brush the inside of a perforated pizza pan or cookie sheet lightly with olive oil. On a heavily floured hard surface, knead dough 1 minute, adding as little flour as necessary to keep from sticking. Press dough out into about half of desired shape, and let rest 1 minute. Transfer dough to oiled pizza pan, and finish pressing out into shape. (Don't worry about making a perfect circle; any shape will do.)

4. Use your fingertip to make indentations in crust at 2-inch intervals. Brush crust top and edges with olive oil, and layer on toppings, beginning with ½ cup Pizza Sauce, then meat and/or vegetables, and ending with cheese. Bake until crust and cheese are deep brown, 13–16 minutes. Serve hot.

. . . .

Pork Chops with Brandy Mustard Sauce
Makes 4 servings.

. . . .

In the sixteenth century, the French and Dutch worked together to find a way to remove water from wine to make shipping easier. Upon receiving the concentrate, the Dutch decided not to add water and took to drinking it as it was, calling the spirit "bradwijn," meaning "burned wine," and later "brandy."

4 (1¼-inch-thick) rib pork chops

Salt, ground black pepper, and paprika

2 tablespoons olive oil

1 tablespoon butter

10 ounces mushrooms, sliced

2 cloves garlic, finely minced

½ cup brandy

½ cup chicken broth

2 tablespoon prepared Creole mustard, or any coarse-grain mustard

½ cup heavy cream

2 tablespoons sliced green onion for garnish

1. Preheat oven to 350°F. Pat pork chops dry and sprinkle both sides with salt, black pepper, and paprika. In a large, oven-proof skillet, heat olive oil over medium heat. Sear pork until deep brown, about 3 minutes each side.

2. Place skillet into oven, and bake until pork is cooked through, when center reaches 150°F, about 7–9 minutes. Remove skillet from oven, and place chops on a platter. Cover and keep warm.

3. In same skillet, melt butter and sauté mushrooms until tender, about 4 minutes. Remove pan from heat, and stir

in garlic. Carefully add brandy. (If pan is too hot, brandy may ignite.)

4. Stir in chicken broth and mustard, and return skillet to medium-high heat. Simmer 3 minutes. Stir in cream and simmer until thick, about 3–4 minutes.

5. Serve sauce over pork chops, and garnish with green onion.

Dr. Talc shuddered at the very thought of Miss Minkoff. In class she had insulted and challenged and vilified him at every turn, egging the Reilly monster to join in the attack. . . . Dr. Talc idly wondered if they had married each other. . . . Perhaps they had both defected to Cuba.

—The undistinguished Tulane University history professor Dr. Talc, remembering the horror of a few years back when Myrna and Ignatius were his students.

The 1962 tensions over Soviet nuclear missiles installed in Cuba that brought the world to the brink of nuclear disaster obviously made an impact on the fictitious Dr. Talc, who views Cuba as opposed to America's cause. But, for New Orleans, the city often described as the northernmost Caribbean city, those ill feelings were relatively new.

For centuries, New Orleans and Cuba had cultural, demographic, and economic ties. From 1762 to 1795, Louisiana's Roman Catholic Church jurisdiction was administered from Cuba. In the 1800s, refugees from Haiti's slave rebellion often ended up in Cuba and

Cuban Pork Roast with Rum Pan Sauce
Makes 6–8 servings.

1 bone-in pork shoulder roast (5–6 pounds)
¼ cup minced garlic, divided
2 teaspoons coarse salt
¼ cup plus 2 tablespoons olive oil
1 cup orange juice
Juice of 1 lemon

then made their way to New Orleans, bringing along music, voodoo, and a love for peppered food. Also during that time, trade in coffee, sugar, and slaves was brisk between the two ports. During the steamship era, ships ferried writers, musicians, and businessmen between the two cities, and investments flowed freely. This exchange was interrupted by the Civil War, when many affluent New Orleans families fled to Cuba to wait things out. By the middle of the twentieth century, more than one-third of the Port of New Orleans's trade was going to Havana, and more than six thousand jobs were directly related to trade with Cuba. Then in 1959, Castro marched into Havana and trade ceased, and a modern generation of refugees flocked to New Orleans.

Creole cuisine has undoubtedly been enriched and spiced up by all this interaction, with Cuban travelers and exiles introducing traditions stemming from the island's Spanish colonial days. That includes a love of rice served with beans, plantains, black bean soup, citrus, tomato, onion, garlic, hot peppers and, of course, rum.

Juice of 1 lime

2 teaspoons dried oregano

1 teaspoon ground cumin

1 teaspoon ground black pepper

½ teaspoon cayenne pepper

1 medium onion, finely chopped

½ cup dark rum

1. Make small slits in pork, and stuff 3 tablespoons garlic into slashes.

2. Make marinade by placing remaining 1 tablespoon garlic and salt in a mortar and pestle. Mash garlic into a smooth paste. Whisk in ¼ cup olive oil, orange juice, lemon and lime juices, oregano, cumin, black pepper, and cayenne. Reserve ½ cup of marinade and refrigerate.

3. Put pork and unrefrigerated marinade into a large plastic food bag. Seal bag and turn to coat all sides of pork. Marinate pork in refrigerator 4–24 hours.

4. Remove pork from refrigerator 1 hour before cooking. Heat oven to 325°F. Place roast and marinade from plastic bag in a roasting pan. Roast pork until center reaches 170°F, about 4–5 hours for pork that's sliceable, or 190°F, 5–6 hours, for pulled pork. (Check liquid level every hour, and add water to maintain ½ inch.)

5. Remove roast from oven, and pour accumulated juices into a bowl. Cover roast while it rests.

6. Heat remaining 2 tablespoons olive oil in a medium saucepan over medium heat, and sauté onion until golden. Stir in rum and reduce by half. Add reserved ½ cup of marinade and 1 cup reserved pan juices. Simmer briskly 5 minutes. Pour sauce over sliced or chopped meat, or serve separately for dipping.

A green hunting cap squeezed the top of the fleshy balloon of a head. The green earflaps, full of large ears and uncut hair and the fine bristles that grew in the ears themselves, stuck out on either side like turn signals indicating two directions at once.

—A description of the everyday Ignatius.

Although he rarely went out without his flapping green hunting cap, it's hard to imagine Ignatius picking up a shotgun or rifle and actually hunting. Hunting is, however, a popular sport in Louisiana, where deer, wild hog, and alligator inhabit fields and marshes, and where an abundance of geese and ducks navigate the Mississippi Flyway, a migration route that generally follows the Mississippi River and, therefore, runs the length of the entire state.

Braised Venison Round Steak
Makes 6 servings.

1 (2-pound) venison round steak, with bones

Salt, ground black pepper, and cayenne pepper

3 tablespoons olive oil

3 tablespoons unsalted butter

2 tablespoons all-purpose flour

1½ cups diced onion

1 stalk celery, diced

½ cup diced green or red bell pepper

2 tablespoons minced garlic

2 cups beef stock

¼ cup red wine

1 teaspoon Creole seasoning (purchased, or use recipe on pages 6–7)

8 ounces crimini or button mushrooms, sliced

¼ cup minced parsley

Cooked rice for serving

¼ cup sliced green onion for garnish

1. Preheat oven to 300°F. Slice venison into 6 equal portions. Working around bones, pound pieces to ⅓ of an inch. Pat pieces dry, and sprinkle with salt, black pepper, and cayenne. Rub seasonings into meat.
2. Heat olive oil in a Dutch oven or large, ovenproof pot over medium-high heat. Sear venison pieces until well browned, and remove to a plate.
3. Make a roux by melting butter in same pot. Add flour and stir over medium-low heat until the color of milk chocolate, 2–3 minutes. Remove pot from heat and stir in onion, celery, bell pepper, and garlic. When sizzling stops, return pot to heat and add stock, wine, and Creole seasoning. Bring to a boil, and simmer 2 minutes.
4. Add browned venison and any accumulated juices to the sauce. Bake, covered, 1½ hours.
5. Stir mushrooms and parsley into sauce. Cover, raise oven temperature to 350°F, and bake an additional 30 minutes.
6. Remove pot from oven, and serve warm venison and gravy over rice. Garnish with green onion.

. . . .

Wild Duck and Andouille Gumbo
Makes 6–8 servings.

. . . .

6 wild ducks

1 tablespoon salt

2 teaspoons ground black pepper

½ teaspoon cayenne pepper

1 large carrot

2 stalks celery, plus 1 cup diced celery

1 large onion, plus 2 cups minced onion

2 bay leaves

1½ cups vegetable oil, divided

1 pound smoked pork andouille, sliced into ½-inch pieces

1 cup all-purpose flour

1 cup diced green bell pepper

1 tablespoon chopped garlic

½ cup chopped fresh flat-leaf parsley

½ cup sliced green onion, divided

Cooked white rice for serving

1. Rinse ducks well, and pat dry with paper towels. In a small bowl, combine salt, black pepper, and cayenne. Rub half of seasoning mix into ducks.
2. Bring a gallon of water to a boil in a large stock pot, and add carrot, 2 stalks celery, 1 large onion, and bay leaves. In a large cast-iron skillet, heat ½ cup of oil, and brown ducks well on all sides. Add duck to boiling stock, and simmer briskly until meat falls off bones, about 1½ hours. Remove ducks from stock, reserving stock. When cool enough to handle, remove meat from bones and discard bones.
3. Cook andouille until brown, and set aside.
4. Add the remaining 1 cup oil and the flour to a heavy-bottomed Dutch oven. Make a roux by stirring mixture constantly over medium heat until dark golden brown.
5. Remove Dutch oven from heat, and immediately stir in diced celery, minced onion, bell pepper, and garlic. Carefully strain duck stock into Dutch oven with roux. Add remaining seasoning mix, and simmer 1 hour.
6. Add duck meat, browned sausage, parsley, and ¼ cup green onion, and simmer 15 minutes. Serve hot gumbo in bowls over cooked white rice, and garnish with remaining green onion.

Duck Breast with Fig Sauce

Makes 2 servings.

Even if you don't hunt, you can always buy duck at the grocery store.

½ cup fig preserves

½ cup orange juice

2 tablespoons balsamic vinegar

1 teaspoon freshly grated ginger

½ teaspoon minced fresh rosemary

¼ cup orange liqueur

Pinch ground white pepper

2 domestic duck breast halves, with skin and
   deboned (½ pound each)

Salt and ground black pepper

1. In a medium saucepan, combine fig preserves, orange juice, vinegar, ginger, rosemary, orange liqueur, and white pepper. Simmer until slightly thickened, about 10 minutes, and keep warm.
2. With a sharp knife, score duck breast skins at ½-inch intervals, forming a diamond pattern and being careful not to cut through to the meat. Dry duck thoroughly, and sprinkle with salt and black pepper.

A frozen banana tree, brown and stricken, languished against the front of the porch, the tree preparing to collapse as the iron fence had done long ago.

—Through the eyes of Patrolman Mancuso, who has just arrived on his motorcycle at the Reilly household on Constantinople Street.

3. Heat a large, heavy-bottomed skillet over medium heat. When hot, add duck, skin side down, and sear until brown, about 8 minutes. Flip duck over, and cook another 7 minutes. For medium rare, cook until internal temperature of 130°F.
4. Slice duck at ½-inch intervals, and serve with warm sauce.

Bananas Foster Sundaes

Makes 4.

In balmy New Orleans, banana trees are common ornamentals. Commercial bananas have historically been big business in the city, especially through ties to the Standard Fruit Company (started in New Orleans, and now Dole) and the even larger United Fruit Company (started in Boston, but with a strong presence in New Orleans, and now Chiquita). In the early twentieth century, these two monopolies were instrumental in the development of plantations in Central America, where corporations exerted influence over local transportation, communications, education, and politics, and which led to the creation of the term "banana republic."

The celebrated dessert Bananas Foster originated in 1951, when the chef of Brennan's Restaurant found himself saddled with a surplus of the fruit. The flaming ice-cream dish was named after Richard Foster, a friend of the restaurant's owner, Owen Brennan. This version of the classic has all the flavor of the original, but without the daunting pyrotechnics.

6 tablespoons butter, cut into bits

½ cup light brown sugar

¼ cup honey

¼ teaspoon cinnamon

⅛ teaspoon freshly grated nutmeg

4 small or 3 large, firm-ripe bananas, peeled and cut
    into ½-inch slices

½ teaspoon pure vanilla extract

2 tablespoons banana liqueur

1–2 tablespoons dark rum (depending on how boozy-
    tasting you want it)

1 quart Vanilla Bean Ice Cream (purchased, or recipe
    pages 192–93)

Chopped pecans

1. In a large saucepan, melt butter over medium heat. Stir
   in brown sugar, honey, cinnamon, and nutmeg, and cook
   just until sugar is totally dissolved.
2. Raise heat to medium-high, add bananas, and stir until
   heated through, about 30–45 seconds. Remove pan from
   heat, and carefully stir in vanilla, banana liqueur, and
   rum. (Be careful: mixture will bubble up.)
3. Place a large scoop of ice cream in a dessert bowl,
   and top with warm bananas, sauce, and pecans. Serve
   immediately.

Triple-Chocolate Belchless Brownies
Makes 24 brownies.

No one knows the actual inventor of brownies. But it is certain that this perennial favorite of twentieth-century bakery shops was created in America, likely in Boston, and that the first recipe for a cake-like brownie appeared in the 1906 edition of *The Boston Cooking-School Cook Book,* edited by Fannie Merritt Farmer.

8 tablespoons (1 stick) unsalted butter,
    plus 1 tablespoon

½ cup canola oil

2 cups sugar

1 cup cocoa powder

1 teaspoon iodized salt

1 teaspoon baking powder

4 large eggs, at room
    temperature

¼ cup strong brewed coffee

> Ignatius belched the gas of a dozen brownies trapped by his valve.
>
> —Ignatius, as he opens the door of his room to his mother, who berates him for wasting money on thing-a-ma-jigs.

2 teaspoons vanilla extract

1½ cups all-purpose flour

1¾ cups (10 ounces) semisweet chocolate chips

1 cup heavy cream

2 cups (12 ounces) bittersweet chocolate chips

1. Preheat oven to 350°F. Butter a 9 x 13-inch baking pan and set aside.

2. Melt 1 stick butter and pour into a large bowl. Stir in canola oil, sugar, cocoa, salt, and baking powder. Let cool 1 minute.

3. Add eggs, one at a time, stirring well after each addition. Add coffee, vanilla, and flour, and beat well until combined. Stir in semisweet chocolate chips.

4. Pour batter into prepared pan, and spread top evenly. Bake 25–30 minutes, or until sides just begin to pull away. Cool completely in pan.

5. To make topping, boil cream in a medium saucepan. Remove from heat. Stir in bittersweet chocolate chips, and cover until chocolate is melted. Stir with a spoon until smooth. Add remaining tablespoon butter, and stir until starting to thicken, about 3 minutes. Spread over cooled brownies. Let stand at cool room temperature until topping is firm. Slice into 24 pieces.

. . . .

Blueberry, Mint, and Rosemary Sorbet
Makes 1 quart.

. . . .

Miss Annie should try ditching the aspirin and chilling out with something refreshing like this sorbet, which contains rosemary, an herb numerous cultures believe helps cure headaches. Sorbet in America is similar to

> "The things I useta hear through my window! 'Put down that skirt' and 'Get off my bed' and 'How dare you? I'm a virgin.' It was awful. I went on aspirins twenty-four hours a day."
>
> —Nosy neighbor Miss Annie describing to Gus Levy what she'd heard eavesdropping on Ignatius when he was entertaining his minx of a girlfriend, Myrna.

fruit-flavored Italian ice. Frozen desserts were popular in early Rome, and were another delicacy brought to France by Catherine de Medici.

½ cup sugar

½ cup water

2 tablespoons minced fresh mint leaves

2 tablespoons coarsely chopped fresh rosemary leaves

2 pints fresh blueberries

2 tablespoons freshly squeezed and strained lemon juice

¾ cup chilled white wine, Champagne, or sparkling wine (or substitute club soda or a lemon-lime soft drink). The alcohol in wine acts like antifreeze and keeps sorbet from freezing rock solid. If you substitute a soft drink for wine, take the sorbet out of the freezer 10 minutes before serving.

1. In a saucepan, bring sugar and water to a boil. Remove from heat, and stir in mint and rosemary. Cover and steep 10 minutes. Strain into a bowl and discard herbs.

2. Puree blueberries and sugar syrup in a blender. Strain and combine with lemon juice and wine. Chill until cold.

3. Process blueberry mixture in an ice cream freezer according to manufacturer's directions. Store covered in freezer at least 8 hours before serving.

5

....

Party Like It's 1960

> "This building is repellingly flamboyant. . . . I would have preferred your renting an American Legion hall or something equally appropriate. This place looks more like the setting for some perverted activity like a tea dance or a garden party."
>
> —Ignatius arriving at Dorian Greene's canary yellow three-story house on St. Peter Street for a kickoff rally to organize a political party for homosexuals.

In the early twentieth century the French Quarter's bohemian atmosphere made the area a magnet for artists. But even before, this, the oldest neighborhood in the city, had long been a clandestine home for homosexuals. The Quarter's gay social world didn't become more public until after Prohibition. This coincided with the 1933 opening of Bourbon Street's Café Lafitte in Exile, a landmark that bills itself as the oldest continually operating gay bar in North America.

By mid-century, gay socializing flourished, with the Fat Monday Luncheon, a private event for local gay men, starting in 1949, and the Krewe of Yuga, the first gay Carnival club, forming in 1958. But, although the community was enjoying more acceptance at the time *Dunces* was written, local politics stifled political organizing, which really didn't take off in New Orleans until the late 1970s.

The gay community's political muscle was tested in 2004, when Louisiana voters overwhelmingly approved a constitutional ban on same-sex marriage. But, in spite of that legislative defeat, New Orleans today is considered one of the most gay-friendly cities in the United States.

Tea dances, late-afternoon tea parties with orchestras, were popular with single men and women in the late 1800s. Within the gay culture, the term is often called a "T-dance" and has been used to describe Sunday or resort afternoon dances. We know that at Dorian's soiree "cigarettes and cocktail glasses held like batons were flying through the air." But while the "seething masses" grooved to Judy Garland and Lena Horne, and while Ignatius was insulting guests and being insulted, what was the host setting out on the buffet table?

Since Dorian gets large checks every month from his "dear family," he might be serving caviar, smoked salmon, and foie gras, the high-end tidbits of the era. The typical 1960s spread, however, was a bit more low-key, and commonly featured finger foods, such as stuffed and marinated vegetables, ham and chicken sandwiches, cheese boards, deviled eggs, kebabs, olives, peanuts, chips and dips. Chex Mix was certainly all the rage, and trendy sweets included Tunnel of Fudge or Red Velvet cakes, ambrosia, or something molded in Jell-O.

For those who wanted something a little fancy, yet affordable, cantaloupe, watermelon, and grapefruit halves often served as bases for chunks of fruit stuck on frilly toothpicks. Shrimp were stylishly arranged and glazed in aspic, fondues were ablazing, and "porcupines" were made from skewered olives and cheese. And, of course, the ultimate in casual elegance were Swedish meatballs and cocktail wieners in a sweet sauce, two dishes that still pop up at local parties.

If he were hosting a sit-down dinner, Dorian could use recipes from Julia Child's popular cookbook *Mastering the Art of French Cooking* (1961). The pioneering chef was also host of the then-new television cooking show *The French Chef.*

French food was also the favorite of the Kennedy White House. In 1961, Jacqueline Kennedy replaced a kitchen run by caterers and Navy stewards with a new chef, French-born René Verdon, who had been working at the Carlyle Hotel in New York. Verdon was noted for serving the president and Mrs. Kennedy their favorite soufflés, and John Kennedy was particularly drawn to *vichyssoise,* chicken in Champagne sauce, *Poulet a l'Estragon* (chicken with tarragon), and quiche. Praised for significantly raising the standard of food served at the White House, Verdon stayed on until 1966, when the Johnsons insisted on saving money by using frozen and canned vegetables.

Cocktails, too, were extremely popular in the 1960s. And the glasses of Dorian's fun-loving guests could be filled with martinis, daiquiris, Manhattans, Bloody Marys, Sidecars, Margaritas, Whiskey Sours, Tom Collins, Gin Rickeys and Rum 'n' Colas. Another popular toddy of the time was New Orleans's own Sazerac, the potent father of all cocktails, and one that might help Ignatius chill out.

....

Tujague's Oysters en Brochette

Makes 4 appetizer servings. Recipe is by chef Richard Bickford, Tujague's Restaurant.

....

Dorian can use some of that beer to impress his wild and crazy guests in this recipe for Angels on Horseback, oysters wrapped in bacon, and a popular hors d'oeuvre of the time. Also called Oysters en Brochette, this classic is an English invention from the 1880s and gained attention in the United States after being served by the Kennedy White House.

This recipe calls for Abita Beer, a brew founded in 1986 in Abita Springs, a small town north of New Orleans across Lake Pontchartrain.

Sauce

  2 tablespoons butter

  1 tablespoon minced garlic

  1 cup Abita Beer, or your favorite beer

  1 cup Worcestershire sauce

> Seated at a table were three women drinking from beer cans. They regarded Ignatius squarely. The one who was crushing a beer can in her hand stopped and tossed the can into a potted plant next to the sink.
>
> —Lesbians Betty Bumper, Frieda Club, and Liz Steele, guests at Dorian's party.

¼ cup hot sauce

2 tablespoons lemon juice

1 tablespoon tomato paste

¼ cup heavy cream

Garlic Toast

4 tablespoons (½ stick) butter

2 teaspoons minced fresh garlic

4 slices French bread, cut on the diagonal

Oysters

16 large oysters, shucked

8 slices thick-cut bacon

4 six-inch wooden skewers

Vegetable oil for frying

½ cup corn flour

1 teaspoon Creole seasoning (purchased, or use recipe
   on pages 6–7)

¼ cup chopped green onion for garnish

1. Make sauce by melting butter in a medium saucepan
   and sautéing garlic until light brown. Deglaze with beer,
   and reduce by half. Add Worcestershire sauce, hot sauce,
   lemon juice, and tomato paste, and simmer 5 minutes. Add
   cream and reduce by half. Set sauce aside and keep warm.

2. Make garlic toast by melting butter and sautéing garlic
   5 seconds. Spread garlic butter on sliced French bread.
   Broil until golden brown.

3. Make oysters by wrapping each oyster with ½ slice of
   bacon. Slide 4 bacon-wrapped oysters onto 1 wooden
   skewer, and repeat with remainder.

4. Heat 2 inches vegetable oil in a deep fryer or heavy pot
   to 350°F. Combine corn flour and Creole seasoning in a
   small bowl. Gently dust the skewered oysters in seasoned flour, and fry until golden brown.

5. To serve, drizzle a little sauce on each of 4 plates. Top
   with garlic toast, and drizzle some sauce on toast. Lay
   one fried oyster skewer on top of toast, and drizzle on
   more sauce. Garnish with green onion, and serve hot.

Oyster Patties

Makes 36 miniature hors d'oeuvres.

Here's another oyster party dish that was extremely popular in New Orleans in the 1960s.

1 pint oysters, with liquor

8 tablespoons (1 stick) unsalted butter, divided

1 cup finely chopped onion

1 clove garlic, minced

1 teaspoon fresh thyme

1 teaspoon freshly squeezed lemon juice

¾ teaspoon salt

½ teaspoon ground black pepper

¼ teaspoon paprika

⅛ teaspoon cayenne pepper

3 tablespoons all-purpose flour

2 tablespoons brandy or cognac

¼ cup heavy cream

2 tablespoons chopped fresh parsley

3 dozen miniature puff pastry shells, insides and tops
removed and discarded

1. Preheat oven to 400°F. Drain oysters and reserve the liquor. Measure oyster liquor, and add enough water to make ½ cup. Reserve any remaining oyster liquor. Chop oysters coarsely, and set aside.

2. Heat a large skillet over medium heat and melt 6 table-spoons butter. Cook onion, stirring occasionally, until tender, 3–5 minutes. Add garlic and sauté 30 more seconds.

3. Reduce heat to low, add thyme, lemon juice, salt, black pepper, paprika, cayenne, and remaining 2 tablespoons butter. When butter is melted, add flour and cook, stirring constantly, for 2 minutes. Stir in cognac and reserved oysters, and simmer 1 minute. Add ½ cup oyster liquid and cream, bring to a simmer, and cook until thick. If necessary, thin with remaining oyster liquid. Stir in parsley and cool 5 minutes.

4. Divide mixture among patty shells, and bake until brown and bubbly, about 12 minutes. Cool a few minutes before serving.

> "When my brain begins to reel from my literary labors, I make an occasional cheese dip."
>
> —Ignatius J. Reilly.

Occasional Chipotle Goat Cheese Dip

Makes 2½ cups.

In the 1960s, party dips were almost always made from dried salad-dressing mix or canned seafood thrown into softened cream cheese. Then came the 1980s' bistro craze, and those old favorite onion and shrimp dips became passé. With today's wider array of available cheeses, however, cheese dips are getting an exciting new look.

1 pound fresh, soft goat cheese (chèvre)

4 tablespoons (½ stick) unsalted butter, softened

⅓ cup crème fraîche or sour cream

1 tablespoon fresh lemon juice

2 tablespoons mashed, canned chipotle chilies in adobo
sauce, plus 1 teaspoon adobo sauce

3 tablespoons finely chopped cilantro, plus additional
whole leaves for garnish

Salt and freshly ground black pepper

Tortilla chips for serving

1. In a food processor, combine goat cheese, butter, crème fraîche, lemon juice, chilies, and adobo sauce. Process until smooth.
2. Add chopped cilantro, and pulse to combine.
3. Scrape into a bowl, and stir in salt and black pepper to taste. Refrigerate at least 1 hour. Garnish with whole cilantro leaves, and serve with tortilla chips.

Herbed Gervais Cheese Ball
Makes 12 hors d'oeuvre servings.

Balls made from processed cheese and rolled in nuts were also a must at 1960s parties. Modernized with fresh herbs and high-quality cheese, cheese balls still make a tasty and impressive display.

4 tablespoons minced fresh green onion, divided

3 tablespoons fresh minced parsley, divided

1 teaspoon fresh thyme leaves

1½ cups (12 ounces) Gervais cheese, or a combination of cream cheese and Neufchâtel

½ teaspoon Creole seasoning (purchased, or use recipe on pages 6–7)

1 clove garlic, finely minced

Crackers for serving

1. In a small bowl, combine 3 tablespoons green onion, 2 tablespoons parsley and thyme. Set aside.
2. In a medium bowl, use a spoon to cream together cheese, remaining tablespoon green onion, remaining tablespoon parsley, Creole seasoning, and garlic.
3. Shape cheese into a ball or a disc about 1½ inches thick. Place on a plate, and gently press herb mixture into

sides and on top. Wrap loosely and chill at least 4 hours. Serve with crackers.

Buffalo Meatballs with Blue Cheese Dip
Makes 60 meatballs.

This recipe is based on the original chicken hot-wing recipe invented in 1964 at the Anchor Bar in Buffalo, New York, where co-owner Teressa Bellissimo tossed disjointed, uncoated chicken wings into the fryer and drowned them in hot sauce. She then served her creation with celery from the antipasto tray and blue cheese dressing originally meant for salad. And chances are excellent the buffalo you'll use in this recipe really won't be buffalo, but bison, which is what used to abundantly roam the American West, and which is a member of the same Bovidae family as African buffalo, but not the same genus or species.

Blue Cheese Dip (makes 2 cups)

¾ cup sour cream

¾ cup crumbled blue cheese

2 tablespoons white vinegar

⅓ cup finely minced red onion

¼ cup finely minced green onion

½ teaspoon salt

¼ teaspoon ground black pepper

¼ teaspoon hot sauce

Meatballs

30 six-inch wooden skewers

2 pounds ground buffalo

2 large eggs

2 tablespoons finely minced garlic

⅓ cup finely sliced green onion

1 tablespoon tomato paste

½ cup breadcrumbs

1½ teaspoons salt

½ teaspoon ground black pepper

8 tablespoons (1 stick) butter, melted

⅔ cup Louisiana-style hot sauce

Celery and carrot sticks for serving

1. Mix Blue Cheese Dip ingredients together, and refrigerate until ready to serve.
2. Preheat oven to 400°F. Lay a sheet of parchment paper on a large cookie sheet or sheet pan, and set aside. Soak wooden skewers in water 15 minutes. (Meatballs can also be cooked unskewered and served in a chafing dish.)
3. While skewers are soaking, make meatballs by mixing together buffalo, eggs, garlic, green onion, tomato paste, breadcrumbs, salt, and black pepper. Use a tablespoon of mixture to form 1-inch balls. Thread 2 meatballs ½-inch apart on the lower half of each skewer. Place in a single layer on prepared pan, and bake until cooked through, 9–15 minutes.
4. In a small, deep bowl, mix together melted butter and hot sauce. Dip skewered meatballs into butter sauce, and place on a rimmed platter, with skewers sticking off edge of platter. Pour remaining hot sauce over meatballs.
5. Serve warm meatballs alongside celery, carrot sticks, and Blue Cheese Dip for dipping.

Daube Glacée

Makes a 2-quart mold, serving 12–16 as an hors d'oeuvre or 8 as an entrée.

If Dorian wants to stick to local specialties, he can whip up Daube Glacée, best described as a jellied mold of spiced meat, and a Creole dish that's been gracing party tables since at least the mid-1800s. This recipe's main ingredient is the French version of daube, a simmered roast, which was originally boiled with calves' and pigs' feet to form the gelatin. Admittedly, the dish is not as popular as it was fifty years ago. And, although it's rarely served in restaurants, it still pops up at home parties.

2 slices thick-cut bacon

1¾ teaspoons salt, divided

1 teaspoon ground black pepper, divided

1 teaspoon sugar

2 tablespoons white vinegar, divided

¼ cup minced parsley

1 clove finely minced garlic

1 (3-pound) boneless beef chuck roast

Creole Seasoning (purchased, or use recipe on pages 6–7)

2 tablespoons vegetable oil

1 medium onion, coarsely chopped

1 carrot, coarsely chopped

½ teaspoon cayenne pepper, divided

4 cups beef stock

3 envelopes unflavored powdered gelatin

Crackers or baguette slices for serving

1. Preheat oven to 325°F. Finely chop bacon, and combine it with 1 teaspoon salt, ½ teaspoon black pepper, sugar, 1 tablespoon vinegar, parsley, and garlic. Make several slits in roast, and stuff them with bacon mixture. Season outside of roast well with Creole Seasoning.

2. In a Dutch oven, heat oil over medium-high heat and sear roast well on all sides. Add onion and sauté 2 minutes. Add carrot, cayenne, and stock. Cover and bake until meat is very tender and falls apart, about 3–3½ hours.

3. Remove beef from pot. Strain cooking juices, reserving juice and discarding vegetables. (You should have about 4 cups juice. If short, add additional stock.) Skim as much fat off top as possible. Stir in remaining ¾ teaspoon salt, ½ teaspoon black pepper, 1 tablespoon vinegar, and ¼ teaspoon cayenne.

4. Dissolve gelatin in 1 cup warm water. Stir into beef juice, and set aside.

5. Remove visible fat from beef and discard. Finely chop beef.

6. Spray a 2-quart mold, bowl, or baking pan with cooking spray. Add half of chopped beef and half of beef juice. Gently add remainder of beef and remainder of juice. Cover tightly and chill at least 12 hours. Remove accumulated fat from top. Unmold onto a platter, and serve with crackers or baguette slices.

Deviled Eggs with Caviar
Makes 12 stuffed eggs.

During this era, stuffed just-about-anything appeared on most party tables, with tomatoes, mushrooms, and eggs leading in popularity. Deviled eggs went out of style for a while, but they've made a resurgence, with modern chefs adding interest with duck and quail eggs, along with innovative seasonings and frills, such as caviar. For this recipe, if fish roe isn't to your taste and you don't want to top your eggs with the usual paprika, dress them up with finely minced chipotle peppers or slivers of red or green bell pepper.

6 large eggs

3 tablespoons mayonnaise

2 tablespoons sour cream

¼ teaspoon ground dry mustard

1 tablespoon finely minced red onion

2 teaspoons minced green onion, tops only

1.75 ounces caviar

1. In a large saucepan, add eggs, and top with enough water so it covers them by at least 1 inch. Over high heat, bring water to a boil, boil 1 minute, and remove pan from heat. Cover pan, and let eggs sit 12 minutes. Run eggs under cold water while peeling.
2. Slice eggs in half crosswise, and remove yolks to a bowl. Mash yolks with a fork, and stir in mayonnaise, sour cream, mustard, red onion, and green onion. Spoon mixture into yolks, cover with plastic wrap, and chill 30 minutes to 8 hours.
3. Just before serving, spoon caviar on top of eggs.

> He [Gus Levy] even got a Christmas card every year from a peanut vendor who worked the parking lot across from Memorial Stadium in Baltimore. He was very well liked.
>
> —Gus Levy's thoughts.

Okay, so the peanut vendor who admires Mr. Levy lives in Baltimore, not New Orleans. But peanuts are a big part of southern cuisine and have been boiled and roasted in Louisiana homes for centuries. And they're also great party food.

Peanuts originated in South America, went to Europe with explorers, and finally found their way to North America. Dr. George Washington Carver, the early twentieth-century African American "stove-top chemist," is heralded for successfully replacing failed U.S. cotton crops with peanuts, and thereby cultivating the domestic industry.

Peppered Party Peanuts

Makes 2 cups.

1 tablespoon light olive oil
2 teaspoons chili powder
¼ teaspoon ground cumin
¼ teaspoon cayenne pepper
¼ teaspoon adobo or hot pepper flakes
½ teaspoon garlic powder
2 cups roasted and shelled unsalted peanuts
1 teaspoon coarse salt

1. Preheat oven to 350°F. Heat oil in a large skillet over medium heat. Stir in chili powder, cumin, cayenne, adobo flakes, and garlic powder.
2. Add peanuts to hot oil in skillet, and cook, stirring constantly, 5 minutes. Sprinkle with salt.
3. Transfer peanuts to a baking sheet, and roast 10 minutes. Serve warm, or cool completely and store in a tightly covered container at room temperature.

Roasted Peanuts

Makes 1 pound.

Plain old peanuts roasted in the shell are great fun at parties, and go especially well with beer.

1 pound raw, jumbo Virginia peanuts, washed and thoroughly dried
1 teaspoon fine salt

1. Preheat oven to 350° F. Spread peanuts in a large, rimmed sheet pan one layer deep. Roast 25 minutes, stirring once after 15 minutes.

2. Remove from oven, and toss peanuts with salt. Leave in pan to cool 10 minutes. (During cooling period peanuts will continue to cook and get crispy.) Serve warm or at room temperature.

. . . .

Retro Date and Pecan Pinwheel Cookies

Makes 4 dozen cookies.

. . . .

This swirly layered sweet is an example of "icebox cookies," cookies that require refrigeration before they can be sliced and baked, and which offer the advantage of baking only a wanted amount. Pinwheel cookies also eliminate the time-consuming need to cut out and decorate, and they were, therefore, extremely popular in the convenience-minded 1960s.

1 cup finely chopped dates

Grated rind of 1 medium lemon

1 teaspoon fresh lemon juice

1¼ cups sugar, divided

½ cup water

1 cup finely chopped pecans

2 cups cake flour

½ teaspoon baking powder

½ teaspoon iodized salt

8 tablespoons (1 stick) unsalted butter, at room temperature

1 large egg yolk

1 teaspoon vanilla extract

3 tablespoons milk

1. In a medium-sized saucepan, mix dates, lemon rind, lemon juice, ½ cup sugar, and water. Simmer, stirring often, until thick but still spreadable, about 5 minutes. Remove from heat, and stir in pecans. Cool to room temperature.

2. In a medium bowl, sift together flour, baking powder, and salt. Set aside.

3. In a large bowl, and using a mixer at medium-high speed, cream together butter and remaining ¾ cup sugar until light colored, about 2 minutes. Beat in egg yolk, vanilla, and milk until light and fluffy, another 2 minutes.

4. Stir flour mixture into butter mixture. Divide dough in half. On a lightly floured hard surface, roll each half into a 10 x 7-inch rectangle. Divide date mixture in half, and spread evenly over dough halves.

5. With the short ends facing you, tightly roll dough halves jellyroll-style. Wrap each dough log in plastic wrap, and chill at least 2 hours.

6. Preheat oven to 375°F. With a thin, sharp knife, slice dough into ¼-inch thick rounds, and bake on parchment-lined cookie sheets until edges are light brown, about 8–9 minutes. Cool on a rack.

. . . .

Mint Juleps for a Crowd

Makes 64 servings. Recipe is by Maureen Detweiler.

. . . .

New Orleanian Maureen Detweiler was a founder of the Tennessee Williams/New Orleans Literary Festival, which at its annual event features *Ignatius on Stage,* a reading of scenes from *A Confederacy of Dunces.* Detweiler also created this mint julep recipe, which has become a festival staple. She explains that she makes the drink's syrup with mint extract instead of fresh because

she would have to "corner the market" on mint to make such a large amount. The use of extract also fits in nicely with a party held in the 1960s, when just about anything processed was favored over fresh.

2 cups sugar

2 teaspoons pure mint extract (not peppermint)

2 drops green food coloring

Chipped ice

Bourbon whiskey

Fresh spearmint sprigs for garnish

1. To make mint syrup, in a 1-gallon container, add sugar, mint extract, and food coloring. Fill container with water to make 1 gallon, and stir until sugar is dissolved.

2. For each drink, fill a cup to the rim with ice. Pour 2 ounces bourbon and 2 ounces mint syrup over the ice. Garnish with a sprig of spearmint (and keep a container of swizzle sticks on the side so your profusion of guests can stir their own).

In the Kitchen with Irene Reilly

"There are wonderful opportunities for advancement, wonderful plans for the alert young man. The salary may soon change."

"You think so? Well, I'm still proud, babe. Take off your overcoat." Mrs. Reilly opened a can of Libby's stew and tossed it in the pot. "They got any cute girls working there?"

Ignatius thought of Miss Trixie and said, "Yes, there is one."

"Single?"

"She appears to be."

Mrs. Reilly winked at Ignatius and threw his overcoat on top of the cupboard.

"Look, honey, I put a fire under this stew. Open you a can of peas, and they's bread in the icebox."

—Ignatius and his mother, Irene, discussing his first day on the job at Levy Pants.

So here's Ignatius, arriving home after his first day at work as a file clerk at Levy Pants, and facing one of his mother's typical meals, one that requires very little cooking. But in this postwar explosion of frozen TV dinners and canned just-about-everything, Irene Reilly is fairly typical of a 1960s homemaker.

But maybe Mrs. Reilly doesn't cook much because she has an antique "Edwardian gas stove." In the 1960s, electric stoves were the thing to have; even Claude Robichaux urges Mrs. Reilly to get a "letrit range." Her refrigerator, too, is ancient. Described as having a cylindrical motor on top, it is likely a General Electric "Monitor Top," the nickname coming from the exposed compressor over the cabinet, and which supposedly resembled the Civil War gunship, the *Monitor*. The Monitor Top was first produced in 1927 and sold for the then-hefty sum of three hundred dollars. The last of this model was made in 1936.

The Bread in the Icebox

Living in the middle of what pop culture calls the "Wonder Bread years," the bread in the timeworn refrigerator could be a commercial loaf of soft, presliced white bread. Or, on the high end of the bread spectrum, Irene could be stashing a loaf of New Orleans–style French bread. If so, that long, unsliced loaf could have been baked at a variety of family-owned bakeries around at the time, including Leidenheimer's, which was founded back in 1896 and is still going strong.

French bread baked in New Orleans has a shatteringly crisp crust, with insides soft as air, and all this for reasons no one can explain scientifically. Is it the city's water? The humidity? Whatever's actually floating around in the air? Who knows? But for way more a century, this uniquely textured bread has been hard to replicate anywhere else.

And locals love New Orleans French bread, with fifty thousand loaves reportedly consumed per day. Much of that serves as the foundation for a proper poor boy. The hefty sandwich was created in 1929 by French Market grocers Clovis and Bennie Martin, two brothers who had tossed together the portable meal to give away free to the "poor boys" who were participating in a streetcar strike.

Interestingly, the creation of New Orleans's most important bakery product, French bread, is attributed to the city's German bakers, like the Leidenheimer family.

Mrs. Reilly's ancient "refrigerator with [a] cylindrical motor on top" was a GE Monitor Top, manufactured from 1927 to 1936.

Photo courtesy Brenda Whitenack

Bread in the seventeenth and eighteenth centuries was crucial to the French diet, and that dependence on *pain* (bread) came along with colonists to Louisiana. French bakers did operate the city's original bakeries, but their bread was relatively heavy and traditionally made in a dome-shaped cap style sold in weights of one, two, four, and five pounds. That all changed in the mid-1800s, when the loaf was made longer and received its trademark light, cotton-soft inside and crunchy, thin crust. And although no one has definite proof of who exactly made the innovation, it's universally credited to the city's Germans who, at the time, were dominating the baking industry.

Making Groceries

When New Orleanians go to the grocery store, they say they're "making groceries." And although we don't know where Irene Reilly buys her food, she could be driving fifteen minutes or so to the Gentilly neighborhood to browse around the 244,000-square-foot Schwegmann Brothers, opened in 1955 as the world's largest supermarket.

And depending on where she shopped for that yummy-sounding meal, she could have been given trading stamps, such as "S&H Green Stamps" and "Top Value Stamps." Back then, in an attempt to attract loyal customers, it was popular for grocers to offer stamps. And shoppers would eagerly take them home, lick the backs, paste the stamps into books, and redeem it all for kitchen appliances and other premiums. This practice continued through 1968, when customers tired of sales gimmicks and supermarkets decided it was cheaper to offer lower prices.

When adjusting for inflation, prices for Irene's groceries have changed either a little or a lot, all depending on what you're buying. Taking a look at a portion of Ignatius's 1963-era meal, the National Food Stores around town were selling a twenty-four-ounce can of Libby's stew for 49 cents. With the annual inflation rate from 1963 through 2014 at 4.07 percent, today that same stew would cost $3.76, about a dollar more than its contemporary price.

And what about those peas? Bell Super Market was advertising a fifteen-ounce can of Leseur green peas for 89 cents, a whopping $6.82 in 2014 dollars. So let's assume the cash-strapped Mrs. Reilly was talking about black-eyed peas (which are actually beans). At the time, Winn-Dixie was selling this revered southern legume for 10 cents a 16-ounce can, which today would cost a budget-friendly 77 cents.

Canned stew and peas aside, Irene Reilly is a 1960s homemaker using shortcuts that were considered nutritious ways to stretch a food dollar, and were extremely common. Even many restaurant chefs and so-called gourmet home cooks didn't think twice about throwing canned ingredients into sophisticated recipes. It wasn't until the early 1970s that California chef Alice Waters popularized the farm-to-table movement, which spurred many serious cooks to curtail their use of processed food. And this shift back to cooking from scratch is gaining steam with each passing day.

Thinking of the electric fryers, gas driers, mechanical mixers and beaters, waffle plates, and motorized rotisseries that seemed to be always whirring, grinding, beating, cooling, hissing, and broiling in the lunar kitchen of his wife, Rita, he wondered what Mrs. Reilly did in this sparse room.

—Officer Mancuso's thoughts while sitting at the Reilly kitchen table.

New Orleans French Bread
Makes 2 loaves.

Among her arsenal of gadgets, it's highly likely Rita Mancuso owns a standing mixer, an appliance that makes kneading any kind of bread a snap. But New Orleans French bread isn't just any kind of bread. Differing from anything found anywhere else, the crispy loaves baked in New Orleans are often compared to France's long, thin loaf known as a baguette (which, by the way, actually originated in Austria, and didn't reach France until the late 1800s). Despite the similarities, the New Orleans loaf is larger than the baguette, and it has a thinner, more brittle crust and cotton-candy soft crumb. New Orleans bakers also use hard wheat flour, whereas "Type 55," the typical flour used for baguettes in France, has a lower protein and gluten content. But both loaves are, however, traditionally cobbled together without preservatives. And in New Orleans that means they'll be stale the next day and just hard enough for making bread pudding and seafood and turkey stuffing.

2 teaspoons yeast

2 teaspoons sugar

1⅓ cups warm water (between 105 and 110°F)

2½–3 cups unbleached bread flour

1 tablespoon vegetable oil

1 teaspoon white vinegar

1 teaspoon iodized salt

1. In a large mixing bowl, combine yeast, sugar, and water. Allow to sit until yeast is foamy, about 5 minutes.

2. To the same bowl, add 2 cups flour. If using a standing mixer, use bread paddle and mix using low speed until flour absorbs moisture. By hand, stir until moisture is absorbed. Add ½ cup more flour, vegetable oil, vinegar, and salt, and knead on medium speed 8 minutes, or by hand on a hard surface 10 minutes. Dough should be very soft, and slightly sticky and tacky. Add more flour only if absolutely necessary and only after kneading a few minutes, which will make dough stiffer.

3. Lightly grease your hands, and roll the sticky dough into a smooth ball. Place into a large greased bowl, and cover surface with greased plastic wrap. Allow to rise in a warm place 1–1½ hours. Dough is ready if you press through the plastic wrap with your finger and the indentation remains.

4. Punch dough down, and roll into 2 loaves, each about 12 inches long. (Commercially sold French bread ranges in size from the 2½-inch roll known as a pistolette to 24-inch poor boy loaves, so shape as you desire.) Line a large cookie sheet with parchment paper, and place loaves on lined sheet. Cover loosely with a slightly damp, lightweight cotton towel (not terrycloth), and allow to rise until at least doubled, 1–1½ hours.

5. Place oven rack on the center of oven. Steam makes the crust crisp, so put a large baking pan on lowest oven rack and preheat oven to 425°F. Five minutes before putting bread in oven, pour 1 cup hot water into the empty baking pan. For an even crisper crust, lightly spray loaves with water. Bake loaves 10 minutes; then lower oven temperature to 350°F. Continue baking until golden brown, about 20–25 more minutes. Remove to a rack to cool.

6. For the crispest possible crust, remove loaves from oven 5 minutes before they're done and allow to cool completely. When ready to serve, heat oven back to 350°F, lay loaves directly on the center oven rack, and bake 5 minutes.

Soft White Rolls

Makes 8 large rolls.

These rolls are reminiscent of the big fluffy ones served in many school lunchrooms during the time Ignatius would have been in elementary and high school.

1 cup whole milk

4 tablespoons (½ stick) butter, divided, plus additional for coating plan

2 tablespoons honey

1 teaspoon iodized salt

1 package (2¼ teaspoons) yeast

2 tablespoons lukewarm water

2½–3 cups sifted bread flour

1. In a small saucepan, bring milk to a boil. Remove from heat, and add 2 tablespoons butter, honey, and salt. Cool to lukewarm.

2. Soften yeast in the lukewarm water, and add to milk mixture.

3. In bowl of a standing mixer, combine milk mixture and 2½ cups flour. With dough hook attachment, beat on low speed, and add enough remaining flour to make a soft dough. (Dough should come clean from sides of bowl but yet be soft.) Raise mixer head to upright position, and put a sheet of greased plastic wrap directly on top of dough. Let rest 10 minutes.

4. Remove plastic wrap and knead dough on medium speed 8 minutes.

5. Put greased plastic wrap directly on top of dough, and let rise in a warm place until doubled in bulk, about 1½ hours.

6. Butter an 11 x 7-inch baking pan. Melt remaining 2 tablespoons butter and set aside. Turn dough onto a floured board, and knead until surface is smooth. Divide dough into 8 equal pieces. Roll each portion into a ball, brush each ball with melted butter, and place in prepared pan. Cover with a towel, and let rise until doubled in bulk, 30–40 minutes.

7. About 10 minutes before rolls have finished rising, preheat oven to 375°F. Brush rolls with remaining melted butter, and bake 15 to 20 minutes, until dark golden brown. Let sit at least 10 minutes before serving.

· ·

Fluffy Buttermilk Biscuits

Makes 8 biscuits.

· ·

If Mrs. Reilly cooks biscuits at all, they probably come out of a twist can, a convenience extremely popular in the 1960s. But canned biscuits just can't compare to properly made scratch biscuits. And they're especially delectable when made from so-called "soft" southern flour made from red winter wheat.

2 cups soft southern wheat flour, such as White Lily or Martha White (substitute 1 cup cake flour and 1 cup all-purpose flour)

2 teaspoons sugar

2 teaspoons baking powder

½ teaspoon baking soda

¾ teaspoon iodized salt

6 tablespoons cold unsalted butter, cut into ¼-inch pieces

¾ cup well-shaken buttermilk

2 tablespoons water

1. Preheat oven to 375°F. Sift together flour, sugar, baking powder, soda, and salt into a large bowl. Add butter, and work it in with a pastry blender or your fingers until mixture resembles coarse meal.

2. Stir buttermilk and water together. With a fork, stir buttermilk mixture into flour until just moist. Transfer dough onto a well-floured, hard surface, and fold dough over itself 4 times. Pat dough out ¾-inch thick.

3. Cut out biscuits with a 2½ -inch floured cutter, pressing straight down and re-flouring for each biscuit. Place on an ungreased baking sheet. Bake until pale golden, 12–15 minutes. Serve warm.

"Mother doesn't cook," Ignatius said dogmatically. "She burns."

—Ignatius to Darlene.

No-Cook Creole Tomato Soup

Makes 1 quart.

This recipe uses one of summer's most popular vegetables, tomatoes, in a soup so easy even Mrs. Reilly won't have an excuse not to make it. And although there is a variety of tomato known as Creole, the famous Creole tomato that appears in markets is actually a medium to large, usually imperfect, tomato that comes from the varieties of species that grow in the unique conditions of the South Louisiana river parishes.

  2 pounds ripe Creole tomatoes, trimmed and quartered
  ½ cup chopped red onion
  ½ cup chopped red bell pepper
  ¼ cup minced fresh cilantro
  2 tablespoons red wine vinegar
  1 teaspoon sugar
  Salt, ground black pepper, and cayenne to taste

Combine all ingredients in a blender, and process until smooth. Cover and chill thoroughly, at least 4 hours and up to 2 days.

Fortuna's Black-Eyed Pea Hummus

Serves 8.

For ages, the black-eyed pea has been eaten in China, India, and Africa, but when this legume reached the antebellum American South, it was used primarily for cattle feed. Now black-eyed peas are a common side dish throughout the South, as well as a "good luck" staple for New Year's dinner.

The black-eyed pea's reputation for good fortune may have started with Sephardic Jews who arrived in Georgia in the 1700s, and who considered the lowly pea a lucky food for the New Year. There's also a totally undocumented legend that the black-eye's popularity among humans rose tremendously after Major General William T. Sherman scorched Georgia from Atlanta to Savannah during the Civil War, and took everything edible except stashes of the assumed nonedible fodder. Supposedly, surviving Georgians felt lucky the "insane" Sherman had left them anything and celebrated New Year's Day 1866 with their left-behind peas.

The following recipe turns a can of plain black-eyed peas into something worthy of the most elegant New Year's party. And it would also make a great starter for Ignatius's meal of canned beef stew.

  ¼ cup well-stirred tahini
  ¼ cup freshly squeezed lemon juice
  1 (15-ounce) can black-eyed peas, drained and rinsed
  1 large garlic clove, minced
  3 tablespoons olive oil
  ½ teaspoon salt
  ¼ teaspoon ground turmeric

Pinch ground white pepper

Few dashes hot sauce

Olive oil, paprika, fresh minced parsley, and pita triangles for garnish

Tortilla chips or raw vegetables for serving

1. Combine tahini and lemon juice in the bowl of a food processor, and process 30 seconds. Scrape sides and bottom, and process 30 more seconds.
2. Add half of black-eyed peas, along with garlic, olive oil, salt, turmeric, white pepper, and hot sauce, and process 30 seconds. Scrape sides and bottom of bowl, add remainder of peas, and process 30 more seconds.
3. If hummus seems lumpy and thick, add water a tablespoon at a time, processing 30 seconds in between. Transfer to a bowl, cover tightly, and refrigerate at least 1 hour for flavors to develop. Can be made and refrigerated up to 3 days ahead.
4. To serve, smooth out onto a plate and top with olive oil, sprinkles of paprika and parsley. Serve with pita triangles, tortilla chips, or raw vegetables.

> "That old lady sure drank up a lotta beer."
>
> —Darlene, talking to Burma Jones about Mrs. Reilly's visit to the Night of Joy.

Irish Channel Beef and Beer Stew

Makes 6 servings.

Beer is a typical ingredient in Irish stew, the one dish just about everyone associates with the waves of Irish immigrants who came to America in the 1800s. The New Orleans Irish Channel is a largely working-class neighborhood just south of the city's refined Garden District. The area was settled mostly by Irish immigrants, who, fleeing British tyranny, began arriving in Catholic-friendly New Orleans at the end of the eighteenth century. Although many were successful and bought property and businesses, the majority were uneducated and ended up doing menial labor. This backbreaking work took a nasty turn beginning in 1830, when the city's American leaders decided to compete with rival French merchants and dig a shipping canal from Lake Pontchartrain through the swamps and to the city's American sector. Since slaves were considered too valuable to do such possibly fatal work, jobs for what was to be called the New Basin Canal went to the Irish, who were paid one dollar a day. By the time the project was completed, cholera, yellow fever, and snakes had killed an estimated 8,000 to 30,000. Many bodies were buried, or just left, right where they'd fallen in the canal.

In 1990, the Irish Cultural Society of New Orleans erected a Celtic cross at the end of West End Boulevard in honor of the fallen workers. So here's to the Irish of New Orleans, not only for their delicious stew, but also for their unimaginable sacrifices.

This recipe calls for beef, a much more popular stew ingredient in Louisiana than the traditional mutton. And, for those who are wondering, even though Mrs. Reilly wasn't serving rice, throughout South Louisiana, stew is virtually always eaten over rice, even if the recipe contains potatoes.

1½ pounds beef chuck, cut into 1½-inch cubes

Salt, ground black pepper, and cayenne pepper

5 tablespoons vegetable oil, divided

¼ cup all-purpose flour

1 medium onion, chopped

1 stalk celery, chopped

1 small bell pepper, seeded and chopped

1 clove garlic, minced

3 cups beef stock

1 cup beer, divided (Guinness is traditional)

1 cup tomato sauce

1 teaspoon fresh thyme

½ teaspoon minced fresh rosemary

4 cups russet potatoes, peeled and cut into 1-inch pieces

2 cups carrot, chopped into ½-inch pieces

¼ cup parsley

Cooked rice for serving (recipes follow)

1. Season beef with salt, black pepper, and cayenne. Heat 2 tablespoons oil in a large, heavy pot over medium-high heat. Add beef, sear all sides, and remove to a bowl.

2. Make a roux by adding remaining 3 tablespoons oil and flour to pot and stirring constantly over medium heat until deep brown, 4–5 minutes. Remove pot from heat, and add onion, celery, and bell pepper. Stir constantly 30 seconds. Return pot to medium heat, and stir in garlic, stock, ½ cup beer, tomato sauce, thyme, rosemary, and reserved beef and accumulated juices. Bring to a boil; then lower to a simmer. Cover and cook 1½ hours.

3. Taste to see if stew needs more salt and pepper. Add potatoes and carrots to pot, and simmer, covered, an additional 30 minutes.

4. Remove cover from pot, stir in remaining ½ cup beer, and simmer until thickened, 10–15 minutes. Taste again for seasoning. Stir in parsley, and serve over hot, cooked rice.

Steamed Plain White or Brown Rice
Makes 3 cups.

Although electric Japanese rice cookers came to Louisiana in the late 1950s–60s, many New Orleans cooks still steam rice the old-fashioned way, in a covered pot on the stove, which produces grains that are slightly sticky.

1 cup raw white or brown rice

2 cups water for white, or 2½ cups for brown

½ teaspoon salt

1. In a medium, heavy-bottomed pot, stir in all ingredients and bring to a fast boil. Lower heat to a bare simmer. Cover tightly, and cook until all liquid is absorbed, when

no more liquid bubbles up between the grains, about 20 minutes for white rice, and 40 minutes for brown rice.

2. To complete steaming process, remove pot from heat and allow to sit, tightly covered, 15 minutes. (Don't be tempted to take off the cover.) Fluff with a fork and serve.

Boiled White or Brown Rice
Makes 3 cups.

This recipe produces grains that stay separate.

1½ quarts water for white, or 3 quarts for brown
1 teaspoon salt
1 cup raw white or brown rice

1. Bring water and salt to a boil, and stir in rice. Cover and simmer 15 minutes for white rice and 30 minutes for brown rice. To lessen chance of gumminess, do not stir rice while it's cooking.

2. Remove from heat, and let sit, covered, 5 minutes for white rice and 10 minutes for brown. Strain well. To completely dry boiled rice, spread warm, well-drained grains on a cookie sheet and let sit 10 minutes.

Patrolman Mancuso's Pork and Beans
Makes 6 servings.

Introduced in the 1880s, pork and beans in a can is often touted as the first canned convenience food.

1½ cups dried navy beans
1½ pounds boneless country-style pork ribs
2 teaspoons Creole seasoning (purchased, or use recipe on pages 6–7)
3 slices thick-cut bacon, cut into ½-inch pieces

Patrolman Mancuso looked at the Plymouth and saw the deep crease in its roof and the fender, filled with concave circles, that was separated from the body by three or four inches of space. VAN CAMP'S PORK AND BEANS was printed on the piece of cardboard taped across the hole that had been the rear window.

—Officer Mancuso at Ignatius's house on Constantinople Street, there to see if he can help that "poor Widow Reilly," who has just wrecked her car.

1 cup chopped onion

½ cup chopped green bell pepper

2 cloves garlic, minced

4½ cups chicken stock

2 tablespoons white vinegar

1 (14.5-ounce) can diced tomatoes,
    with liquid

2 tablespoons tomato paste

3 tablespoons molasses or honey

2 tablespoons Creole mustard, or any
    coarse-grain mustard

2 teaspoons chili powder

4 teaspoons minced fresh sage

1. Pick out anything that doesn't look like a bean from beans. Rinse beans, and transfer to a large pot. Cover with 2 inches cold, unsalted water; bring to a boil, and cook 2 minutes. Cover pot, remove from heat, and allow to sit 1 hour. (Alternatively, let beans soak overnight.) Drain beans and rinse again. Set aside.

2. Preheat oven to 300°F. Slice pork into 1-inch pieces, and sprinkle all over with Creole seasoning.

3. In a Dutch oven set over medium heat, render bacon until oil is released but bacon is not brown. Remove bacon, and sear pork in bacon fat until lightly brown, about 3 minutes. Add onion and bell pepper, and sauté 1 minute. Add garlic, and sauté 15 seconds.

4. Stir in stock and soaked beans, scraping up any bits that may have formed. Add bacon, vinegar, tomatoes and liquid, tomato paste, molasses, mustard, chili powder, and sage. Bake, covered and stirring occasionally, until beans are tender. Depending on how long the beans have been sitting around dried, this should take 2–3 hours. Serve warm.

"You know that poor old colored lady sells them pralines in front the cemetery? Aw, Ignatius. I really feel sorry for her. The other day I seen her wearing a little cloth coat full of holes, and it was cold out. . . .

So, you know what I done, Ignatius. I give her a quarter and I says, 'Here, darling, go buy you a trinket for your little grandchirren.'"

—Irene Reilly to Ignatius.

In Old New Orleans, the African American woman selling her creamy, caramel-tinged candy on the street would have been known as a *pralinière*. And, although the woman in *Dunces* is certainly impoverished by today's standards, in the nineteenth century she would have been hailed as an entrepreneur who was taking advantage of a unique merchandising opportunity legally available to *les gens de couleur libres*, New Orleans's free people of color.

The praline itself was created as a sugar-coated almond confection in seventeenth-century France and is generally attributed to Clement Lassagne, personal chef to César, Duc de Choiseul, Comte du Plessis-Praslin. It is believed that, when the Ursuline nuns came to New Orleans in 1727, they brought the French recipe for pralines and substituted native pecans for the almonds. Perfecting the recipe supposedly became a required lesson for a group of students known as "casket girls," young women brought from France and intended to marry French colonists. The story goes that, as they married and scattered throughout South Louisiana, these new brides spread the knowledge of praline-making.

Perfectly Creamy Pralines

Makes 2 pounds candy.

1½ cups granulated sugar

1½ cups light brown sugar

1 cup evaporated milk

½ teaspoon salt

¼ teaspoon cream of tartar

4 tablespoons (½ stick) unsalted butter

1 tablespoon vanilla extract

3 cups pecan halves

1. Lay 2½ feet of parchment paper on a hard surface. In a 3-quart, heavy-bottomed saucepan, combine sugars, evaporated milk, salt, and cream of tartar. Stir while bringing to a boil over medium-high heat. Lower heat to medium, and simmer, without stirring, until mixture reaches the soft-ball stage, or 238°F.

2. Remove pan from heat, and stir in butter and vanilla. Keep stirring and, when mixture starts to get creamy, stir in pecans.

3. Quickly drop candies onto parchment paper by the tablespoonful. Allow to cool until firm. Store in an airtight container up to 2 weeks.

Figs and Proscuitto with Boursin

Makes 24 canapés.

Although figs seem as southern as pecans, they're actually native to the eastern Mediterranean around the region of western Turkey. It is likely the fig was the first plant humans grew, with evidence of fig consumption going back to as early as 3000 BC. In the sixteenth century, the Spanish brought fig trees to the New World, where they quickly adapted to semitropical Louisiana and today grow happily and without much attention. And if Mrs. Reilly's fig trees are only dormant and eventually come back to life, she can try out this recipe, which requires very little cooking skill.

Boursin is the trademarked name of a soft, fresh, herbed and spiced cheese invented in 1957 by a cheesemaker named Francois Boursin in Normandy, France. If Boursin isn't available, try making your own version with a variety of minced herbs and well-drained homemade Creole cream cheese (recipe follows).

In the back yard he [Patrolman Mancuso] found Mrs. Reilly hanging a spotted and yellowed sheet on a line that ran through the bare fig trees.

1 carton (5.2 ounces) Boursin cheese (herb or pepper)

24 small plain crackers, such as Melba toast

8 thin slices proscuitto di Parma (ham)

12 ripe figs, stemmed and halved lengthwise

24 mint leaves

1. Spread 1 teaspoon Boursin on top of each cracker.
2. Cut each slice of proscuitto lengthwise into 3 pieces each, for a total of 24. Wrap pieces of proscuitto around crackers and Boursin, overlapping on top.
3. Press a fig half into top of each proscuitto-wrapped cracker. Garnish with a mint leaf. Serve immediately.

Creole Cream Cheese

Makes 5 cups.

Creole cream cheese is a single-curd, mildly tart artisan cheese that in the nineteenth century was sold by female African American street vendors known as cream cheese women. And until the advent of refrigeration it was a staple in humid South Louisiana, where resourceful home cooks made the most of unpasteurized milk that had soured and curdled into clabber. Many locals still remember hanging cloth pouches full of milk curds in cool spots, such as under live oak trees and porches.

In the time of Igantius, the 1960s, Creole cream cheese would have still been extremely common on New Orleans breakfast tables, where it was traditionally served with cream, sugar, and strawberries. It was around the 1970s that pasteurization laws and dietary habits changed and Creole cream cheese went out of fashion. Local cooking personality Poppy Tooker has been credited with bringing back the Creole cream cheese tradition by teaching classes on making the spe-

cialty and by encouraging local farmers to once again produce and market it.

1 tablet rennet, or 4 drops liquid rennet

1 cup cultured buttermilk, at room temperature

1 gallon whole or skimmed milk, at room temperature and preferably not homogenized

5 (1- to 2-cup) molds made from plastic cups or plastic food tubs, optional

Cheesecloth

1. Combine rennet and buttermilk until mixed well. Stir buttermilk mixture and milk together in a large stainless-steel or glass bowl. Cover and let sit undisturbed at warm room temperature (75–80 degrees) for 24 hours. The milk should have separated into a large curd (the coagulated milk) and whey (the watery part).
2. Line a large colander with 3 layers of cheesecloth that hang over the colander rim by at least 3 inches all around. Scoop curds into colander, and allow to drain 30 minutes. Gather edges of cheesecloth over cheese, tie a knot over cheese, and hang the pouch in a cool place to drain, either on a sink faucet or over a bowl. The longer the cheese drips, the firmer it will be.
3. Cheese can be consumed and stored at this stage. To make it even more firm, punch several holes in the bottom of the 5 plastic containers and line each with a layer of cheesecloth. Pack the drained curds into the molds. Place filled molds in a rimmed pan, cover each mold, and refrigerate at least 8 hours. Creole cream cheese can be refrigerated up to 2 weeks.

Ignatius was feeling around in the cookie jar.

—While Ignatius and his mother are trying to figure out how to get more than a thousand dollars to pay for damages her automobile accident caused to a building.

Praline-Topped Sweet Potato Cookies

Makes 3 dozen.

A dollop of praline icing tops these soft, puffed, gingery cookies made with sweet potatoes, one of Louisiana's most important agricultural crops. Sweet potatoes originated in Central America and are often called yams, but aren't even closely related to what is actually a much larger African tuber. Louisiana's commercial sweet potato growers started using the term "yam" as a marketing tool in 1937, when scientists at Louisiana State University developed a moist, sweet variety that was an improvement over the drier, more mealy varieties grown in America's East.

2¼ cups all-purpose flour

2 teaspoons baking powder

½ teaspoon iodized salt

1½ teaspoons ground ginger

1 teaspoon ground cinnamon

1 teaspoon ground allspice

10 tablespoons (1¼ sticks) unsalted butter, at room temperature

¾ cup light brown sugar

¼ cup granulated sugar

2 large eggs, room temperature

1 cup cooked, mashed sweet potato

1 teaspoon vanilla extract

½ cup finely chopped candied ginger

Praline Icing (recipe follows)

1. Preheat oven to 350°F, and line a cookie sheet with parchment paper. In a medium bowl, sift together flour, baking powder, salt, ground ginger, cinnamon, and allspice. Set aside.

2. In a large bowl, use medium electric mixer speed to cream together butter, brown sugar, and granulated sugar until fluffy, about 3 minutes. Beat in eggs 1 at a time, scraping down sides and beating well after each addition. Add sweet potato and vanilla, and beat on medium speed 1 minute. Stir in candied ginger.

3. Gently stir in flour mixture until it is completely absorbed. Chill dough ½ hour.

4. Drop by rounded tablespoons 2 inches apart onto prepared cookie sheet, and bake until just brown around the edges, 14–18 minutes. (Refrigerate dough between batches.)

5. Remove cookies to a rack and cool completely before spreading tops with Praline Icing.

Praline Icing   Makes 2½ cups

8 tablespoons (1 stick) unsalted butter

1½ cups light brown sugar, packed

½ cup half-and-half

¼ teaspoon salt

1 teaspoon pure vanilla extract

2 cups powdered sugar

1 cup finely chopped pecans

1. In a large, heavy-bottomed saucepan over medium heat, stir together butter, brown sugar, half-and-half, and salt. When mixture comes to a full boil, immediately set heat at low and cook exactly two minutes without stirring.

2. Remove from heat, and stir in vanilla and powdered sugar. Beat with a wooden spoon until frosting reaches spreading consistency but is not completely cool. Stir in pecans. If icing seems too stiff, add more half-and-half. Ice cookies immediately.

Santa Battaglia, or How to Cook Like a Sicilian

"I'm only happy when I'm scrubbing my floors and cooking my food," Santa told her guests. "I love to fix a big pot of meatballs or jumbalaya with shrimps."

—Santa Battaglia, hosting her matchmaking party for Mr. Robichaux and Mrs. Reilly.

By far, the most accomplished cook in *A Confederacy of Dunces* is Irene Reilly's friend Santa Battaglia, who has "strong Italian blood." Santa is obviously descended from the large waves of Sicilians who immigrated to New Orleans from 1880 to 1920, an influx that had at one time made New Orleans home to the largest population of Sicilians in the United States.

In the early days, most Italians in New Orleans worked producing or selling cotton, seafood, and vegetables. Many even created large produce businesses, which eventually grew to dominate the local industry. Sticking tightly together, they lived in the French Quarter and in the neighborhoods known as the Ninth Ward and the Irish Channel. A huge portion, too, settled in the Independence area north of New Orleans, where they farmed produce, including their celebrated strawberries.

The Sicilians also brought with them the expertise to craft hearty breads, including *taralli* (sort of like a crunchy Italian bagel). They taught New Orleans to love red tomato sauce, locally known as "red gravy," a staple still on Sunday dinner tables. Santa's ancestors were also experts at making sweets, such as *cannoli, sfingi* (deep-fried dough rolled in sugar), and *pignolati* (pastry balls rolled in hot honey). Then there's the multitude of cookies, such as *biscotti* and *amaretti,* and cookies made with anise, sesame seeds, and dried fruits. And don't forget the grotesquely named *Fave dei Morti,* beans of the dead, and *Orso di Mortis,* bones of the dead, both served for All Saints Day and All Souls Day.

Another tradition Sicilians introduced to New Orleans is the custom of building elaborate, food-laden St. Joseph's Altars. Today still, on every March 19 local Italians give thanks to the Catholic "San Giuseppe" for having prevented a famine in the Middle Ages. A palm branch over the door to a church or home means everyone is invited in to taste. Among a breathtaking myriad of foods are all sorts of pastas, as well as breads shaped like sandals, ladders, saws, palms, or wreaths, and elaborately decorated cookies. These traditional foods are placed on an altar shaped like a cross, with three levels honoring the Holy Trinity. Chances are extremely good Santa Battaglia and her family participate in a St. Joseph's Altar.

The Italians were prominent in the seafood industry, and through Battaglia's heavily Yat-inflected words we learn how to crack open "ersters" or, to anyone outside Orleans Parish, "oysters." Remember Toole's splendid description of a Yat—"that accent that occurs south of New Jersey only in New Orleans, that Hoboken near the Gulf of Mexico." The term "Yat" comes from the salutation "Where y'at?" a greeting lower- and middle-class Irish, Italian, and German-descended New Orleanians supposedly used ad nauseum, although no one today remembers ever hearing it. Anyway, the Yat accent still is certainly heard around town. And it's a good bet the speakers or their family knows a thing or two about cobbling together big pots of meatballs, as well as how to magnificently cook seafood and sweets.

Marinated Garlic Olives

Makes 2 cups.

Instead of serving a ho-hum jar of stuffed green olives, Santa should serve an antipasto that includes olives spiced up with a simple marinade.

> A fork stuck out of the open bottle of olives that she had placed on a tin tray on top of the covered and folded rollaway bed.
>
> —Hors d'oeuvres at Santa Battaglia's party.

16 ounces kalamata or large green olives, with brine

⅓ cup olive oil

1 tablespoon minced garlic

1 tablespoon minced fresh oregano

1 rosemary sprig

Drain olives, reserving ½ cup brine. In a quart jar, combine reserved brine, olive oil, garlic, oregano, and rosemary. Pack olives in marinade. Cover and refrigerate at least 24 hours. Keeps 1 month in the refrigerator.

Refrigerator Okra Pickles

Makes 3 pints.

Easy-to-make pickled okra would be a great addition to Santa's tin hors d'oeuvre tray. Okra is another one of those vegetables that came with the slave trade. The African word for okra in the Bantu language of Central Africa is *quingombo,* which, over time, was likely shortened to the word for the famous New Orleans soup, gumbo.

1 dry quart small, fresh okra (3–4 inches long)

3 cloves peeled fresh garlic

3 sprigs fresh oregano

2 cups apple cider vinegar

2 cups water

2 tablespoons, plus 1 teaspoon salt

1 tablespoon sugar

1 tablespoon dry mustard seeds

1 teaspoon black peppercorns

¾ teaspoon dried red pepper flakes

1. Pack cleaned okra, caps down and pointed tips up, into 3 sterilized 1-pint canning jars. To each jar add 1 clove garlic and 1 sprig oregano.
2. In a medium saucepan, bring to a boil vinegar, water, salt, sugar, mustard seeds, black peppercorns, and red pepper flakes. Lower to a simmer, and cook 5 minutes. Pour hot liquid into jars over okra and all the way to the top. Close jars loosely with tops.
3. Let okra stand at room temperature at least 2 hours. Close jars tighter; then refrigerate at least 2 weeks and up to 1 month.

Basic Tomato Bruschetta

Makes 12. Recipe is by Sofia Rizzo, who was born in Sicily and immigrated to New Orleans in the 1920s.

Santa could really wow her guests with a colorful, yet simple-to-put-together tray of bruschetta, the popular Italian grilled bread. This starter's name actually originates from the Italian verb *bruscare,* to roast over coals, and it began hundreds of years ago in Italy's Tuscan region as merely toasted, stale bread drizzled with olive oil. To fancy up this recipe, add chopped olives, or roasted or sautéed vegetables.

Half a loaf Italian bread, cut into 12 slices, ¾-inch each

2 medium tomatoes, seeded and diced

1 clove garlic, minced

¼ teaspoon salt

½ teaspoon fresh oregano, or ¼ teaspoon dried

3 tablespoons olive oil

1 tablespoon balsamic vinegar

1. Toast bread slices under a broiler on both sides until golden brown.
2. In a medium bowl, combine tomatoes, garlic, salt, oregano, olive oil, and vinegar. Top bread slices with tomato mixture, and serve.

Bon Ton Café's Bayou Jambalaya

Makes 4 servings. Adapted from a recipe from Wayne Pierce of the venerable Bon Ton Restaurant, on Magazine Street since 1953.

Jambalaya is a takeoff of the Spanish one-pot rice dish paella. As with Santa's "jambalaya with shrimps," New Orleans jambalaya historically contains seafood, and it is typically colored red from tomatoes. In the rural Cajun parishes, the dish is often made with game and sausage and no tomato, and is usually dark brown. More and more, the spicier, heartier, brown version is served in New Orleans restaurants.

The Bon Ton's jambalaya recipe takes the traditional New Orleans Creole shrimp-and-rice concept and enhances it with crawfish. It also deviates from the typical New Orleans–style jambalaya by being made without tomatoes and calling for precooked rice, thus eliminating the chance of the grains cooking unevenly and the seafood being overcooked. Even though the technique is not so common any more, early jambalayas were often cooked with leftover and, therefore, "precooked" rice.

The name "jambalaya" may have come from the Provençal chicken and rice stew called *jambalaia.* Or it could have originated with the words for a prime ingredient in early jambalayas, ham, in Spanish, *jamón,* and in French *jambon,* along with the African word for rice, *ya-ya.*

12 tablespoons (1½ sticks) unsalted butter

¾ cup chopped green onion

¾ cup chopped yellow onion

1 tablespoon chopped garlic

1 pound fresh medium Gulf shrimp, peeled and deveined

1 pound Louisiana crawfish tails, with the natural fat

1 teaspoon sweet paprika

Salt and ground black pepper

4 cups cooked white rice

¼ cup chopped parsley

1 cup water

Fresh parsley sprigs and lemon slices for garnish

1. Melt butter over medium heat in a large skillet or pot. Remove ¼ cup of melted butter, and set aside. Simmer remaining butter in skillet 30 seconds. Add green and yellow onions, and sauté until yellow onion is limp. Add garlic and sauté 30 seconds.

2. Add shrimp, and stir until shrimp are just cooked through, when curled and pink, about 3 minutes. Stir in crawfish, along with fat, and paprika, and salt and pepper to taste. Mix well, and check for seasoning.

3. Fold in cooked rice, chopped parsley, reserved ¼ cup melted butter, and water. Over low heat, stir mixture until rice absorbs the liquid. Check again for seasoning.

4. Serve on a warm plate, and garnish with a fresh sprig of parsley and lemon.

Garlicky Crab, Crawfish and Shrimp-Stuffed Eggplants

Makes 4 entrée servings.

The Spanish brought eggplants to America in the seventeenth century. At the time, Europeans knew enough about members of the nightshade family of plants to know the leaves are toxic, so they assumed the poison went all the way to the plant's fruit. That erroneous thinking changed in the early twentieth century, when the Italians came en masse and showed America it was safe to eat eggplant, which had, until then, been mostly grown here as an ornamental.

2 eggplants (¾–1 pound each)

3 tablespoons olive oil

1 cup chopped onion

½ cup chopped bell pepper

½ pound peeled crawfish tails, with fat (or substitute shrimp)

1 pound raw shrimp, peeled, deveined, and coarsely chopped

1 tablespoon minced fresh garlic

¼ cup dry white wine

1½ cups breadcrumbs, preferably made from stale French bread, divided

½ teaspoon salt

½ teaspoon ground black pepper

¼ teaspoon cayenne pepper

2 teaspoons minced fresh oregano, or 1 teaspoon dried

1 tablespoon minced fresh basil

¼ cup minced fresh parsley

¼ cup, plus 2 tablespoons grated Parmesan cheese

1 egg, beaten

½ pound crab meat

1 tablespoon unsalted butter, melted

1. Preheat oven to 350°F. Halve eggplants lengthwise, keeping stems intact. Using a paring knife, score the cut insides in a crisscross pattern, making sure to not cut down through skin. Using same knife or a grapefruit

"Aarff," Santa belched. "I think I put too much garlic in them stuffed eggplants, but I got a heavy hand with garlic. Even my granchirren tell me, they say, 'Hey, Maw-maw, you sure got a heavy hand with garlic.'

"Ain't that sweet," Mrs. Reilly said of the gourmet grandchildren.

"I thought the eggplants was fine," Mr. Robichaux said.

spoon, scoop out the pulp, leaving ¼ inch on the skin. Chop pulp into ½-inch pieces, and reserve both pulp and skin.

2. Heat oil in a large skillet or Dutch oven over moderately high heat, and sauté onion and bell pepper until softened. Add crawfish and shrimp, and sauté until just cooked through, about 1 minute. Stir in eggplant pulp, garlic, and wine, and sauté, stirring constantly, until eggplant is just tender and most of liquid is evaporated, about 2 minutes.

3. Remove skillet from heat, and stir in 1 cup breadcrumbs, salt, black pepper, cayenne, oregano, basil, parsley, ¼ cup Parmesan cheese, and beaten egg. Gently stir in crab meat.

4. Mound stuffing into eggplant shells, and top with a mixture of remaining ½ cup breadcrumbs, 2 tablespoons Parmesan, and melted butter. Place in a lightly oiled baking pan, and bake until brown, about 30 minutes. Let cool 5–15 minutes before serving.

Garlic and Crumb-Stuffed Artichokes with Garlic Dipping Sauce

Makes 4 whole stuffed artichokes. Adapted from a recipe by Phyllis "Mama" Monistere Fresina.

The artichoke has been cultivated in Sicily for more than two thousand years, and is thought to be that region's only indigenous vegetable. But it was the French who first brought this thistly member of the *asteraceae* family to New Orleans. The Gallic colonials had learned about the artichoke from their former queen, that food-obsessed Catherine de Medici, who convinced her loyal French subjects it was an aphrodisiac. It was New Orleans's later influx of Sicilian immigrants, like the Fresinas, who raised the artichoke to rock star status, particularly with this eye-popping stuffed creation.

It's also interesting that in Sicily you'd be hard-pressed to find stuffed artichokes. Apparently, when the Sicilians arrived in New Orleans they discovered the French cooking artichokes stuffed with meat. So the Italians started stuffing every single leaf with a garlicky, cheesy breadcrumb-and-olive-oil mixture that screams "Italy," and now most everyone just assumes the dish had to have originated in Sicily.

4 medium artichokes

6 slices whole-wheat bread

¾ cup shredded Romano cheese

¾ teaspoon crushed dried basil

½ teaspoon garlic powder

¼ teaspoon crushed, dried oregano

1¼ teaspoons salt, divided

¼ teaspoon black pepper

¾ cup minced garlic

1 medium onion, chopped

11 tablespoons extra virgin olive oil, divided

Garlic Dipping Sauce

5 cloves garlic, crushed

Pinch of salt

1 cup water

1 tablespoon olive oil

¼ teaspoon crushed black pepper

"I like to cook," Mr. Robichaux said. "It helps out my daughter sometimes."

"I bet it does," Santa said. "A man who can cook is a big help around the house, believe me." She kicked Mrs. Reilly under the table. "A woman's got a man that likes to cook is a lucky girl."

1. Slice off bottom stem of each artichoke. Remove hard bottom leaves. If artichokes are large, with a large serrated knife, slice ½ inch off tops. Snip off ½ inch from tip of each leaf. There is no need to remove the fuzzy inner choke.
2. To loosen leaves, hit the top of each artichoke lightly on a hard surface 4 times. Wash each under cold water, and place upside down on a drain board or hard surface to drain.
3. Toast bread, grate fine, and measure 1¾ cups. Reserve remaining crumbs for another use. Mix breadcrumbs with cheese, basil, garlic powder, oregano, ½ teaspoon salt, and pepper.
4. Grind garlic and onion in a food processor until finely minced. Add to breadcrumb mixture, and stir in 6 tablespoons olive oil.
5. Divide breadcrumb mixture into four portions. Stuff the center of each artichoke with a heaping tablespoon of breadcrumb mixture. One at a time, fill the second layer of leaves from the top by spooning 1 tablespoon breadcrumbs into each leaf. Continue process until all leaves have been filled. Wet hands, and go around artichoke to remove excess breadcrumbs.
6. Place artichokes upright, and close together in a 4-quart pot. Pour 1 inch water into pot, and add 1 tablespoon olive oil and ¾ teaspoon salt. Drizzle 1 tablespoon olive oil on each artichoke, and sprinkle lightly with salt. Bring water to a rapid boil; then lower to medium-low. Cover pot tightly, and cook until tender, about 1½ hours. Artichokes are done when leaves pull off easily. Check water level occasionally and, if necessary, add more boiling water.
7. Combine all sauce ingredients, and use as a dip for individual leaves, or pour over cooked artichokes. Serve artichokes slightly cooled.

How to Eat an Artichoke: Pick off a leaf, put the soft, fleshy leaf bottom in your mouth, and pull the leaf through your teeth. Remove the fuzzy "choke" in the center of the artichoke, and eat the heart underneath.

. . . .

Fried Cabbage "Sicilian Style" (Frittata)

Makes 4 servings. The frittata, an open-faced vegetable omelet, translates to "egg cake" in Italian. Phyllis "Mama" Monistere Fresina says, "If you have already tried this recipe and you are not Italian, then you must have a good friend who is."

. . . .

1 large cabbage
Salt
2 eggs
1 tablespoon all-purpose flour
2 tablespoons extra virgin olive oil, *fruitato* (fruity), divided
½ cup Italian seasoned breadcrumbs
½ cup Romano cheese, grated
Pepper and garlic powder to taste

1. Core and chop cabbage into 1-inch pieces. In a large pot, add 1 tablespoon salt to 3 quarts water, and bring to a rapid boil. Gradually add cabbage, pushing down after each addition, and cook at a rolling boil until tender, about 3–5 minutes. Drain thoroughly.
2. In a medium bowl, beat eggs. Add flour, and beat until smooth. Set aside.
3. Coat the bottom of a medium nonstick skillet with

1 tablespoon olive oil, and heat over medium heat. Add cabbage and fry, stirring constantly, 4–5 minutes.

4. Add breadcrumbs and cheese. Sprinkle with salt, pepper, and garlic powder. Stir gently.

5. To make a smooth egg base, slowly drizzle half of egg mixture on top of cabbage, coating all cabbage, and cook 1 minute. Place a flat plate on top of cabbage, and flip cabbage onto plate.

6. Add remaining tablespoon olive to the skillet, and slide cabbage off plate into oil. Slowly drizzle remaining egg mixture on top of cabbage, coating all cabbage. Shake skillet back and forth until bottom is brown.

7. Place plate over cabbage again, and flip cabbage onto plate. To brown other side, slide cabbage into skillet and shake back and forth, about 3–4 minutes. Remove from skillet, cut into wedges, and serve warm.

. . . .

Braciole

Makes 6 servings. Adapted from a recipe by Sophia Rizzo.

. . . .

As a New Orleans Sicilian, Mrs. Battaglia surely would have been familiar with braciole. The plural of the word braciola, braciole literally means "chops" or "cuts" of meat, and is a smaller version of braciolone, a do-ahead dish made from a whole, thick steak of beef or veal rolled with a filling that can include just about anything.

The following recipe is simple, but can be embellished with garlic, breadcrumbs, mushrooms, spinach, proscuitto, or even raisins or boiled eggs. If you make the larger braciolone, tie up the rolled meat with string instead of toothpicks.

6 slices, about 1½ pounds, beef top round steak, very thinly sliced

Salt and ground black pepper

½ cup grated Parmesan cheese

¼ cup chopped fresh Italian flat-leaf parsley

¼ cup olive oil

28 ounces (3½ cups) tomato puree

¼ cup chopped fresh basil

Cooked pasta or gnocchi for serving

1. Place beef slices between sheets of plastic wrap, and pound slightly, until about ⅛-inch thick. Lightly season both sides of all pieces with salt and black pepper.

2. In a small bowl, combine cheese and parsley. Divide mixture into six portions, and spread one portion over top of each meat slice. With a short end facing you, neatly roll meat slices jellyroll fashion and secure with wooden toothpicks.

3. Heat olive oil in a large pot over medium-high heat and sear braciole until brown on all sides.

4. Lower heat to medium, add tomato puree, and cook 10 minutes. Lower heat to a simmer. Cover and simmer 1 hour and 20 minutes. Check occasionally and, if sauce appears too thick, stir in a little water. Stir in basil, and simmer another 10 minutes. Serve warm braciole and sauce over pasta.

Heavy odors of Mediterranean cooking floated across the congested neighborhood from the opened kitchen windows in every apartment building and double house.

—As Irene Reilly walks through Santa Battaglia's Ninth Ward neighborhood.

"Potatis" Salad

Makes 6–8 servings. Recipe is by Maureen Detweiler (who has been using this local recipe for more than fifty years).

So maybe Santa needs a few elocution lessons. And maybe potato salad isn't exactly an Italian invention. (The French get credit for mayonnaise, and most folks agree the Germans turned potatoes into a salad.) But, if this little matchmaker makes hers along the line of traditional Southern potato salad, with just potatoes, eggs, onion, celery, a little mustard, and pickle, then she will indeed impress Mr. Robichaux.

And chances are good the mayonnaise Santa uses in her potato salad is Blue Plate, a brand manufactured in the New Orleans area since 1929. Today Blue Plate is owned by New Orleans's own William B. Reilly III, whose grandfather founded the popular Luzianne brand of coffee and iced tea.

2 pounds red potatoes (about 6 medium)

3 hard-boiled eggs

1 cup Blue Plate mayonnaise

½ cup yellow mustard

1 cup finely chopped onion

1 cup finely chopped celery

1 cup well-drained and finely chopped dill pickle

¼ cup finely chopped parsley

Salt and pepper to taste, or use Creole seasoning (purchased, or use recipe on pages 6–7)

1. Boil whole, unpeeled potatoes just until fork tender. When potatoes are cool enough to handle, peel and dice into bite-sized pieces and set aside.

2. In a large bowl, mash eggs and blend well with mayonnaise and mustard. Stir in onion, celery, pickles, and parsley.

3. Stir potatoes into dressing, making sure potatoes are coated well. Add salt and pepper or Creole seasoning. Cover, and chill before serving.

Daube and a Big Pot of Meatballs with Boiled Eggs and Spaghettis

Makes 10–12 servings. Adapted from a recipe by Stevie Mack.

The Sicilians took French daube, a braised cut of tough beef roast usually stuffed with pork fat, and tweaked the recipe by stuffing the roast with garlic and simmering it in red gravy (tomato sauce). They then served it over spaghetti, thereby creating a Creole-Italian masterpiece.

Spaghetti with meatballs is mostly an American idea, with the first recipe published by the National Macaroni Association (now the National Pasta Association), and appearing in 1920. Spaghetti and meatballs are certainly both common in Italy, but there the meatballs are usually small and they're rarely served on the same plate with pasta.

Not only is red gravy over pasta the Sunday dinner dish for Louisianians of Sicilian descent, but lots of these folks also celebrate Christmas and Thanksgiving with red gravy and spaghetti served right alongside turkey and dressing. The custom of tossing boiled eggs into the pot goes back to southern Italy, where Catholics used eggs in place of meat on Fridays, and where eggs also made a good substitute for expensive meat.

Red Gravy and Daube

½ cup olive oil, divided

3 medium onions, chopped

6 large garlic cloves, minced, plus 6 whole peeled cloves

1 (16-ounce) can whole imported Italian tomatoes

6 (6-ounce) cans tomato paste

1 tablespoon sugar

4 bay leaves

Dried red pepper flakes

Salt and ground black pepper

1 (3½-pound) beef rump roast or bone-in pork picnic roast

2 teaspoons fresh oregano or 1 teaspoon dried

8–12 hard-boiled eggs

2 pounds dried spaghetti

Meatballs

Makes about 3 dozen 1½-inch balls.

2 pounds ground beef chuck

1 cup Italian breadcrumbs

½ cup grated Pecorino Romano cheese

1 tablespoon olive oil

4 tablespoons minced fresh parsley

1 medium onion, chopped

8 cloves garlic, minced

5 eggs

1 teaspoon salt

¾ teaspoon ground black pepper

1. Heat ¼ cup olive oil in a large Dutch oven with a heavy bottom, and sauté onion until soft, but not brown. Add minced garlic, and sauté 2 minutes.

2. Use your hands to crush tomatoes, and add to the pot. Cook 10 minutes. Add tomato paste, and cook another 10 minutes, stirring constantly. Add 4 quarts water, sugar, and bay leaves, and red pepper flakes, salt, and black pepper to taste. Cook 1½ hours, uncovered, stirring occasionally.

3. While gravy is cooking, prepare roast. If using pork picnic roast, remove hard, fatty rind. Make slits in roast, and stuff with remaining 6 whole garlic cloves. Season with salt and pepper. Heat remaining ¼ cup olive oil over

medium-high heat in a large, heavy skillet, and sear roast on all sides. After gravy has cooked 1½ hours, add roast and cook an additional 3–4 hours, or until meat is extremely tender.

4. Combine all meatball ingredients, and form into 1½-inch balls. Add oregano, boiled eggs, and meatballs to gravy during the last 1½ hours of cooking time.

5. Cook spaghetti in 2 large pots, each containing 6 quarts water and 2 tablespoons salt. Drain cooked spaghetti, and remove bay leaves from gravy. Serve spaghetti topped with warm slices of daube, meatballs, and boiled eggs.

Meat and Spinach–Stuffed Pasta Tubes

Makes 8 servings. Recipe is from Dr. Robert Cangelosi.

This recipe calls for grinding anise-scented, Sicilian-style daube and mixing it with spinach to form a pasta stuffing. With rows of pasta snuggled side-by-side, this eye-catching dish is today certainly considered elegant, but back a hundred years or so in southern Italy, it would have been considered peasant food.

Dr. Cangelosi grew up in the French Quarter, where he says in the old days it was easy to find his favorite pasta for stuffing, tufoli, a 2-inch-long tube. Times have obviously changed, and it's almost impossible to purchase tufoli shells anywhere in the United States. For this recipe, however, you can use any large pasta tube, such as cannelloni, manicotti, rigatoni, or even paccheri, a short, wide shape that can be placed in the baking dish standing up.

½ cup olive oil, divided
1 stalk celery, minced
1 carrot, finely chopped
2 cups finely chopped sweet onion
1 cup finely chopped green bell pepper
1 teaspoon anise seed, or to taste
2 cloves garlic, minced
2 tablespoons minced fresh basil
1 bay leaf
1½ teaspoons salt
1½ teaspoons ground black pepper
½ teaspoon paprika
1 (1-pound) veal roast
1 (1-pound) beef roast
1 (1-pound) pork roast
1 (6-ounce) can tomato paste
2 cups (16 ounces) tomato sauce
2 cups beef stock
1 cup freshly grated Parmesan cheese, plus optional
    cheese for topping
1 tablespoon sugar
1 pound fresh spinach
16 ounces large tube pasta

1. In a heavy-bottomed Dutch oven, heat ¼ cup olive oil over medium-high heat and sauté celery, carrot, onion, bell pepper, and anise seed until vegetables are soft. Add garlic, basil, bay leaf, salt, black pepper, and paprika. Stir 30 seconds and remove from heat.

2. In a large skillet, preferably cast-iron, heat remaining ¼ cup olive oil over medium-high heat and sear the 3 roasts until brown on all sides.

3. To sautéed vegetables, add browned meats, tomato paste, tomato sauce, beef stock, cheese, and sugar. Simmer, uncovered and stirring occasionally, until meat is tender, about 2–3 hours.

4. While meat is cooking, boil spinach in a small amount of water until wilted. Drain and squeeze out excess water. When cool enough to handle, chop spinach finely and set aside.

5. When meat is cooked, discard bay leaf and remove meat from gravy. With a meat grinder or in a food processor, grind meat finely and mix with spinach.

6. Preheat oven to 350°F. Boil pasta until barely al dente, 6–8 minutes. With a small spoon, stuff each piece of pasta with meat mixture. Lay a single row of stuffed pasta on the bottom of a 13×9-inch baking pan. Cover with gravy. Repeat process by layering on remaining stuffed pasta and gravy. Cover with foil, and bake until completely heated through and bubbly, about 30–40 minutes. Remove foil and, if desired, sprinkle on additional cheese and bake 10 more minutes. Serve hot.

> Santa picked up the photograph lying face down on the mantelpiece and showed it to her two guests. "My poor dear momma. The police took her out the Lautenschlaeger Market four times for disturbing the peace. . . . You think she cared? Not her."
>
> —Santa to Mrs. Reilly and Mr. Robichaux

Biscotti all'Anaci (twice-baked anise biscotti)

Makes 24. Adapted from a recipe by Mary Lavigne.

These crunchy dipping cookies originated centuries ago in the Italian city of Prato.

2 cups all-purpose flour
2 teaspoons baking powder
¼ teaspoon iodized salt
8 tablespoons (1 stick), plus 1 tablespoon unsalted butter, at room temperature
¾ cup sugar
3 large eggs
3 drops anise oil or 1 teaspoon anise extract
1 cup coarsely chopped pistachios, pecans, or assorted nuts

1. Preheat oven to 350°F. Place a sheet of parchment paper on a large cookie sheet. Sift together flour, baking powder, and salt, and set aside.

2. In a large bowl, cream together 1 stick butter and sugar on medium mixer speed until light and fluffy, about 3 minutes. One at a time, add eggs, beating well after each addition. Stir in anise.

3. Using a spoon, gradually work flour mixture and pistachios into wet mixture and stir until you have a soft dough. Divide dough into two.

4. On a well-floured surface and using floured hands, roll each piece into a 12-inch log. Transfer logs to prepared sheet, and spread each into two 4×12-inch rectangles, at least 2 inches apart. Bake until the tops are pale brown, 20–30 minutes. Remove from oven, and cool 10 minutes.

5. Cut loaves into 1-inch slices. For toasted biscotti, turn oven to broil. Place another sheet of parchment paper on the cookie sheet, and oil it with remaining tablespoon butter. Lay slices of biscotti, a cut side up, on buttered parchment, and toast until both sides are lightly brown, turning once every minute, totaling about 4 minutes. For hard cookies, place sliced biscotti on a baking sheet and bake in a 300°F oven 20 minutes, turning every 5 minutes. Cool completely, and store in an airtight container.

Giugiuleni ("joo-joo-lay-knee," Italian Sesame Seed Cookies)

Makes 100 cookies. Adapted from a recipe by Mary Costanza Gennaro.

This crisp seed-covered cookie is one of the many Italians traditionally make for Christmas gift-giving.

2 cups sesame seeds

4 cups all-purpose flour

2 teaspoons baking powder

¼ teaspoon salt

½ teaspoon ground cinnamon

½ teaspoon ground cloves

½ teaspoon ground allspice

16 tablespoons (2 sticks) unsalted butter, room temperature

1¼ cups sugar

3 large eggs, divided

¼ cup whole milk

1 tablespoon pure vanilla extract

½ teaspoon anise extract, optional

1. Preheat oven to 350°F. Line two cookie sheets with parchment paper, and set aside.

2. Place sesame seeds in a shallow bowl or baking pan, and set aside. In a large bowl, whisk together flour, baking powder, salt, cinnamon, cloves, and allspice. Set aside.

3. In another large bowl and using a wooden spoon, cream together butter and sugar. Add 2 eggs, milk, vanilla extract, and optional anise, and beat until combined. Blend in flour mixture to form the dough.

4. Make an egg wash by beating the remaining egg with 1 tablespoon water. Divide dough into 4 rough balls. On a hard surface, roll a dough ball into a long rope with a ½-inch diameter. (Flour hard surface only if absolutely necessary, and cover surface of remaining dough with plastic.) From the rolled rope, cut off pieces of dough 2 inches long. Dip each piece in the egg wash, then roll in sesame seeds, pressing them to adhere. (If desired, you can roll pieces into an "S" shape.) Repeat with remaining dough.

5. Place cookies 1 inch apart on prepared sheets, and bake until the bottoms and sides are lightly toasted, 18–20 minutes. Let sit on cookie sheet 1 minute; then transfer to wire racks to cool completely. Store tightly covered up to 1 week.

Cuccidati (goo-chee-DAH-tee, Italian Fig Cookies)

Makes 56 cookies (or many more if you make them small).

An extremely unscientific survey of New Orleans–area residents of Sicilian descent hints that the favorite pastry of this wide-ranging community is the iced fig cookie known in Italian as *cuccidata*. This cookie, too, is a staple at holiday time, and large versions cut into fancy lace-work are popular on St. Joseph's altars.

Filling

2½ cups packed, dried figs, stems removed

1 cup pitted dates

½ cup orange marmalade

2 tablespoons orange juice

1 cup finely chopped pecans

½ cup finely chopped walnuts

⅓ cup bourbon

¼ cup honey

Finely minced zest from a large orange

2 teaspoons ground cinnamon

½ teaspoon freshly grated nutmeg

½ teaspoon vanilla extract

Dough

4 cups all-purpose flour

1 tablespoon baking powder

¾ teaspoon iodized salt

16 tablespoons (2 sticks) unsalted butter, at room temperature

⅔ cup sugar

3 large eggs, beaten

⅓ cup milk

2 teaspoons pure vanilla extract

¼ teaspoon almond extract

Icing

1½ cups confectioners' sugar

2 tablespoons freshly squeezed orange juice

1 teaspoon pure vanilla extract

Multicolored nonpareils

1. *Make filling:* In a food processor, pulse together figs and dates until finely chopped. Combine marmalade and orange juice in a small pan, and over low heat cook, stirring occasionally, until marmalade is melted. In a bowl, combine fig and date mixture, melted marmalade, and remaining filling ingredients. Cover tightly and refrigerate 2–24 hours.

2. *Make dough:* Sift together flour, baking powder, and salt, and set aside. In a large bowl, cream together butter and sugar on medium mixer speed until light and fluffy, about 3 minutes. Add flour mixture, eggs, milk, vanilla extract, and almond extract, and stir with a spoon until a soft dough forms. Knead until smooth, about 2 minutes. Cover with plastic wrap, and let dough rest in refrigerator 1 hour.

3. Place a rack in center of oven, and preheat oven to 350°F. Divide dough into 4 equal portions, and divide filling into 4 equal portions. (For smaller cookies, divide dough into 6, or even 8 pieces.) On a floured hard surface, roll 1 piece dough into a 21 x 4-inch strip. (Refrigerate remainder until ready to use.) Roll a portion of filling into a 21-inch log, and place down center of dough. Fold sides of dough over filling, and pinch to seal. Cut roll into 2 pieces, and for each piece, turn filled dough seam-side down and gently roll into a log to seal seam.

4. Cut logs into 1½-inch cookies. Place seam-side down 1 inch apart on an ungreased cookie sheet, and bake until edges are brown, 15–20 minutes. Cool on a rack. Repeat process with remaining dough and filling.

5. *Make icing:* Beat together confectioners' sugar, orange juice, and vanilla extract. If too stiff to dribble off a spoon, add more orange juice. Pour icing over cooled cookies while they're still on the rack, and immediately sprinkle on nonpareils. Allow cookies to sit until icing firms up.

Escaping to the Movies and Bowling Alley

> Social note: I have sought escape in the Prytania on more than one occasion, pulled by the attractions of some technicolored horrors, filmed abortions that were offenses against any criteria of taste and decency, reels and reels of perversion and blasphemy that stunned my disbelieving eyes, that shocked my virginal mind, and sealed my valve.
>
> —Ignatius, in his journal.

Safe Haven at the Prytania

Almost every night, to the chagrin of theater managers and staff, Ignatius Reilly's valve risks rupture as he loudly critiques movies at local theaters. His favorite movie house is the Prytania, the real-life theater at 5339 Prytania Street. Opened in 1915, it's just a few blocks from Ignatius's fictitious home. And in the 1960s, it was just one of the many theaters that served as entertainment hubs found in nearly every neighborhood.

The New Orleans love affair with theaters began in 1791, with construction of a tiny theater on St. Peter Street that featured performances spoken in French. Another noteworthy early theater was the St. Charles, built in 1835 and the largest, most opulent theater to date in the United States. There was also the elegant French Opera House, built in 1859, and the Varieties, the name later changing to the Grand Opera House, the latter one of the most dazzling performance venues in the South.

Movies became part of mainstream entertainment beginning July 26, 1896, when the four-hundred-seat Vitascope Hall opened at 623 Canal Street as the world's first for-profit theater dedicated solely to showing motion pictures. During the 1920s, theaters showing stage plays as well as silent movies opened in the same glitzy downtown area, and included the Saenger, Loews State (State Palace), and the Orpheum, the theater where Ignatius Reilly lost control over a "soft-focus love scene." The Joy, an art deco movie palace, opened in the same area as the Orpheum in 1947.

In 1940, the city's first drive-in went up in the Lakeview neighborhood, but complaints about noise forced the theater to close five years later. However, the city was soon dotted with drive-ins, which were especially popular before the advent of air-conditioning.

But, in spite of the popularity of grand movie houses and drive-ins, going to "the show" at neighborhood

movie theaters such as the Prytania is what New Orleans natives most remember. An ode to those relatively smaller theaters was written by René Brunet Jr., who has been in the movie theater business more than seventy years. In his book *There's One in Your Neighborhood: The Lost Movie Theaters of New Orleans,* Brunet and coauthor and preservationist Jack Stewart touch on the conversion of silent to talking pictures, the introduction of various types of color and 3-D, as well as CinemaScope and stereophonic sound. The meat of the book, however, is the meticulously written histories of a myriad of smallish theaters that were a part of everyone's life.

In addition to featuring the latest releases, it was in these sometimes inglorious structures that Depression glass was given away on "Ladies' Night" or money on "Bank Night." The local movie theater was also the place to walk to meet friends or take a date. And in many cases they were an area's central meeting place, especially during World War II, when moviegoers expected to see newsreels, and go through blackout and air-raid tests.

Many still nostalgically remember the excitement of going to movies at theaters such as the Ashton, the Fox, the Tiger, the tiny Fine Arts, the Coliseum, the relatively sleek Napoleon, and the Tivoli. The Carver was for "Negro Patrons," as was the Gallo, the premier Uptown theater for African Americas. Another theater of note was the Martin Cinerama, advertised as having the largest indoor screen in the world.

When television came along in the 1950s, movie attendance dropped by one-third in less than a decade. However, the 1960s' popularity of the automobile made drive-ins faddish, but by the 1970s, high land values and Daylight Savings Time made their luster fade. Today, drive-ins have completely vanished in Louisiana.

In the suburbs, the sixties saw the advent of the now-familiar multiplex. But in the city, changing demographics, maintenance costs, and an inordinate number of fires forced just about all of the dying movie houses to close, even those that had resorted to showing X-rated films.

But, against all odds, the Prytania is still open. Ignatius's favorite cinema is now the only single-screen theater in Louisiana and is the oldest still operating in the New Orleans metro area. Since it aired its first movie, the landmark has survived a couple of fires and various threats of closing, and has also undergone several massive renovations. Brunet, the movie buff who literally wrote the book on New Orleans movie theaters, currently holds a long-term lease on the Prytania, which today shows first-run films, classic movies, weekend midnight movies, and G-rated flicks for children. The Prytania also hosts annual events, such as the New Orleans Film Festival. It's also home to the regional French Film Festival, with movies that have enough romance and exposed flesh to make Ignatius's valve explode.

Aside from those that catered exclusively to African Americans, New Orleans movie theaters relegated blacks to balconies until the early 1970s, when René Brunet did away with balcony seating for African Americans at the Circle Theater at St. Bernard and North Galvez. For his effort, several black publications dubbed Brunet as "The man who let us out of the balcony."

Bowled Over

The 1950s through early 1960s was the grand era of bowling, so it is not surprising that the threesome of Mancuso, Battaglia, and Reilly are headed to the lanes. Bowling alleys became popular after Prohibition, when beer companies started sponsoring bowling teams, tour-

Fazzio's Bowling Alley on North Rampart Street, as it
looked in the early 1960s (now condominiums).

Charles L. Franck/Franck-Bertacci Photographers Collection
in The Historic New Orleans Collection

naments, exhibitions, and promotional giveaways. Snack bars, of course, were found in just about every one of those early bowling alleys, with these usually bare-bones operations not so surprisingly selling more beer than food.

By the time World War II rolled around, bowling was the biggest participation sport in the United States. Bowling became even more popular with the innovation of the mechanical pinsetter, the formation of the Professional Bowlers Association in 1959, televised bowling shows, and with the utilization of animated neon, such as the bowler in action that perpetually rolled a strike on top of O'Shaughnessy's on Airline Highway.

According to Sam Fazzio, the bowling alley Toole references in *A Confederacy of Dunces* was Fazzio's father's three-story bowling alley at 1301 North Rampart. The building was originally built in 1926 for Colonial Home Furnishing Company, and in 1938, Dom Fazzio leased it and installed bowling lanes on the bottom floor. Business mushroomed, so Fazzio constructed lanes on the second floor and, a few years later, on the third, making Fazzio's one of the largest bowling centers in the country. Fazzio's snack bar was located on the first floor and, besides chili, it dispensed typical bowling alley food of the day, such as hot dogs, sandwiches, popcorn, candy bars, potato chips, and beer.

The original Fazzio's on North Rampart closed in 1960 and is now condominiums. Through the years, the Fazzio family also owned bowling alleys on St. Charles Avenue, in New Orleans East, and in the neighboring communities of Arabi and Algiers.

The United States Bowling Congress reports that today there are only 4,666 certified bowling alleys in the United States, down from around 11,000 in the 1960s. But, although bowling's heyday seems to have come and gone, New Orleans still has plenty of lanes. And Mrs. Reilly would surely be impressed by them, especially the new upscale Fulton Alley, a "boutique" establishment with polished hardwoods, leather couches, and state-of-the-art flat-screen monitors. Then there's the unique Mid-City Lanes Rock 'n' Bowl, a vintage, second-floor bowling alley that features live music. Just about every night, Rock 'n' Bowl hosts bands that play rock, swing, New Orleans Funk, Latin, and zydeco, the foot-stomping music of the black Creoles of southwest Louisiana, entertainment that would make Mrs. Reilly tap her feet and maybe help get rid of that arthritis.

Golden Years of Junk Food

Many food historians dub the 1960s the "decade of junk food." Television ads, vending machines, and grocery store shelves were certainly filled with the stuff. And in bowling alleys and theaters you could find a profusion of sugary or salty snacks that cost only a nickel each. Some favorites were Bit-O-Honey, Boston Baked Beans, Pixy Stix, and candy cigarettes. And who can forget candy necklaces, Now and Laters, Swedish Fish, Starbursts, Jawbreakers, Lemonheads, Necco Wafers, Sweetarts, and wax bottles and wax lips. On the salty side there were Cheese-Nips, Ruffles, Chee-tos and, of course, potato chips, with Doritos brand tortilla chips making its debut in 1964. Then there's popcorn, which has been around for thousands of years and, as a whole grain, can actually be nutritious if you don't drown it in butter and salt.

The decade was also memorable for chewing gum. Bubblegum cigars and baseball-card collecting were certainly still popular. And Trident, the first sugar-free gum, came on the scene in 1964. But what's most noteworthy is that by then most chewing-gum makers had switched from using chicle, a natural gum tapped from trees, to butadiene-based synthetic rubber, which is cheaper to manufacture.

We all know way too well that junk food is still a big part of the American diet. And even though most snackers also know that carrot sticks and broccoli are more healthful, there's still that craving inside, the same longing that plagued Ignatius, that uncontrollable desire for a candy bar or chips. No one would argue that it wouldn't be a good idea to ignore that hankering. Or maybe just give in once a year, on July 21, National Junk Food Day.

Grownup Molasses-Coated Popcorn and Peanuts

Makes 3 quarts.

A snack made of popcorn and peanuts sweetened with molasses appeared at the Chicago World's Fair in 1893, and the trademark name Cracker Jack was registered three years later. In 1912, the coveted toy was added to the box that features Sailor Jack and his dog Bingo. Aside from movie theaters, Cracker Jack is a staple at baseball parks. Considered by some as the nation's first junk food, the snack became especially popular after 1908, when Jack Norworth wrote his famous song "Take Me Out to the Ballgame," and the lyrics included the words "buy me some peanuts and Cracker Jack."

3 quarts popped corn (page 95)
1½ cups toasted, shelled peanuts
1 cup pecan halves
1 cup shelled macadamia nuts
6 tablespoons unsalted butter, cut into
    ½-inch pieces
1 tablespoon white vinegar
1½ cups light brown sugar
½ cup light corn syrup
3 tablespoon molasses
½ teaspoon salt
3 tablespoons bourbon
1 teaspoon vanilla extract
¼ teaspoon baking soda

1. Preheat oven to 325°F. Line a sheet pan or large cookie sheet with parchment paper, and set aside. Combine popped corn, peanuts, pecans, and macadamia nuts in a large bowl, and set aside.

2. In a medium, heavy-bottomed saucepan, melt butter over medium heat, stirring constantly, until butter just starts to turn tan. Remove from heat, and stir in vinegar, brown sugar, corn syrup, molasses, and salt. Return to heat, bring to a boil, and cook, without stirring, over medium-low heat until mixture reaches 250°F, about 5 minutes.

3. Remove pot from heat, and stir in bourbon, vanilla, and baking soda. Pour syrup over popcorn and peanuts, and stir until syrup is evenly distributed. (Be careful: syrup is extremely hot.) Spread popcorn on sheet pan, and bake 15 minutes.

4. Remove from oven, and stir well, making sure to scrape up and blend in any accumulated syrup. Spread popcorn evenly in pan again, and bake 15 more minutes. Remove from oven, stir well, and allow to cool. Break into pieces. Store tightly covered at room temperature up to 2 weeks.

Popcorn

Makes 3 quarts.

Popcorn originated in Mexico, and archaeological digs prove natives of North and South America have been enjoying this whole grain for thousands of years. History also tells us American colonists topped their popcorn with cream and sugar and ate it for breakfast.

3 tablespoons peanut or canola oil
½ cup fresh popping corn

1. Pour oil into a large, heavy-bottomed Dutch oven or pot with a lid, and heat over medium-high heat until oil is hot but not smoking. Add popcorn in a single layer. Cover pot, but leave a slight opening to keep popcorn crisp.
2. When first popcorn pops, shake pot back and forth, still leaving cover slightly ajar. Shake every 20 seconds until the sound of corn popping slows down to once every 2–3 seconds. Remove pot from heat, and allow to sit, partially covered, until popping sound stops completely. Serve hot.

Creole Popcorn

Makes 3 quarts.

6 tablespoons unsalted butter
1 teaspoon Worcestershire sauce
1½ teaspoons onion powder
1 teaspoon garlic salt
2 teaspoons paprika
½ teaspoon dried thyme leaves
¼ teaspoon ground black pepper
¼ teaspoon Tabasco brand sauce
3 quarts popped corn (see recipe above)

1. Preheat oven to 350°F. In a small saucepan, melt butter. Stir in Worcestershire sauce, onion powder, garlic salt, paprika, thyme, black pepper, and Tabasco sauce.
2. Pour seasoned butter over popcorn, and stir to coat. Spread popcorn in a baking pan, and bake 3 minutes. Stir and bake 3 more minutes. Serve warm or at room temperature.

"Mr. Mancuso and his aunt, they gonna pick me up in a few minutes. We going down by Fazzio's to bowl."

"What?" Ignatius screamed. "Is that true?"

"I'll be in early. I told Mr. Mancuso I can't stay out late. And his aunt's a grammaw, so I guess she needs her sleep."

"This is certainly a fine reception that I am given after my first day of work," Ignatius said furiously. "You can't bowl. You have arthritis or something. This is ridiculous. Where are you going to eat?"

"I can get me some chili down by the bowling alley." Mrs. Reilly was already going to her room to change clothes.

. . . .

Bowling Alley Chili

Makes 4 servings.

. . . .

This recipe brings back memories of the days when bowling alleys often sold Frito pie, a slit bag of Fritos corn chips topped with chili and cheese.

2 tablespoons olive oil

2 cups chopped yellow onion

½ cup chopped green bell pepper

1 tablespoon minced garlic

1½ pounds ground beef

1 can (24 ounces) crushed tomatoes

1 can (10 ounces) diced tomatoes and green chilies, undrained

1 can (8 ounces) tomato sauce

1½ cups beef stock

3 tablespoons mild chili powder

2 tablespoons ground cumin

1 teaspoon salt

1 teaspoon paprika

½ teaspoon ground black pepper

¼ cup chopped fresh cilantro

1 can (15¼ ounces) kidney beans, drained

Grated Cheddar cheese, chopped white onion, and corn chips for serving

1. In a large pot, heat olive oil over medium-high heat. Sauté onion and bell pepper until onions are brown, about 5 minutes.
2. Stir in garlic and sauté 1 minute. Add ground beef, and cook until brown, about 5 minutes.
3. Stir in crushed tomatoes, diced tomatoes, and green chilies, tomato sauce, stock, chili powder, cumin, salt, paprika, black pepper, and cilantro. Bring to a boil; then lower to a simmer and cook 45 minutes, uncovered, and stirring often.
4. Stir in drained kidney beans, and simmer until thick,

about 15 minutes. Serve chili in bowls, and top with Cheddar cheese, white onion, and corn chips.

Fulton Alley Fried Brussels Sprouts with Pepper Jelly Glaze

Makes 8 side-dish servings. Recipe is from Executive Sous Chef Danny Laguaite, Fulton Alley Bowling Lanes.

Fulton Alley is considered a "boutique" bowling alley, and with its upscale food and drinks, Mr. Robichaux could really impress his future girlfriend Mrs. Reilly.

2–3 pounds Brussels sprouts

3 tablespoons canola oil

Kosher salt

2 tablespoons Pepper Jelly (recipe follows, or purchased and diluted with 1 tablespoon apple cider vinegar)

1. Trim Brussels sprouts, and cut in half or, if large, in fourths. In a large cast-iron or heavy-bottomed skillet, use medium-high heat to bring oil to 350°F, or until very hot but not smoking. Cook Brussels sprouts cut side down, flipping once, until golden brown and slightly tender, about 3–5 minutes.

2. Remove sprouts from skillet. If necessary, blot lightly with paper towels to remove excess oil. Transfer to a large bowl, and stir in a liberal pinch of salt.

3. Gently stir in pepper jelly, and serve immediately.

Pepper Jelly   Makes 3–4 cups

This recipe makes much more than you'll need to glaze the above Fried Brussels Sprouts recipe, but it keeps well in the refrigerator and is great for basting meats, on turkey sandwiches, in coleslaw, on blocks of cream cheese, and as a dip for fried vegetables.

5 red bell peppers

10 fresh jalapeño peppers

2 cups apple cider vinegar

2 cups apple juice

1 pack (3 ounces) liquid pectin

1 teaspoon kosher salt

6 cups white sugar

1. Remove stems and seeds from all peppers. Combine peppers, vinegar, and apple juice in a blender, and blend until smooth. Pour into a glass bowl, cover, and allow to sit at least 6 hours, and preferably overnight.

2. Transfer pepper mixture to a large saucepan, and stir in pectin, salt, and sugar. Bring to a boil over low heat, and stir until the sugar is dissolved. Boil another 1 minute, stirring constantly.

3. Cool completely; then store, covered, in the refrigerator up to 3 months.

Rock 'n' Bowl Meat Pies

Makes 20. Recipe is by chef Bradley McGehee of Johnny Blancher's Front Porch Grill at Rock 'n' Bowl.

The Rock 'n' Bowl, originally known as Mid City Lanes, started in 1941. And along with bowling, zydeco, and mixed drinks, this unique entertainment complex now serves its version of the Natchitoches meat pie.

This savory, hand-sized fried turnover first appeared in the center-western portion of the state in what is now the city of Natchitoches, and what, in the eighteenth century, was a center of outposts and missions run by the Spanish. It is, therefore, not surprising that the meat pie favors the empanada. But research also shows this meaty treat may also share a history with the French *tourtière*, a baked meat pie. During the time-period Mrs. Reilly was dining at bowling alleys, the Natchitoches meat pie had almost become extinct throughout the state, even in Natchitoches. But thanks to a few restaurateurs and determined home cooks, the portable meal is once again popular, or at least it is at the Rock 'n' Bowl.

2 pounds lean ground beef (Rock 'n' Bowl uses grass-fed)

1 medium yellow onion, small diced

2 tablespoons butter

2 tablespoons Creole seasoning (purchased, or use recipe on pages 6–7)

1 tablespoon sriracha chili sauce

Salt to taste

20 (5 x 5-inch) cold puff pastry squares, from four 10 x 15-inch sheets packaged pastry, thawed if frozen (or use recipe for Easy Puff Pastry on page 155)

Vegetable oil for frying (if frying instead of baking)

2 eggs, well beaten (if baking instead of frying)

1. Brown beef over medium-high heat in a heavy 12-inch sauté pan. Drain off fat. Add onion and butter, and sauté until onion is translucent. Remove from heat.

2. Stir in Creole seasoning, sriracha sauce, and salt. Chill in refrigerator 30 minutes or until cold.

3. Place cold puff pastry squares on a clean, hard work surface, and place 2 tablespoons filling onto center of each pastry square. Using your index finger, brush egg wash around the edges of the pastry. Fold pastry over into triangles, and crimp with your fingers to seal the meat into the pies.

4. Using a large, round cookie cutter (4–5 inches), or free-handed with a knife, cut the triangle pies into half-circles. If desired, crimp edges with the back of a fork.

5. Deep fry (recommended): Preheat at least 2 inches vegetable oil to 350°F in a deep-fat fryer or large, heavy pot. Fry pies on both sides until golden brown and flaky, approximately 4 minutes total.

6. To bake pies: Preheat oven to 425°F. Brush tops of meat pies with beaten egg, and arrange on a baking sheet 1 inch apart. Bake until golden brown and flaky, 20–25 minutes. Serve pies hot.

Ignatius Eatery's Strawberry Salad with Lemon Vinaigrette and Grilled Chicken

Makes 4 servings. Recipe is by chef Blake McDonald, Ignatius Eatery.

Lemon Vinaigrette — Makes ¾ cup

½ cup olive oil

3 tablespoons fresh lemon juice

2 teaspoons balsamic vinegar

2 teaspoons Creole mustard

Combine all ingredients in a bowl, and whisk together until emulsified. Can be made 1 day ahead, chilled, and covered. Bring to room temperature before using.

4 boneless skinless chicken breasts

Salt and ground black pepper

2 bunches spinach (about 1½ pounds), coarse stems removed and leaves washed and spun dry

Lemon Vinaigrette (recipe above)

16 strawberries

½ cup pecans, chopped coarse

⅓ cup crumbled feta cheese

If Ignatius were around now, whenever his mother goes out bowling, he could mosey down to Magazine Street for dinner at his namesake restaurant, Ignatius Eatery. Opened in 2006, the Louisiana-centric restaurant is festooned with art featuring quotes from *A Confederacy of Dunces,* along with drawings of Mrs. Reilly's "boy" and an agglomeration of votive candles worthy of Santa Battaglia's mantelpiece.

1. Prepare a grill at medium-high heat. Season chicken with salt and pepper, and grill until cooked through, turning occasionally, about 5 minutes each side. Transfer to work surface, and cut crosswise into thin slices.

2. Toss spinach with Lemon Vinaigrette and divide among 4 entrée-sized bowls. Arrange strawberries around spinach. Sprinkle on pecans and feta, and top with warm grilled chicken.

"Mother! Is this offensive display of ill manners one of the results of your association with those bowling Sicilians?"

—Ignatius to Mrs. Reilly, who is determined to find him a job and snatches the want ads out of his hands.

Ignatius Eatery's Mac 'n' Cheese with Fried Shrimp

Makes 4 servings. Recipe is by chef Blake McDonald, Ignatius Eatery.

3 slices bacon

¼ cup minced onion

2 tablespoons minced garlic

½ pound elbow macaroni

1⅔ cups heavy whipping cream

8 ounces sharp cheddar cheese, coarsely grated, divided

Salt and ground black pepper to taste

Peanut oil for frying

2 cups all-purpose flour

½ teaspoon chili powder

1 tablespoon garlic powder

1 tablespoon onion powder

½ teaspoon paprika

1 teaspoon salt

2 tablespoons minced fresh parsley

12 jumbo fresh shrimp, cleaned and deveined, with tail intact

1. Preheat oven to 350°F. In a skillet, fry bacon until crisp. Leaving drippings in skillet, remove cooked bacon, crumble, and drain on paper towels. Sauté onion in bacon drippings until translucent. Add garlic and sauté 30 seconds. Remove skillet from heat.

2. In a pot of salted boiling water, cook macaroni until just al dente, about 7 minutes. Drain well.

3. Whisk whipping cream into onion mixture, and bring to a boil. Set aside ½ cup shredded cheddar, and whisk remaining cheese into cream mixture. When cheese is melted, add salt and pepper to taste and gently stir in macaroni.

4. Divide macaroni among 4 gratin dishes. Sprinkle tops with remaining ½ cup cheese and bacon pieces. Bake until bubbly and brown, 25–30 minutes.

5. While macaroni is baking, pour enough peanut oil into a large, heavy pot to reach a depth of 2 inches, and heat to 375°F. In a shallow bowl, mix together flour, chili powder, garlic powder, onion powder, paprika, salt, and parsley. Add shrimp to bowl, and toss to coat. Working in batches, add shrimp to hot oil and fry until golden, about 1½ minutes. Transfer to paper towels to drain. Keep warm.

6. When macaroni comes out of oven, top each dish with 3 fried shrimp and serve.

Milky Way Soufflés

Makes 4 servings.

Ignatius's favorite candy bar melts inside individual soufflés, forming creamy caramel and nougat centers, and eliminating the need for a sauce.

2 regular-sized Milky Way candy bars (1.84 ounces each), chilled

4 tablespoons unsalted butter, softened, divided

¼ cup sugar, plus 2 tablespoons for coating ramekins

8 ounces semisweet or milk chocolate chips

½ teaspoon vanilla extract

3 large egg yolks

4 large egg whites, at room temperature

¼ teaspoon cream of tartar

⅛ teaspoon iodized salt

Confectioners' sugar for garnish

1. Place a rack on the lower third of oven, and preheat oven to 400°F. Cut Milky Way bars into halves, and each half into thirds. Set aside. Rub insides of 4 individual 6-ounce ramekins with 1 tablespoon butter and coat with 2 tablespoons sugar. Refrigerate ramekins.
2. Melt chocolate and 3 remaining tablespoons butter in a large metal bowl over simmering water, stirring occasionally. Remove bowl from heat, and stir in vanilla. Cover and set aside.
3. In a separate medium bowl, whisk egg yolks and ¼ cup sugar until creamy and light yellow, about 3 minutes. Fold into chocolate mixture.
4. In a separate large bowl and using medium-high mixer speed, beat egg whites, cream of tartar, and salt until stiff and glossy. Gently fold into chocolate mixture.

5. Pour soufflé mixture halfway into prepared ramekins, and top each with 3 Milky Way bar slices. Top with remaining soufflé mixture.
6. Bake until puffy and exterior is firm, about 23–25 minutes. Dust tops with confectioners' sugar, and serve immediately.

Chunky Peanut and Raisin Dark Chocolate Fudge

Makes 16 pieces.

Remember when you used to "open wide" for Chunky? This recipe is a take on the Nestlé Company's fat square (trapezoid, actually) of chocolate studded with peanuts and raisins, which is still a movie theater favorite.

3 cups sugar
½ cup cocoa powder
2 ounces unsweetened baking chocolate, chopped
1¼ cups evaporated milk
¼ teaspoon salt
¼ teaspoon cream of tartar
3 tablespoons unsalted butter
1 teaspoon vanilla extract
¾ cup shelled, roasted peanuts
¾ cup raisins

1. Coat the insides of an 8 x 8-inch baking pan well with butter. In a large heavy-bottomed saucepan, combine sugar, cocoa, baking chocolate, evaporated milk, salt, and cream of tartar. Stirring constantly, bring to a boil over medium heat. Lower heat to a simmer, and cook to softball stage, 234°F. Gently stir with a heat-proof

spatula every 3–4 minutes so candy doesn't stick to bottom of the pot.

2. Remove from heat. Without stirring, add butter and vanilla. To prevent a grainy texture, allow to cool undisturbed until mixture reaches 130°F.

3. Stir in peanuts and raisins with a wooden spoon just until mixture thickens and begins to develop a dull sheen. Quickly pour into prepared pan, level off top, and cool at room temperature until firm. Cut into 2-inch pieces. Store tightly covered at room temperature up to 2 weeks.

Suddenly Mrs. Reilly remembered the horrible night that she and Mr. Reilly had gone to the Prytania to see Clark Gable and Jean Harlow in *Red Dust*. In the heat and confusion that had followed their return home, nice Mr. Reilly had tried one of his indirect approaches, and Ignatius was conceived. Poor Mr. Reilly. He had never gone to another movie as long as he lived.

—As she sits at the kitchen table sipping muscatel, Mrs. Reilly recalls an evening out with her now-deceased husband.

9

. . . .

Goodies from the German's

> "I got a cake from the German's, too, but I can't remember right off where I put it."
>
> —Mrs. Reilly to Ignatius.

The fictitious "German's" on Magazine Street, the bakery where Mrs. Reilly purchases Ignatius's jelly-filled doughnuts and cakes, could have been based on a number of places since, during this era, New Orleans had a plethora of neighborhood bakeries, and many were run by Germans.

It's been suggested that the model for Mrs. Reilly's "German's" was a pastry shop called the Swiss Bakery. A check of city directories of the time shows, however, no such place existed on Magazine Street. The legendary Swiss Confectionery, noted for its spectacular wedding cakes, has been in business more than ninety years, but it's on St. Charles Avenue and miles away from the Reilly home. And when Toole wrote *Dunces,* Swiss Confectionery was located on Frenchmen Street, and even further away.

Toole's actual inspiration was just around the corner from Constantinople. According to George Gurtner, a noted local author and former resident of the Irish Channel and who occasionally hung out with Toole, *Dunces*'s German bakery was modeled on Schwabe's, a small family store on Magazine Street between Napo-

leon Avenue and General Pershing. Toole was certainly familiar with Schwabe's, and it was the bakery that, according to Gurtner, made the best jelly doughnuts in the world. And a look at the city directory from 1960 shows they made much more than doughnuts and cake:

SCHWABE'S BAKERY, We Specialize in Cakes for Banquets, Weddings, Parties and Special Occasions, Fresh French Bread, Cookies, Pastries, Whipped Cream Goods, Pies Baked Fresh daily, Open 7 Days a Week, 4229 Magazine, Tel TWinbrook 1–1833

Baking is reportedly the oldest industry in New Orleans. The earliest record available shows that a commercial bread baker, a Frenchman named François Lemesle working under the alias Bellegarde, was selling his goods in the year 1722. The number of bake shops steadily increased over the next few years, and their products apparently remained decidedly French. Ursuline Nun Madeleine Hachard even chronicled that by 1728 one could find the same pastries in New Orleans as in Paris.

French-style baked goods remained favored in New Orleans after Spain took over in 1769, and even following the American influx after 1803. Then, in the 1830s, talented Germans started overtaking the industry. But things still remained the same, with German bakers wishing to keep the local peace and going out of their way to accommodate French preferences. This included learning to master the Creole favorite *pâte feuilletée,* a flaky puff pastry, as well as petit fours, Napoleon squares, cream puffs, éclairs, Charlotte Russe, and babas, also known as savarins, similar to the modern wine cake. Naturally, Germans did introduce goods from their homeland, including Vienna, rye, and pumpernickel breads, along with cookies such as the spiced *pfeffernuss,* coffee cake, strudel, specialized pies, apple turnovers, fruitcake, and the iced, flat ginger cake known as the stage plank, some of which became locally popular.

It is also certain that German bakers brought their tradition of making doughnuts to New Orleans, and that Creoles immediately deemed the solid fried dough squares taboo for being too rubbery and greasy. This pooh-poohing is understandable, since the local French had long been attached to their holeless, square beignet, a much lighter puff of sweet fried dough that had come to Louisiana from France in the 1700s.

Mostly arriving after the Civil War, another group of talented bakers, the Italians, started introducing their home country specialties. But this new breed of baker left the production of French specialties to the Germans and, in addition to making their own familiar breads and cakes, the Italians decided to bake goods that catered to American and English tastes.

In the early twentieth century, New Orleans had more than 138 bakeries and an active Master Bakers Association. But, with the rise of supermarkets, malls, mechani-

> "Have a nice jelly doughnut. I just bought them fresh this morning over by Magazine Street. Ignatius says to me this morning, 'Momma, I sure feel like a jelly doughnut.' You know? So I went over by the German and bought him two dozen. Look, they got a few left."
>
> —Mrs. Reilly to Officer Mancuso, who has just dropped by for a visit.

zation, and the trend to extend shelf life with preservatives, master bakers and neighborhood bakeries faded.

One high-profile bakery chain sorely missed is McKenzie's, known for Blackout Cake and the Buttermilk Drop, a confection resembling a large doughnut hole. A few of the old stalwarts are, however, still around, including Leidenheimer's, established in 1896, and still baking fresh French bread for the New Orleans and Gulf South wholesale trade. And in 2012, after 100 years in business, the fried sweet pie manufacturer Hubig's was shut down by a fire, but its management is vowing to return.

For the retail trade, Alois Binder Bakery started as a family business in 1914 and still produces outstanding French bread, along with square German-style doughnuts. Angelo Brocato's opened in 1905 and bakes everyone's favorite Italian pastries, while Gambino's has been baking king cakes and doberge cakes for more than fifty years. Haydel's, opened in 1959, is also renowned for king cakes and holds the distinction of being the first local bakery to insert a *feve,* a porcelain trinket, inside. Too, the city is seeing a resurgence in artisanal bakeries. Of special note are Vietnamese bakers, who turn out exceptional baguettes. So, although the inspiration for *Dunces*'s German bakery shut down its ovens long ago, today Mrs. Reilly would not have a problem finding freshly baked goods for her little Ignatius.

. . . .

Nice Glazed Jelly Doughnuts
Makes 24.

. . . .

The earliest known recipe for a jelly-filled doughnut traces back to Germany, where instructions for making *Gefüllte Krapfen* was published in 1485 in the cookbook *Kuchenmeisterei* (Mastery of the Kitchen).

The following recipe is simpler than it looks, requiring only a total 2½ hours rising time, and the dough can be made up to 12 hours ahead of frying. The result is a yeast-raised doughnut as light as any you'll find at a bakery.

Sponge Starter

2 teaspoons active dry yeast

1 teaspoon sugar

1½ cups warm water (105–115°F)

1½ cups bread flour

2 tablespoons nonfat dry milk powder

Dough

1½ teaspoons active dry yeast

½ cup warm water (105–115°F)

1 tablespoon nonfat dry milk powder

½ cup sugar

2 large eggs, plus 2 large egg yolks, at room temperature

8 tablespoons (1 stick) unsalted butter, at room temperature

¼ teaspoon freshly grated nutmeg

4 cups bread flour

1 teaspoon iodized salt

Vegetable oil for frying

3 cups jelly or jam

Doughnut Glaze

2½ cups confectioners' sugar, sifted

¼ cup water

1 teaspoon vanilla extract

1. *Make starter:* In a medium bowl, dissolve yeast and sugar in warm water. Stir in bread flour and milk powder. Cover bowl, and allow to sit in a warm place 30 minutes.

2. *Make dough:* In the bowl of a standing mixer, combine yeast, warm water, and milk powder. Stir in starter; then stir in sugar, eggs, butter, and nutmeg. Using mixer bread paddle on low speed, mix in flour and salt. Knead on medium-low speed 7 minutes. Dough should be very soft

and sticky. Place in a large greased bowl. Completely cover surface with plastic wrap, and allow to sit in a warm place 30 minutes.

3. To make sure all dough surface is covered, remove plastic from dough and replace plastic again. Refrigerate 1–12 hours.

4. On a lightly floured sheet of parchment paper, roll dough out to ¼-inch thick. Cut out doughnuts using a round floured 2 to 3-inch cookie cutter. Place doughnuts on a sheet pan lined with lightly floured parchment paper. Cover lightly with a cloth, and allow to rise in a warm spot until doubled in volume, about 30 minutes.

5. Heat 3 inches vegetable oil in a fryer or Dutch oven to 350°F. Using a thin-bladed spatula, drop doughnuts into oil, without crowding, and fry until golden on both sides, about 5–6 minutes total, flipping often. Drain on paper towels.

6. Allow doughnuts to cool 10 minutes. Stir jelly until smooth and scoop into a pastry bag fitted with a large, plain tip. With the tip, poke a deep hole through the side of each doughnut and squeeze in 2 tablespoons jelly.

7. *Make glaze:* In a shallow soup bowl, mix together confectioners' sugar, water, and vanilla until smooth. Dip tops of doughnuts in glaze, and set on a wire rack to firm up, about 15 minutes. Serve immediately.

> Ignatius . . . picked up the telephone, and in an assumed voice rich with Mayfair accents said, "Yus?"
>
> "Mr. Reilly?" a man asked.
>
> "Mr. Reilly is not here. . . ."
>
> "This is Gus Levy. . . ."
>
> "I'm terribly sorry," Ignatius enunciated. "Mr. Reilly . . . is at the state mental hospital in Mandeville. . . . Since being so viciously dismissed by your concern, he has had to commute back and forth regularly from Mandeville."
>
> "He cracked up?"
>
> "Violently and totally. . . ."
>
> "Can he have visitors at Mandeville?"
>
> "Of course. Drive out to see him. Bring him some cookies."
>
> —Telephone conversation between Ignatius and Mr. Levy.

Updated Chocolate Chip Cookies with Walnuts

Makes 4 dozen.

In 1939, Ruth Graves Wakefield, a trained dietician, cookbook author, and co-owner of the Toll House Inn, in Whitman, Massachusetts, tossed walnuts and pieces of a Nestlé semisweet chocolate bar into cookie dough, and created what she originally called the Chocolate Crunch Cookie. Her concoction eventually became a huge national sensation, and Wakefield ended up giving her recipe to Nestlé for a lifetime supply of chocolate.

Today, chocolate chip cookies are the most popular cookie in America, with seven billion consumed annually. In this revised version of the old favorite, the addition of whole-wheat flour makes a richer-flavored cookie that is less apt to fall apart.

1½ cups all-purpose flour

½ cup whole-wheat flour

1 teaspoon baking soda

¾ teaspoon iodized salt

14 tablespoons (1¾ sticks) cold, unsalted butter

1 cup light brown sugar, packed

½ cup white sugar

1 teaspoon vanilla extract

¼ teaspoon almond extract

2 large eggs

1 (12-ounce) bag chocolate chips

1 cup chopped walnuts

1. In a medium bowl, stir together flours, soda, and salt. Set aside.
2. Cut butter into ½-inch pieces. In a large mixing bowl, cream butter and sugars on medium speed until light-colored, about 3 minutes. Scrape down sides. Add extracts and eggs, and beat on medium another minute. Lower mixer speed, and gradually add flour mixture. Mix until well combined. With a wooden spoon, stir in chocolate chips and walnuts. Refrigerate 1–24 hours.

> "Perhaps you are the hope for the future," Ignatius said....
>
> "Oh, what a fun day this has been. You're a gypsy. Timmy's a sailor. The marvelous policeman's an artist.... It's just like Mardi Gras.... I think I'll go home and throw something on."
>
> —Dorian Greene and the pirate-garbed Ignatius, who wants to discuss the idea that homosexuality might be the key to world peace. But all Dorian wants to do is party.

3. When ready to bake, preheat oven to 375°F and line a cookie sheet with parchment paper. Drop dough by rounded tablespoons onto prepared cookie sheet, and bake until edges are just brown, 9–10 minutes. Cool 1 minute on cookie sheet; then cool completely on a rack.

. . . .

Cinnamon-Filled King Cake (Gâteau du Roi, or Twelfth Night Cake)

Makes 1 cinnamon-filled cake.

. . . .

Maybe Ignatius can get Dorian to discuss world peace over fat slices of king cake, the traditional dessert of Mardi Gras season, the time of year it's sold in just about every bakery, grocery store, and convenience store in town.

The king cake is a large ring of sweet brioche or Danish-style dough with a baby trinket hidden inside, and it originated in southern France around the twelfth century. The *galette de roi,* which has relatively recently become popular in New Orleans, is a more elegant round cake made from puff pastry filled with frangipani, a ground almond cream, and it originated in northern France.

The New Orleans ring-type cake is usually iced in the Mardi Gras colors, purple for justice, green for faith, and gold for power, which, in traditionally Catholic Louisiana, represent the three kings, or Magi who brought gifts to Jesus's manger.

King cakes appear in bakeries beginning January 6, known as Twelfth Night, or Epiphany, the feast of the Three Kings. Throughout Lent, king cakes are pretty much a fixture at offices and social gatherings. At parties, whoever gets the slice with the plastic baby, which originally was a bean, is deemed king or queen. Often, the "lucky" baby recipient is also obliged to host the next king cake party. In office or family settings, whoever gets the baby buys the next cake.

Originally, New Orleans king cakes were a simple oval of dough with minimal decoration. All that changed in the 1980s when bakers started filling cakes with sweets such as cream cheese, pie fillings, nuts, raisins, and whatever else they could think of. But, in the 1960s, when Ignatius was dressed as though he was ready for Mardi Gras, the king cake would have still been fairly plain.

⅔ cup whole milk

¾ teaspoon iodized salt

10 tablespoons unsalted butter, softened, divided

⅓ cup sugar

1 envelope (2¼ teaspoons) active dry yeast

3 tablespoons warm water

¼ cup canola oil

2 whole eggs, plus 1 for glaze

2 egg yolks

3–3½ cups bread flour

½ cup dark brown sugar, packed

1 tablespoon ground cinnamon

Green, purple, and gold-colored sugars for sprinkling

1 small, plastic baby trinket, or a dried bean (be sure to inform guests that a hard object is inside the cake)

King Cake Glaze

2 cups confectioners' sugar

1 tablespoon butter, melted

¼ teaspoon vanilla extract

3 tablespoons water

1. To make cake, bring milk to a boil in a small saucepan, and remove from heat. Add salt, 6 tablespoons butter and sugar, and stir until butter melts. Cool to lukewarm (110°F).

2. While milk is cooling, dissolve yeast in warm water in a small bowl. Let sit 5 minutes.

3. In a standing mixer, combine milk mixture, yeast mixture, canola oil, 2 eggs, egg yolks, and 2 cups flour. On low mixer speed, add remaining flour a few tablespoons at a time until a soft dough forms and pulls cleanly away from the sides of the bowl. Cover top with plastic wrap, and let sit 10 minutes.

4. Using the mixer dough hook, knead dough at medium speed 5 minutes. Turn dough onto a hard floured surface and form into a smooth ball. Place dough in a greased bowl, cover with plastic wrap, and allow to rise in a warm place 1 hour.

5. Punch dough down, and fold it over itself 4 times. On a

lightly floured hard surface, roll dough out to a 22 x 10-inch rectangle. Spread with remaining 4 tablespoons butter. Mix together brown sugar and cinnamon, and sprinkle over butter. With a long side facing you, roll dough jellyroll fashion. Pinch the seam together well (so filling doesn't ooze out). Seam side down, place on a parchment-lined baking sheet. Bring the two dough ends together to form an oval or a circle, and pinch seam together. Cover lightly with a towel, and allow to rise 45 minutes.

6. Preheat oven to 350°F. Bake cake until golden brown, about 20 minutes. Beat remaining egg with 1 tablespoon water and brush cake with egg wash. Bake an additional 5 minutes.

7. Remove cake to a rack, and let cool. Mix together glaze ingredients, and pour over cake. Sprinkle on colored sugars, and insert baby into cake from underneath. Cake keeps, covered at room temperature, up to 3 days.

Lattice Peach and Blackberry Pie with a Cornmeal Crust

Makes one 9-inch pie.

Fruit pies always have a commanding presence in bakery showcases. This specialty is made with two of Louisiana's favorite summer fruits.

1 recipe Crunchy Cornmeal Double Pie Crust
　　(recipe page 110)
2½–3 pounds firm, ripe peaches
⅓ cup all-purpose flour
¾ cup sugar, plus 1 tablespoon
½ teaspoon cinnamon
¼ teaspoon freshly grated nutmeg
¼ teaspoon salt
1 tablespoon freshly squeezed lemon juice
1½ cups fresh blackberries
1 egg, beaten with 1 tablespoon water

1. Place a rack in lower third of oven, and preheat oven to 350°F. Roll half of pie crust to an 11-inch circle. Line a 9-inch pie pan with the rolled dough circle, allowing excess to hang over edges. Wrap remaining half with plastic, and refrigerate both pieces of crust.

2. Remove peach peels by bringing a large pot of water to boil. Cut an X in the bottom of each peach, and drop peaches into boiling water. Simmer 1 minute, and remove to a bowl of ice water. When cool enough to handle, slip peeling off peaches. Remove stones and cut into ¾-inch slices.

3. In a large bowl, combine flour, ¾ cup sugar, cinnamon, nutmeg, salt, and lemon juice. Stir in peach slices, and allow to sit 15 minutes.

4. Gently stir blackberries into peaches. Remove unrolled pie crust disc from refrigerator, and roll between 2 sheets of floured wax paper into an 11-inch circle. Slice dough into ½-inch wide strips.

5. Remove pie pan with crust from refrigerator, and brush insides lightly with beaten egg. Pour peaches and blackberries into crust. Top with strips of dough, forming a lattice. Crimp edges decoratively. Brush lattice top with remaining egg, and sprinkle with remaining tablespoon sugar.

6. Place pie on a foil-line baking sheet to catch drips, and bake until brown and bubbly, about an hour and 10 minutes. Remove from oven, and cool at least 1 hour before serving.

Crunchy Cornmeal Double Pie Crust

Makes one 9-inch double-crust pie

A touch of cornmeal is the secret to making this crispy crust, and it's a shell that pairs extremely well with any fruit pie.

    2½ cups all-purpose flour
    ¼ cup finely ground cornmeal
    1 tablespoon sugar
    1 teaspoon iodized salt
    16 tablespoons (2 sticks) cold unsalted butter,
        cut into small pieces
    8–10 tablespoons ice water

1. In a large bowl, stir together flour, cornmeal, sugar, and salt. Using your fingers, work in butter until the mixture resembles coarse cornmeal.
2. Stir in enough ice water so that dough holds together. Divide dough in half, and form each dough half into a disc. Wrap each disc with plastic. and refrigerate at least 1 hour, and up to 1 day ahead.

Deep Dark Chocolate Meringue Cream Pie

Makes one 9-inch pie.

This perennial favorite is adapted to modern tastes with less sugar and the addition of lots of luscious bittersweet chocolate. And the meringue is stabilized, made more firm with a cornstarch paste, and so the pie slices more attractively.

(9-inch) single pie crust (recipe follows)
⅓ cup cocoa powder (not Dutch process)
1¼ cups sugar, divided, plus 1 tablespoon
6 tablespoons cornstarch, divided
½ teaspoon salt
4 large eggs, yolks and whites separated
3 cups whole milk
4 ounces fine quality bittersweet chocolate, melted
2 tablespoons unsalted butter, softened
1½ teaspoons vanilla extract, divided
¼ teaspoon cream of tartar

1. Bake unfilled pie crust, and set aside.
2. Preheat oven to 325°F. In a 3-quart heavy saucepan, whisk together cocoa powder, ¾ cup sugar, 5 tablespoons cornstarch, and salt until well combined. Whisk in egg yolks and milk, and bring to a boil over moderate heat. Reduce to a simmer, and cook 1 minute, whisking constantly. (Mixture will be thick.)
3. If you kept up with your whisking, there shouldn't be any lumps. But if lumps do appear, force filling through a fine-mesh sieve into a bowl. Whisk in melted chocolate, butter, and 1 teaspoon vanilla, and pour into prepared crust.
4. Make meringue by first mixing remaining 1 tablespoon cornstarch and 1 tablespoon sugar in a very small saucepan. Stir in ⅓ cup water. Bring to a boil over medium heat, and boil 15 seconds, stirring constantly, until mixture forms a thick, translucent paste. Remove from heat, and cover.
5. In a large bowl, beat egg whites on medium speed until foamy. Beat in remaining half-teaspoon vanilla and cream of tartar until soft peaks form. Very gradually beat in remaining ½ cup sugar. When stiff peaks form, reduce speed to low and beat in cornstarch paste 1 tablespoon at a time. When all paste is incorporated, increase speed to medium and beat 10 seconds.

6. Cover pie with meringue, and bake until golden brown. Cool completely at room temperature, and refrigerate at least 4 hours before serving.

Single Pie Crust
Makes one 9-inch crust

Refrigerating the dough twice results in a super-flaky crust.

- 1¼ cups all-purpose flour
- 1 teaspoon sugar
- ½ teaspoon iodized salt
- 8 tablespoons (1 stick) cold unsalted butter, cut into cubes
- 2–3 tablespoons ice water

1. Combine flour, sugar, and salt in a large bowl. Add butter, and blend in with a pastry blender or your fingers until mixture is the texture of coarse meal.
2. Stir in enough water to hold dough together. Form into a disc, wrap in plastic, and refrigerate 1 hour.
3. Roll dough between 2 sheets of lightly floured wax paper to form an 11-inch circle. Fit into a 9-inch pie pan. Trim and crimp edges. Prick bottom and sides of shell with a fork, and chill 30 minutes.
4. Preheat oven to 375°F. Blind bake (pre-bake) the shell by first lining inside of pie crust with aluminum foil and filling with pie weights, raw rice, or dried beans. Bake in center of oven 20 minutes. Remove weights and foil. Prick insides of crust again. Return to oven, and bake until golden brown, about 10–15 more minutes. Remove from oven and allow to cool.

Lemon Cream Tart with Mixed Berry Topping

Makes one 9-inch tart.

For an authentic Louisiana topping, choose strawberries or blackberries, or even blueberries, which are not indigenous to the state, but now successfully grow here, and are popular at u-pick-it farms.

- 1¼ cups all-purpose flour
- 1 tablespoon light brown sugar
- ¾ teaspoon iodized salt
- 8 tablespoons (1 stick), plus 2 tablespoons cold unsalted butter, cut into small bits
- 3–4 tablespoons ice water
- 2 tablespoons cornstarch
- ¾ cup sugar
- ½ cup heavy cream
- 1 tablespoon finely minced lemon zest
- ½ cup freshly squeezed lemon juice
- 3 large eggs, plus 2 egg yolks
- 3 cups mixed fresh berries
- ¼ cup apple jelly

1. Make crust by combining flour, brown sugar, and salt in a large bowl. With a pastry cutter or your fingers, work 1 stick butter into flour mixture until it resembles coarse meal. Stir in just enough water for dough to come together. Form dough into a disc, wrap with plastic, and refrigerate 30 minutes to 8 hours.
2. To finish crust, heat oven to 375°F. Roll dough between two sheets of lightly floured wax paper to an 11-inch round. Press rolled dough onto bottom and up sides of

a 9 x 1-inch round fluted tart pan with removable bottom. Blind bake by lining inside of dough with aluminum foil and weighing down with pie weights, raw rice, or dried beans. Bake 15 minutes. Remove weights and foil and prick insides with a fork. Bake until medium brown, an additional 10 minutes. While crust is finishing baking, prick any bubbles that form with a fork. Remove from oven, and cool completely in pan.

3. To make filling, set up a double boiler with barely simmering water, making sure water will not touch bottom of top pan. Before assembling double boiler, in top double-boiler pan, whisk together cornstarch, sugar, cream, lemon zest, lemon juice, eggs, and egg yolks. Put pan over simmering water, and cook, whisking constantly, until mixture thickens, about 6–7 minutes.

4. Remove entire pan from heat, leaving bowl over hot water. Add remaining 2 tablespoons butter, and whisk until butter melts. Remove top from double boiler, and let filling cool at room temperature 5 minutes. Pour filling into cooled crust. Refrigerate at least 3 hours.

5. Up to 8 hours before serving, melt jelly in a small saucepan. Scatter berries over top of tart, and generously brush with melted jelly. Refrigerate until set, about 1 hour. Remove from tart pan, and serve.

> Ignatius imagined . . . his mother's family, a group of people who tended to suffer violence and pain. There was the old aunt who had been robbed of fifty cents by some hoodlums, the cousin who had been struck by the Magazine streetcar, the uncle who had eaten a bad cream puff.
>
> —Ignatius arriving home from his first day at Levy Pants, wondering what terrible thing his frazzled mother was about to spring on him.

Good Cream Puffs
Makes 10.

The cream puff started out in the thirteenth century in southern Germany and France as a puff pastry filled with cheese mixtures. Over time, the recipe for the puffed bun became standardized, using flour, water, egg, and fat, and the dough was given the name *choux.* The filled dessert became known in mid-nineteenth-century England and France as the profiterole, and the French still call a puff filled with pastry cream a profiterole. Americans, on the other hand, tend to think of a profiterole as a pastry puff filled with ice cream and topped with chocolate, and it's our cream puffs that are filled with pastry cream. Cream puffs were extremely popular New Orleans bakery items in the 1960s, as they are still.

Pastry Cream Filling

 2 cups whole milk

 ½ cup sugar

 5 tablespoons all-purpose flour

 ⅛ teaspoon salt

 1 vanilla bean, split lengthwise

 3 large egg yolks, lightly beaten (save 2 whites
  for brushing pastry)

 2 tablespoons butter

 1 teaspoon vanilla extract

Choux Pastry Puffs

 1 cup water

 1 tablespoon sugar

 ½ cup (1 stick) unsalted butter

 ¼ teaspoon iodized salt

 1 cup all-purpose flour

 4 large eggs, at room temperature

 2 egg whites

 Confectioners' sugar for garnish

1. *Prepare Pastry Cream Filling:* In a large saucepan, add milk, sugar, flour, and salt, and whisk until flour is completely dissolved. Slice vanilla bean in half lengthwise, and scrape seeds. Add both seeds and bean pod halves into pan. Bring to a boil and simmer, stirring constantly, over low heat 1 minute. Remove from heat, and remove vanilla bean pods.

2. Whisk ½ cup hot milk mixture into egg yolks. Put pan with milk mixture on low heat, and slowly whisk in egg mixture. Cook 2 minutes on low heat, whisking constantly.

3. Remove from heat and, if lumps have formed, force through a coarse strainer into a bowl. Stir in butter and vanilla extract. Press a piece of buttered plastic wrap directly onto top of pastry cream, and refrigerate until firm. (Can be made a day ahead.)

4. *Prepare Choux Pastry Puffs:* Preheat oven to 400°F and set racks in center and bottom of oven. Line 2 sheet pans with parchment paper, and set aside.

5. In a large saucepan over high heat, bring water, sugar, butter, and salt to a full rolling boil. Using a wooden spoon, stir all the flour into boiling liquid and cook, stirring constantly, until the mixture starts pulling away from sides of the pan, about 30 seconds. Remove pan from heat, and pour mixture into a large bowl.

6. Stir batter 30 seconds; then mix in eggs, 2 at a time, and beat well with a hand mixer or large spoon, until thick, smooth, and glossy. Scoop dough into a piping bag fitted with a large tip, and pipe out balls of dough the size of golf balls 2 inches apart onto parchment-lined sheets. If you don't have a pastry bag, drop a rounded ¼ cup of dough onto pans.

7. Bake until light brown, rotating pans halfway through, for a total of 25–30 minutes. Prick through tops with a wooden toothpick, brush lightly with egg whites, and continue baking until crisp and golden brown, about 5 more minutes. Remove baked puffs to a rack, and cool completely at room temperature.

8. To assemble, slice top third off puffs and scoop out any uncooked dough. Fill with chilled pastry cream, place tops back on, and liberally sift each cream puff with confectioners' sugar. Serve immediately, or refrigerate up to 2 days.

Caramel Doberge Cake

Makes one 9-inch, 8-layer cake.

In 1933, pastry chef Beulah Ledner opened a bakery in her own home in Uptown New Orleans, and from that business she forever changed the local cake scene with her invention of the doberge (DOUGH-bash) cake. This colossal multilayered, multifrosted confection is based on the Hungarian dobos torte, and it's filled with custard instead of buttercream, and is iced with both buttercream and fondant. Named "doberge" because the word sounds French, Ledner's creation is still extremely popular and is often sold as an eye-catching cake that is half lemon and half chocolate. Doberge cake is also what most New Orleanians wants for their birthday.

Caramel Custard Filling (recipe follows, and preferably made a day ahead)

3½ cups cake flour

3 teaspoons baking powder

½ teaspoon iodized salt

1 cup buttermilk, room temperature

2 teaspoons pure vanilla extract

½ teaspoon almond extract

12 tablespoons (1½ sticks) unsalted butter, room temperature

2 cups sugar

5 egg yolks

4 egg whites, stiffly beaten

Caramel Frosting (recipe follows)

Poured Caramel Icing (recipe follows)

1. Make Caramel Custard Filling, and allow to cool until firm.
2. Preheat oven to 350°F. Oil three 9 x 2-inch round cake pans. Line the bottom of each pan with parchment paper rounds. Oil the tops of the paper, and dust insides of pans with a few tablespoons all-purpose flour.
3. Sift together flour, baking powder, and salt. Set aside. In a separate bowl, mix together buttermilk, vanilla and almond extracts, and set aside.
4. In a large mixing bowl, cream butter and sugar on medium mixer speed until light and fluffy, at least 3 minutes. Add egg yolks, one at a time, and blend until smooth.
5. Using low mixer speed, add sifted dry ingredients, alternating with buttermilk mixture, beginning and ending with flour. Gently fold in egg whites by hand. Batter will be thick.
6. Pour ¾ cup batter into each of the 3 prepared pans, and use a spoon to spread tops evenly. Rap cake pans on a hard surface several times to release any air bubbles. Bake until center is set, about 12–15 minutes. (Tops will

not be brown.) Remove layers from pans and cool. Repeat baking process, to make 8 thin layers.

7. When cake layers are cool, spread ⅔ cup of Caramel Custard Filling between each layer.

8. Ice with Caramel Frosting and refrigerate at least 1 hour. (Save leftover frosting to pipe a decoration around cake base when everything is done.)

9. Complete by placing iced cake on a large rack set over a baking sheet to catch drips. Pour Poured Caramel Icing over cake, and spread onto sides. If caramel hardens before pouring, add a little milk and heat gently. Let icing cool until firm before removing cake to a platter. If desired, pipe rosettes around base with leftover Caramel Frosting. Store cake in the refrigerator up to a week.

Caramel Custard Filling

1 quart whole milk
1½ cups dark brown sugar, packed
½ teaspoon salt
¼ cup all-purpose flour
5 egg yolks, well beaten
¼ cup cornstarch
1 tablespoon vanilla extract

1. In a large, cold, heavy-bottomed saucepan, add milk, brown sugar, salt, and flour, and whisk until flour is dissolved. Bring to a boil over medium heat, turn heat to low, and simmer 1 minute, whisking constantly. Remove from heat.

2. Slowly pour 1 cup hot milk mixture into egg yolks, whisking constantly. Whisk cornstarch into egg mixture until cornstarch is completely dissolved. Over low heat, whisk egg mixture into milk mixture, and cook, whisking constantly, 2 minutes.

3. Remove from heat, stir in vanilla, and cool at room temperature, stirring occasionally. Cover and chill until firm. Can be made up to 2 days ahead and refrigerated. Stir well before filling cake.

Caramel Frosting

2¼ cups light brown sugar, packed
18 tablespoons (2¼ sticks) unsalted butter, divided
2 tablespoons dark corn syrup
½ cup evaporated milk
¼ teaspoon salt
1½ teaspoons vanilla extract
1 box (1 pound) confectioners' sugar

1. In a large, heavy-bottomed saucepan over low heat, stir together brown sugar, 2 sticks butter, corn syrup, evaporated milk, and salt. Just as mixture comes to a full rolling boil, cook exactly two minutes, without stirring.

2. Remove from heat, and stir in remaining 2 tablespoons butter, vanilla, and confectioners' sugar. Beat with a hand mixer on medium speed until smooth and beginning to firm. Continue beating with a wooden spoon until icing reaches spreading consistency but is not completely cool. Spread on cake immediately.

Poured Caramel Icing

2½ cups light brown sugar, packed
¾ cup dark brown sugar, packed
2 cups half-and-half
3 tablespoons light corn syrup
½ teaspoon salt
3 tablespoons unsalted butter
2 teaspoons pure vanilla extract

1. In a medium-sized, heavy-bottomed saucepan, add light and dark brown sugars, half-and-half, corn syrup, and

salt. Stir over medium heat until simmering. Reduce heat to low. Stirring occasionally, cook until a candy thermometer reaches 232°F.

2. Remove from heat, and immediately add butter and vanilla. Stir with a wooden spoon until thick but still warm and pourable, from 5–15 minutes, depending on the humidity that day. Pour on cake immediately.

· ·

Russian Cake (Creole Trifle)

Makes one 9-inch cake.

· ·

Russian cake supposedly got its start in New Orleans in 1872, when the Grand Duke Alexis of Russia visited New Orleans for Mardi Gras. The story goes that a baker assigned to make sweets for His Highness had run short of ingredients. So he mixed pastry scraps with a booze-tinged syrup and pressed the mishmash between two split cake layers, forming a dense patchwork dessert. Extremely popular in New Orleans in the 1950s and 1960s, Russian cake still can be found in a few bakeries.

½ cup white grape, apple, or pineapple juice

¼ cup dark rum

2 tablespoons grenadine syrup

½ teaspoon anise extract, optional

8 cups of ½-inch pieces stale pastries (cakes, doughnuts, cookies, and so forth, frosting included, but nothing cream-filled)

1 Yellow Butter Cake (recipe follows)

½ cup seedless raspberry jam

2 cups confectioners' sugar

8 tablespoons (1 stick) unsalted butter, room temperature

3 tablespoons half-and-half

1 teaspoon pure vanilla extract

¼ teaspoon almond extract

Multicolored nonpareils

1. In a large, deep bowl, whisk together grape juice, rum, grenadine, and anise extract. Add stale pastry pieces, and stir gently until liquid is completely absorbed.

2. Oil the bottom and sides of a 9-inch springform pan. Slice cooled butter cake in half horizontally and place bottom half inside pan. Spoon ⅓ of moistened cake pieces on top of cake in pan, and press everything down hard and evenly with a wooden spoon. Spread on half of raspberry jam. Top with another ⅓ of cake pieces, press hard again, and spread on remaining ¼ cup jam. Top

with remaining ⅓ of cake pieces, press hard, and lay remaining butter cake half on top.

3. Cover cake with a sheet of plastic wrap, then top with a 9-inch cardboard cake round, a 9-inch cake pan, or anything that's round and flat and fits into the pan. Lay foil-wrapped bricks or canned goods on top of cake, and let sit 12–24 hours in the refrigerator.

4. To make icing, combine confectioners' sugar, butter, half-and-half, vanilla and almond extracts in a large bowl and beat over medium speed of an electric mixer until fluffy, about 4 minutes. Spread icing over cake top, and sprinkle top with nonpareils. Remove cake from pan, and serve. Store unused cake in the refrigerator. Keeps tightly covered up to a week.

Yellow Butter Cake

Makes one 9-inch cake layer

1⅓ cups cake flour
1¼ teaspoons baking powder
½ teaspoon iodized salt
¼ teaspoon baking soda
8 tablespoons (1 stick) unsalted butter, room temperature
1 cup sugar
2 large eggs, room temperature
⅔ cup buttermilk, room temperature
1½ teaspoons pure vanilla extract
½ teaspoon almond extract

1. Preheat oven to 350°F. Grease and flour a 9-inch round cake pan with 2-inch sides. With a fork, stir together flour, baking powder, salt, and soda, and set aside.

2. In a large bowl, use medium mixer speed to cream together butter and sugar until light and fluffy, about 3 minutes. Add eggs, one at a time, beating 30 seconds between each addition.

3. In a separate bowl, combine buttermilk, vanilla, and almond extract. Using low mixer speed, alternate flour and buttermilk mixture into butter, beginning and ending with flour. Spread batter into prepared pan, and bake until center springs up when touched, about 30–35 minutes. Cool cake in pan 5 minutes. Remove to a rack, and cool completely.

Ignatius was forced to go to work because Mrs. Reilly wrecked
her 1946 Plymouth. In 1946, Chrysler's Plymouth line was offered

Setting Trends at Levy Pants

"The company says it's going to give me a nice boiled ham for Easter," Miss Trixie told Ignatius. "I certainly hope so. They forgot all about my Thanksgiving turkey."

—Miss Trixie, hoping that Levy Pants makes good on its promise.

It was a traumatic day for Ignatius when Irene Reilly plowed her 1946 Plymouth into a building and the resulting damage settlement forced him to look for work. Luckily, Levy Pants was hiring.

According to John Kennedy Toole's mother, Thelma, the fictitious Levy Pants is based on Haspel Brothers, a clothing manufacturer formerly at St. Bernard Avenue and Broad Street, and where her son worked briefly. Haspel was founded in New Orleans in 1909 by Joseph Haspel Sr., and the company became famous for creating the "wash and wear" seersucker suit.

As every fashion-minded New Orleans male knows, seersucker is a puckered cotton fabric made of alternating smooth and rough stripes. The lightweight material was originally popular in the steamy regions of Colonial British India, with its name deriving from the Persian word *shīr-o-shakar,* literally meaning "milk and sugar," referring to the fabric's textures.

Joseph Haspel first made a national name for himself by attiring southern workers in overalls made of then-economical blue and white seersucker. And, in those days before air-conditioning, businessmen, too, soon started wearing the cool, easy-care fabric. Then, in the vein of reverse snootiness, Princeton undergrads donned seersucker in the 1920s, and by the 1930s the puckered, striped garb was the thing to wear in the elite Northeast.

This fashionably rumpled look jumped to the big screen in 1962, when Gregory Peck wore a seersucker suit in the movie *To Kill a Mockingbird,* and a year later when Cary Grant wore one in *Charade.* Seersucker even found a niche in government, with female Marines wearing seersucker uniforms for summer service during World War II. Later, in the late 1990s, Mississippi Senator Trent Lott decided to show the populace the U.S. Senate could be bipartisan and hip, and he designated Seersucker Thursday in the second or third week of June. In 2004, California's Senator Dianne Feinstein jumped on the seersucker bandwagon by gifting female senators with seersucker suits to wear on that dashing day, which, in 2012, became voluntary.

In *A Confederacy of Dunces,* Ignatius ends up trying to ignite the African American factory workers at Levy

Pants to riot in a "Crusade for Moorish Dignity," but he fails and gets fired. And Levy Pants never does fork over a turkey or ham to Miss Trixie. But the Haspel Clothing brand, now based in Baton Rouge, is a company that gives something valuable to the whole world, a breezy suit of summer wear that, for generations, has been a staple in southern closets.

Miss Trixie's Orange-and-Bourbon-Glazed Ham

Makes 1 glazed ham, serving 15–20.

It may be considered old-fashioned to score a ham and stud it with cloves, but hardly any technique or spice does a better job of magnifying the flavor of a ham, that entrée so closely associated with the South.

⅓ cup orange juice

2 tablespoons honey

1 cup orange preserves or marmalade

1 (8- to 9-pound) bone-in cured or smoked ham

Whole cloves

2 tablespoons bourbon

1. In a small saucepan, stir together orange juice, honey, and preserves. Bring to a boil, and simmer over low heat 5 minutes. Remove glaze from heat, and set aside, uncovered.

2. Preheat oven to 325°F. Score fat layer of ham horizontally and vertically at 1-inch intervals, and stud the centers of the resulting squares with whole cloves. Place ham on a rack over a foil-lined roasting pan. Bake 1 hour.

3. Stir bourbon into glaze. Baste ham with half of glaze, and bake 15 minutes. Raise oven temperature to 350°F. Spread on remaining half of glaze, and bake 15 more minutes. Remove ham from oven, and allow to cool at least 20 minutes before slicing.

Shrimp and Ham–Stuffed Mirlitons

Makes 8 servings.

Miss Trixie can use leftover ham to make this stuffed specialty, a savory side that's ubiquitous on New Orleans holiday menus. The mirliton, aka vegetable pear or chayote, is a pear-shaped, squash-like vegetable with one large, edible seed. It actually belongs to the gourd family and grows enthusiastically on vines that gardeners trail along backyard fences. Locals are so taken with this distinctive vegetable that the Bywater section of the city holds an annual Mirliton Festival.

4 mirlitons

2 tablespoons olive oil

¾ cup finely chopped onion

½ cup finely chopped bell pepper

1 stalk celery, finely chopped

2 teaspoons minced garlic

1 cup peeled, deveined shrimp, coarsely chopped

1 cup cooked ham, cut into ½-inch cubes

1 teaspoon minced fresh oregano

½ teaspoon fresh thyme

½ cup half-and-half

1 cup fine breadcrumbs, divided

½ teaspoon salt

¼ teaspoon black pepper

¼ teaspoon Crystal hot sauce

1 large egg, beaten

2 tablespoons minced fresh flat-leaf parsley

1 tablespoon melted butter

1. Steam or boil mirlitons until just tender, about ½ hour for steamed and 1 hour for boiled. Drain well. When mirlitons are cool enough to handle, scoop out the seeds and discard. Scoop out mirliton pulp, reserving, and leaving a ¼-inch margin in the shell. Turn shells upside down on paper towels to drain. Chop pulp into ¼-inch dice, and set aside.

2. Preheat oven to 350°F. In a large skillet, heat olive oil over medium heat. Add onion, bell pepper, and celery, and sauté until onion is lightly brown. Add garlic, and sauté 30 seconds.

3. Add the reserved mirliton pulp, shrimp, ham, oregano, thyme, half-and-half, ½ cup breadcrumbs, salt, black pepper, and hot sauce. Cook, stirring often, until most of the liquid is evaporated and mixture is thick, about 5 minutes. Remove from heat, and stir in the egg and parsley.

4. Mound shrimp mixture into reserved mirliton shells. Combine remaining ½ cup breadcrumbs with melted butter, and sprinkle over mirlitons. Place mirlitons in a lightly oiled baking dish, and bake, uncovered, until tops are deep brown, about ½ hour. Serve warm.

Arnaud's Chicken Pontalba

Makes 4 servings. Adapted from a recipe from Katy Casbarian, owner, Arnaud's Restaurant.

Miss Trixie can also use her leftover ham in this New Orleans classic of chicken and potatoes cloaked in béarnaise sauce. Originally created by chef Paul Blange of Brennan's restaurant in the 1950s, this dish is named for the dramatic and sophisticated Baroness Micaela Pontalba, who lived in New Orleans in the 1800s. This version is what's served at Arnaud's, the romantic French Quarter restaurant opened in 1918 by a colorful French wine salesman known as "Count" Arnaud Cazenave.

8 tablespoons (1 stick) lightly salted butter

1 medium onion, finely chopped

12 green onions, white and light green parts only, thinly sliced

1 clove garlic, very finely chopped

2 white potatoes (not Idaho), about 1½ pounds, peeled and cut into ½-inch cubes

4 ounces lean ham, cut into ¼-inch dice

4 ounces white or cremini mushrooms, brushed clean and sliced

½ cup dry white wine

1 tablespoon finely chopped flat leaf parsley

1 cup all-purpose flour

1 teaspoon kosher or sea salt

½ teaspoon freshly ground black pepper

⅛ teaspoon cayenne pepper

2 pounds boneless chicken breasts, legs, and thighs

1 cup vegetable oil

1½ cups béarnaise sauce (recipe follows)

1. Preheat oven to 200°F. Over medium-low heat, melt butter in a heavy, 12-inch sauté pan or deep skillet. When foam has subsided, add the onion, green onions, garlic, and potatoes, and cook over low heat until the vegetables are browned, about 15 minutes, stirring frequently.

2. Add the diced ham, mushrooms, wine, and parsley, and cook, stirring occasionally, until the wine is evaporated and the potatoes are fork-tender, about 8 minutes.

3. Remove the pan from heat. Allowing excess butter to drain back into the pan, use a slotted spoon to transfer

Béarnaise Sauce

Makes 1½ cups. Can be made 1 hour ahead.

½ cup red wine vinegar

¼ cup chopped fresh tarragon leaves

2 large shallots, finely chopped

½ teaspoon coarsely ground black pepper

5 large egg yolks

1¼ cups clarified butter (recipe page 123)

Kosher or sea salt

Freshly ground white pepper

1. In a medium saucepan, combine vinegar, tarragon, shallots, and black pepper. Place pan over high heat, bring to a boil, and cook until the liquid has almost completely evaporated, leaving a moist but not wet

mixture. Remove from heat, and set aside at room temperature until just barely warm.

2. Transfer mixture to the top of a double boiler. Over gently simmering water, add the egg yolks and whisk until the mixture is pale yellow and slightly thick, when the base of the pan is visible as you whisk, about 2 minutes.

3. Add clarified butter very slowly in a thin stream, whisking constantly. After ⅓ of the butter has been incorporated, add butter a little more quickly. Season to taste with salt and white pepper. Keep at room temperature until serving. If making ahead, when ready to serve, stir in 1 tablespoon hot water.

mixture to a large gratin dish attractive enough to bring to the table. Put dish into oven. (At this point, the vegetable mixture can be cooled to room temperature and refrigerated overnight. Be sure to retain excess butter.)

4. In a wide, shallow bowl, combine flour, salt, black pepper, and cayenne pepper. Cut up the larger pieces of chicken, and pound them so none are thicker than ½ inch. Dredge chicken in seasoned flour, gently shaking off the excess.

5. Add vegetable oil to the butter in the original pan, and place the pan over medium-high heat. When sizzling gently, add chicken and fry, turning frequently, until cooked through and golden brown, about 10 minutes. Remove chicken, and drain on paper towels. Arrange evenly over vegetables in gratin dish. Return dish to oven while preparing béarnaise sauce, if you have not already done so. To serve, spoon the sauce evenly over the entire top of the dish and bring to the table hot.

Clarified Butter

Makes 1½ cups

1 pound (4 sticks) unsalted butter

1. Place butter in a heavy-bottomed saucepan, and melt over low heat. As butter melts, skim off the white residue (milk solids) that rise to the top.
2. After no more foam rises, about 10 minutes, remove from heat. Very carefully pour the golden liquid, the clarified butter, into a bowl, leaving solids in the pan. Alternatively, strain through a cheesecloth-lined strainer. Keeps 3–6 months refrigerated.

> Mr. Gonzalez took the opportunity of her disappearance to retrieve his stamp pad from the bag and discovered that it was covered with what felt and smelled like bacon grease.
>
> —Mr. Gonzalez, searching in one of Miss Trixie's mysterious and ever-present paper bags.

Green Beans in Bacon Grease Stock

Makes 4 servings.

If Mr. Gonzalez actually had a clean supply of bacon grease, he'd have one of the key ingredients needed to prepare a dish common throughout the South. It wasn't so long ago that just about every Louisiana home cook saved the drippings from the breakfast bacon. This smoky flavoring ingredient was often stored in a coffee can on the stove, and a generous part of it could end up simmered with green beans cooked until they were just about falling apart. By today's standards, this dish certainly isn't considered a health food. But it sure does taste good.

3 tablespoons bacon grease, or 1 tablespoon butter
and 2 tablespoons olive oil

½ cup finely chopped onion

6 cups water

½ teaspoon salt

½ teaspoon ground black pepper

1¼ pounds fresh green beans, ends trimmed

1. In a medium pot, add bacon grease and onion, and sauté over medium heat until onion is translucent.
2. Add water, salt, and black pepper. Bring to a boil, and simmer 5 minutes.
3. Add green beans, and cook at a bare simmer, uncovered, until very soft, about 1–1½ hours. Drain and serve warm.

. . . .

Toothsome Cubano Sandwiches

Makes 4 servings.

. . . .

Luncheon meat, or cold cuts, defines any brined, smoked, or otherwise cured meat that is ready to eat. Most luncheon meat is molded, and often sliced and prepackaged, and typically ends up inside a sandwich. Spam is

a luncheon meat, as are the packages of bologna, sliced turkey, and ham dangling in your grocer's deli case. And, although the sandwiches Ignatius is serving sound lowbrow, luncheon meat can certainly be dressed up, as in the following recipe.

In Cuba, the *cubano* is pressed and toasted in a *plancha,* a machine similar to a panini press, but without the grooved surfaces. If you don't have a fancy sandwich press, a couple of heavy skillets work just fine.

1 loaf Cuban, French, or Italian bread, at least
28 inches long

Yellow or Creole mustard

1 pound sliced deli honey-glazed ham

1 pound deli-roasted pork, or Cuban Pork Roast
(recipe on pages 46–47)

½ pound sliced Swiss or Provolone cheese

Thinly sliced dill pickles

2 tablespoons butter, divided

1. Slice bread in half horizontally, and spread mustard on insides of bread.
2. Layer ham evenly on bottom half of bread, and top with pork. Top pork with cheese and pickles, and place bread top on sandwich. Press down firmly all along sandwich, and cut into 4 portions, about 7 inches each.
3. Melt 1 tablespoon butter in a large, heavy skillet over medium-low heat. Lay 2 sandwiches in skillet, and place another large, heavy skillet on top of sandwiches. (For added pressure, top with a couple cans of beans.) Grill 1

> "I have discovered that Miss Trixie considers luncheon meat a rather toothsome delicacy."
>
> —Ignatius, to Mr. Gonzalez.

minute, and turn over. Place skillet on top of sandwiches again, and cook until cheese is melted. Sandwich should be flattened to less than half its original size. Repeat with remaining tablespoon butter and sandwiches. Slice portions diagonally, and serve.

. . . .

Prime Rib of Beef with Pan Sauce
Makes 6 servings.

. . . .

Let's pretend that trollop Trixie *is* determined to get a roast out of Mr. Levy, and that nothing less than prime rib will do. Also known as a standing rib roast, this pricy cut of beef comes from the primal rib, and can contain two to seven ribs. Prime rib is actually graded by the USDA as select, choice, and prime, with prime the highest grade, since it has the most marbling, and is therefore buttery tender.

> One 3-rib (5-pound) prime rib beef roast, with bones
>   Frenched (meat trimmed to expose the bones)
> Salt and pepper
> 2 tablespoons olive oil
> ½ cup cognac
> 1 tablespoon unsalted butter
> 1 tablespoon balsamic vinegar
> ½ teaspoon cornstarch

1. Remove roast from refrigerator 2 hours before preparing.
2. Preheat oven to 275°F. Liberally season roast with salt and pepper.
3. Heat olive oil over medium-high heat in a cast-iron skillet large enough to hold the roast, or in a heavy-bottomed roaster. Sear roast well on all sides, about 15 minutes total.

> "The Trixie trollop had a fixation about a turkey or a ham. Or was it a roast?"
> —Ignatius, to Mr. Levy.

4. Place skillet in oven, and roast the beef, uncovered, until a thermometer inserted into thickest portion registers 115°F for rare, about 20 minutes per pound. Roast to 125°F for medium-rare, and 135°F for medium. Place roast on a cutting board, cover loosely with aluminum foil, and let stand 30 minutes. (Roast will continue cooking while standing.)
5. While roast is resting, prepare sauce by skimming fat from drippings in skillet. To skillet add cognac, and deglaze over moderately high heat until reduced by half. Add butter and vinegar, and stir until butter is melted. Dissolve cornstarch in 2 tablespoons water, and whisk into sauce. Simmer 1 minute, and serve over slices of warm beef.

. . . .

Herb-Smoked Turkey
Makes 10–12 servings.

. . . .

Smoking is one of the tastiest ways to prepare a turkey, and as a bonus it frees up the oven at holiday time. This recipe breaks all the rules with herb-stuffed slits cut straight into the breast, which allows the seasoning to better permeate the meat.

1 turkey (10–12 pounds)

1 tablespoon salt

¼ cup olive oil

2 tablespoons freshly squeezed lemon juice

1 teaspoon ground black pepper

½ teaspoon cayenne pepper

½ cup finely minced fresh herbs, such as rosemary, parsley, thyme, oregano, and chives

2 cloves garlic, finely minced

3 stalks fresh rosemary

4 cups hickory wood chips

1. Remove wing tips, neck flap, and giblets from turkey. In a bowl, combine salt, olive oil, and lemon juice, and whisk or stir until salt is dissolved. Stir in black pepper, cayenne, herbs, and garlic. Make at least 4 deep slits into the breast and a slit on top of each thigh, and fill cuts with marinade. Using your fingers, carefully separate skin from breast and work any remaining marinade under the skin and onto the top of skin and inside the cavity. Stuff rosemary stalks into cavity. Place the turkey in a roasting pan, cover with plastic wrap, and marinate in the refrigerator 4–24 hours.

2. Remove the bird from the refrigerator 1 hour ahead of cooking time. Soak wood chips in water 1 hour. Prepare an electric or charcoal smoker or a water smoker according to manufacturer's directions, and bring to 240°F. Toss 1½ cups drained wood chips onto the coals or in the smoker pan.

3. Oil the grill grate, and place the turkey, breast side up, on top rack. Cover the smoker and close vents ⅓ of the way. After 1½ hours, check to see if smoker needs additional wood chips. A charcoal smoker will require adding 12–24 briquettes every 1½ hours. Maintain a 240–250°F temperature throughout cooking.

4. Turkey is ready when the juices run clear from the thigh, or when a thermometer inserted into the thickest part of the inside thigh meat reaches 165°F. This should take about 30–40 minutes per pound. Allow turkey to sit 30 minutes before carving.

Bacon-Wrapped Turkey Breast
Makes 6–8 servings.

Miss Trixie should be willing to compromise, and then maybe she can wrangle a turkey breast out of Levy Pants. She can cook her prize using this simple recipe, which produces flavor-packed, super-moist meat that doesn't require basting, and will therefore limit interruptions on naps.

½ turkey breast (2–2½ pounds), with skin and bones

Salt, black pepper, cayenne pepper

Garlic powder

8 fresh sage leaves

6 slices thick-cut bacon

1 tablespoon unsalted butter, melted

1 tablespoon olive oil

Turkey Neck Gravy for serving (recipe follows)

1. Season turkey with salt, black pepper, cayenne pepper, and garlic powder. Arrange sage leaves over breast top. Wrap bacon strips closely together around turkey breast, tucking bacon ends underneath. Place turkey in a resealable plastic food bag, and refrigerate 24 hours, or up to 2 days.

2. Remove turkey from refrigerator, and heat oven to 400°F. Add butter and olive oil to a Dutch oven. Place turkey breast, skin side up, on top of oil. Cover and bake 30 minutes.

3. Reduce heat to 325°F, and continue baking, covered, until a probe thermometer registers 165°F, about 20 additional minutes.

4. Remove turkey breast from pot, and cover with aluminum foil until ready to serve.

5. If serving with Turkey Neck Gravy, skim fat from drippings and heat remaining drippings with prepared gravy.

Turkey Neck Gravy

Makes 2 cups

If Miss Trixie can conjure up a little energy, she can easily make this rich gravy to spoon over her roasted turkey breast.

2 pounds turkey necks

2 teaspoons Creole Seasoning (purchased, or use recipe on pages 6–7)

3 tablespoons vegetable oil

1 medium onion, chopped

1 medium bell pepper, seeded and chopped

1 stalk celery, chopped

2 cloves garlic, chopped

5 cups chicken broth

2 cups water

2 tablespoons unsalted butter

3 tablespoons all-purpose flour

1. Season turkey necks with Creole Seasoning. Over medium-high heat, heat oil in a large, heavy-bottomed saucepan. Brown seasoned turkey well on all sides.

2. Transfer turkey to a bowl. To the same saucepan add onion, bell pepper, and celery, and sauté 3 minutes, stirring occasionally.

3. Add garlic, chicken broth, water, and browned turkey necks. Bring to a boil, and simmer briskly, uncovered, 45 minutes. Strain mixture and discard solids.

4. Melt butter in a medium-sized, heavy-bottomed saucepan. Add flour, and make a light brown roux by stirring constantly over medium heat, about 2 minutes. Remove from heat.

5. Carefully whisk 1 cup reserved broth into hot roux (it will splatter). Whisk in remaining broth, return to heat, and bring to a boil. Adjust for seasoning and serve.

Turkey Pot Pie

Makes 4 servings.

It's a safe bet that, if the single Miss Trixie actually receives a whole turkey, she will have leftovers, which would be excellent in this old-time favorite.

2 tablespoons vegetable oil

1 cup diced carrot

1 cup chopped onion

⅔ cup diced celery

½ cup coarsely chopped mushrooms

½ cup chopped red bell pepper

¼ cup frozen green peas

3 tablespoons all-purpose flour

2½ cups chicken stock

½ cup diced potatoes

2 cups cooked and cubed turkey

⅓ cup heavy cream

1 teaspoon chopped fresh sage
   (or ½ teaspoon dried)

1 tablespoon brandy

Salt and pepper

2 tablespoons chopped parsley

6 sheets phyllo dough, thawed

4 tablespoons (½ stick) melted butter

1 egg beaten with 1 tablespoon water

1. Preheat oven to 350°F. In a heavy saucepot, heat oil over medium-high heat and sauté carrot, onion, celery, mushrooms, bell pepper, and peas until soft, 2 minutes. Stir in flour, and cook over low heat, stirring constantly, 1 minute.

2. Add stock, and bring to a boil. Add potatoes, and simmer until carrots and potatoes are just tender, about 10 minutes.

3. Stir in turkey, cream, and sage, and cook until slightly thickened. Add brandy, salt, and pepper to taste, and parsley. Bring to a boil, and remove from heat.

4. Spoon mixture into 4 oven-proof soup bowls or ramekins. Prepare tops by laying 1 sheet phyllo dough on a hard surface and brushing with butter. Lay another sheet on top, brush with butter, and repeat process until all sheets are used. With a sharp knife, cut pastry to fit on top of bowls. Brush with egg wash, and bake until golden brown and bubbly, about 20–25 minutes. Cool 5 minutes before serving.

Keeping Susan and Sandra Alive for Peanuts Asian Coleslaw

Makes 4–6 servings.

4 cups Napa or green cabbage, shredded

1 cup bok choy, julienned

1 large carrot, grated

¼ cup minced green onion

Honey Sesame Dressing (recipe follows)

½ cup roasted peanuts

In a large bowl, combine cabbage, bok choy, carrot, and green onion. When ready to serve, toss with Honey Sesame Dressing and top with peanuts.

Honey Sesame Dressing   Makes about ⅔ cup

¼ cup rice vinegar

3 tablespoons canola oil

2 tablespoons honey

2 tablespoons toasted sesame oil

2 teaspoons tamari or soy sauce

1 teaspoon freshly grated ginger

½ teaspoon red pepper flakes, or to taste

Combine all ingredients in a covered glass jar, and shake well.

"Thank goodness my mother has some money. I always knew I'd have to go back to her someday. . . . You can't keep Susan and Sandra alive for peanuts."
"Oh, shut up."

—Mrs. Levy deriding Mr. Levy for a lawsuit filed against Levy Pants—and Mr. Levy's response.

Mocha Chocolate Ice Cream
Makes 1½ quarts.

The empty cartons Ignatius uses for growing beans could have once held ice cream made by Brown's Velvet, a dairy in New Orleans since 1905, and now owned by Dean Foods, which doesn't make ice cream. Or the cartons could have come from K&B, the drugstore chain that had its own brand of ice cream, and advertisements that revolved around the color purple.

2 cups whole milk

1⅓ cups sugar

⅓ cup unsweetened cocoa powder (not Dutch process)

1 tablespoon cornstarch

¼ teaspoon salt

4 large egg yolks

1 can (12 ounces) evaporated milk, chilled

½ cup heavy cream, chilled

½ cup strong, brewed coffee, chilled

2 teaspoons pure vanilla extract

2 tablespoons plain vodka (to keep the ice cream
    from freezing too hard)

1. In a large, heavy-bottomed saucepan, whisk together
   whole milk, sugar, cocoa powder, cornstarch, and salt.
   Bring to a boil, and simmer over low heat 1 minute,
   whisking constantly. Remove pan from heat.

2. In a medium bowl, whisk egg yolks until thick, about 2
   minutes. Slowly add 1 cup hot chocolate mixture into
   eggs in a stream, whisking the entire time. In a slow
   stream, pour egg mixture into chocolate in pan,
   whisking constantly.

3. Whisking constantly, cook mixture over low heat until
   slightly thickened, about 3 minutes. Remove pan from
   heat, and whisk in evaporated milk, cream, coffee, and
   vanilla. If lumps have formed, strain. Pour into a bowl,
   and place bowl in a larger bowl of ice water. Allow to
   come to room temperature, whisking occasionally.
   Cover and refrigerate custard overnight.

4. When ready to process, stir in vodka. Churn in an ice
   cream freezer according to manufacturer's directions.
   Before serving, freeze tightly covered in the freezer at
   least 2 hours. Store tightly covered in the freezer.

> In several empty ice cream cartons on top
> of the filing cabinets beans were already
> sprouting little vines.
>
> —Mr. Gonzalez, happily surveying the Levy Pants
>   office and the results of Ignatius's handiwork.

> Miss Trixie was sitting up on the couch. Her face
> had been cleaned. Her mouth was an orange smear.
>
> —One of Mrs. Levy's attempts to perk Miss Trixie up. (Instead
>   of wearing orange-colored lipstick, the unconcerned octoge-
>   narian would probably be happier actually eating something
>   made with a real orange.)

Mimosa Sorbet

Makes 1 quart.

Just below New Orleans in Plaquemines Parish, farmers
have been growing citrus commercially since the 1800s.
Although hurricanes, insects, disease, and hard freezes
occasionally hamper production, Plaquemines Parish
growers still manage to produce some of the South's juic-
iest and most intensely flavored satsumas, grapefruit,
and oranges.

1 tablespoon orange zest

½ cup sugar

2½ cups chilled, freshly squeezed orange juice,
    divided

1 tablespoon fresh lemon juice

1 cup chilled Champagne or sparkling wine

¼ cup orange liqueur

1. In a small saucepan, combine zest, sugar, and ½ cup orange juice. Stir over low heat until sugar dissolves. Pour
   syrup into a small bowl, and chill until cold. Strain and
   discard zest.

2. In a medium bowl, combine chilled syrup, remaining 2
   cups orange juice, lemon juice, Champagne, and orange
   liqueur.

3. Freeze mixture in an ice cream maker according to manufacturer's directions. Scoop into a freezer-safe container, cover, and freeze until firm.

. . . .

Stroopwafels (Dutch Syrup Waffles)
Makes 24 cookies.

. . . .

If you ask Dutch residents to name their most popular cookie, the answer would probably be the *stroopwafel,* a common street food in the Netherlands. This "Dutch cookie" is made of two thin waffles filled with cinnamon-flavored caramel, and it's often enjoyed at breakfast, after it's been warmed over a hot drink in a cup. It's especially popular in Gouda, where a baker supposedly created the treat from leftover crumbs and syrup in 1784. The waffle part of a *stroopwafel* can be made on a waffle cone iron, a pizzelle press, or a *stroopwafel* iron.

1 teaspoon active dry yeast

½ cup lukewarm milk

4 cups all-purpose flour

3 teaspoons ground cinnamon, divided

½ cup granulated sugar

¼ teaspoon iodized salt

14 tablespoons (1¾ sticks) room temperature butter, plus 8 tablespoons (1 stick), cut into ½-inch pieces

2 large eggs

1¼ cups packed light brown sugar

½ cup dark corn syrup

1. Make waffle batter in a small bowl by mixing together yeast and milk. In a large bowl, mix flour, 1 teaspoon cinnamon, sugar, and salt. Use your fingers to work 14 tablespoons butter into flour until mixture resembles coarse meal. Beat in yeast mixture and eggs.

2. Knead dough 1 minute. Roll into a ball, and place in a bowl. Press plastic wrap onto exposed top of dough, and let sit 30 minutes.

3. To make filling, fill a large saucepan ⅓ full with hot water. Set aside. In a slightly smaller saucepan, combine remaining 8 tablespoons butter, brown sugar, remaining 2 teaspoons cinnamon, and corn syrup. Cook over medium heat, stirring constantly, until mixture reaches the soft ball stage, 234–235°F. Remove pan from heat, and place, uncovered, in the larger pan of hot water.

4. Heat waffle iron and oil lightly only once. Divide dough in half, and keep dividing dough pieces into halves until

you have 24 equal pieces. Roll each piece into a ball, and cover them all with plastic wrap. Slightly flatten a ball and place in center of the hot waffle iron. Press top down and cook until golden brown, 30 seconds to 1 minute, depending on your waffle iron.

5. Remove cookie from waffle iron, and immediately place flat on a hard surface. If it cools, it will break, so with a thin, sharp knife quickly slice in half horizontally to make 2 thin cookies.

6. Spoon a tablespoon of filling onto the cookie bottom. Let cool 30 seconds; then press on top half, spreading out filling evenly. If using a waffle cone iron, use a 3-inch cookie cutter to trim the cookie. Cool on a rack, and repeat process with remaining batter and filling. Store in an airtight container.

. . . .

Danish Vanilla Butter Cookies (Vanillekranse, "Vanilla Wreaths")

Makes 4 to 5 dozen cookies. Recipe is by Anna Jorgensen, originally from Denmark, and courtesy of her daughter, Lise Duda.

. . . .

It's possible the "Dutch" cookies the Levys bought are actually a box of Danish Butter Cookies, which appear at cut-rate prices all over New Orleans during the holiday season. Although the Netherlands is not considered part of Scandinavia, the Dutch and their neighbors to the north share a tradition of baking crisp, rich butter cookies. Try this easy recipe, and you'll never buy that blue tin of cookies again.

> Sitting there in the sports car before the main building at Mandeville with the huge box of Dutch cookies on her lap, she must have made the authority a little suspicious, Mr. Levy thought.
>
> —Mr. and Mrs. Levy on their way to visit Ignatius, who they believe is in the mental hospital.

3 sticks salted butter, softened

1 egg, beaten

¾ cup sugar

1 teaspoon vanilla

4 cups all-purpose flour

1. Using an electric mixer, cream together butter, egg, sugar, and vanilla in a large bowl. Gradually add flour until dough forms, working in all 4 cups. Wrap dough tightly, and chill 1 hour.

2. When ready to bake, preheat oven to 350°F and lightly grease or line a baking sheet with parchment paper. To make traditional wreath cookies, use a cookie press and feed dough through the tube with the ribbed disk attachment and form 4-inch strips of dough into circles. Or if you're not a practiced Danish grandmother, press the dough out in your favorite shape. Even easier, you can divide the dough in half, and on a floured surface roll each dough half into a long tube shape, about 2 inches in diameter. Using a sharp knife, cut dough into ½-inch cookies.

3. Transfer cookies to baking sheet about 1 inch apart, and bake 10 to 12 minutes or until lightly golden brown. Store tightly sealed up to 2 weeks.

In a Seafood State of Mind

> "Hello," she said into the telephone.
>
> "Hey, Irene?" a woman's hoarse voice asked. "What you doing, babe? It's Santa Battaglia."
>
> "How you making, honey?"
>
> "I'm beat. I just finished opening four dozen ersters out in the backyard," Santa said in her rocky baritone. "That's hard work, believe me, banging that erster knife on them bricks."
>
> "I wouldn't try nothing like that," Mrs. Reilly said honestly.
>
> "I don't mind. When I was a little girl I use to open ersters up for my momma. She had her a little seafood stand outside the Lautenschlaeger Market. Poor Momma. Right off the boat. Couldn't speak a word of English hardly. There I was just a little thing breaking them ersters open. I didn't go to no school. Not me, babe. I was right there with them ersters banging away on the banquette."

It is certainly not surprising that Santa Battaglia's mother was a seafood vendor, an occupation chosen by many Sicilians arriving in New Orleans in the early 1900s. And the Lautenschlaeger Market, which actually existed, was one in a network of municipal public agricultural markets the Spanish had started back in 1779. Extremely popular until after World War II, these open-air versions of the modern grocery store rented stalls to farmers, hunters, and fishermen, and grew to become economic engines for local neighborhoods. The still-bustling French Market in the New Orleans French Quarter was founded in 1791 as a Native American trading post, and it is the nation's oldest continuously running public market.

Named for City Councilman John A. Lautenschlaeger, the nearby market where Santa's mother had her stand was located at 1930 Burgundy Street at Touro, and had been constructed in 1903. The facility was enclosed in 1929, sold to a private entity in 1946, and later became a fish market. In 2003, the structure was converted to condominiums.

Since Louisiana is 16 percent water and sits on the coast of the Gulf of Mexico, the seafood industry itself is, naturally, important to the state. New Orleans's first public market handling fish started in 1784. But production really took off in the years before the Civil War, when a railroad started servicing Shell Beach along the coast in St. Bernard Parish, and ice manufacturing became a reality. Although descendants of the French and of African slaves certainly still work in the industry, over the years, the backbreaking work of actually fishing seafood out of the Gulf of Mexico has mostly been dominated by recent immigrants.

While Louisiana was still under Spain's rule, the government feared the City of New Orleans was militarily vulnerable, and so recruited a group of fishermen from the Canary Islands to do the necessary defending. The Isleños, as they've come to be called, settled eighty miles south in the coastal marshes and not only guarded New Orleans but supplied the city with a seemingly inexhaustible supply of fish, shrimp, and crab.

Another ethnic group, the Croatians, get the nod for creating the state's oyster industry, which took off when this group of fishermen hailing from the Adriatic Sea started cultivating oysters in Louisiana around the year 1840. Fast-forward to the mid-1970s, when yet another ethnic group, twenty-five thousand Vietnamese bent on escaping communism at the end of the Vietnam War, settled in Louisiana. The majority live around the section of the city called New Orleans East, and many have gravitated to the fishing and shrimping trades they knew at home.

Today, in spite of challenges from Mother Nature, foreign suppliers, and the oil industry and its spills, one out of every seventy jobs in Louisiana is seafood related, with a total economic impact of more than $2.4 billion. Louisiana leads the nation in production of both hard- and soft-shelled crabs, shrimp, oysters, and freshwater crawfish. Adding to those impressive statistics, Louisi-ana's commercial fishing industry produces 25 percent of all the seafood in America, and also holds the record for the greatest catch ever, 1.9 billion pounds in one year.

Most of this bounty is caught and processed by small operations, by fishermen who continue the traditions of fathers, grandfathers, and great-grandfathers, and even of great-grandmothers. And who knows, maybe a few families started in the business by selling ersters in a little seafood stand on the corner of Burgundy and Touro, just outside an old open-air market known as Lautenschlaeger.

For mountainous platters of boiled and fried seafood, New Orleanians in the 1960s motored to the casual restaurants overlooking Lake Pontchartrain in an area known as West End Park. Separated by the Seventeenth Street Canal, West End is a shoreline neighbor with Bucktown, originally a fishing village and named in the 1800s either for the "young bucks" who caroused its bars, gambling halls, and houses of prostitution or so named for the area's good deer hunting—take your pick. Live jazz, too, was a big draw to this whole area.

For one reason or another, the West End seafood stalwarts started losing favor around the 1980s. The final blow came with hurricanes that have hopelessly leveled the historic restaurants. Of note, in 1998, Hurricane Georges destroyed Fitzgerald's, a massive seafood joint, which had operated on and off since the 1940s. Georges also severely damaged the laid-back Bruning's, on the lake since late 1859. After Georges, Bruning's reopened in a nearby location, but six years later both it and the old place were fully destroyed by Hurricane Katrina.

If Santa and her entourage had chosen to catch their own crabs, they could have thrown nets out along the seawall and taken their haul home to boil. Crabbing in

Lake Pontchartrain is best between June and August, and in clear water when the tide is moving, either rising or falling. Before the use of outdoor propane tanks and burners and fancy commercial-sized kettles, the typical cook would throw the day's catch into a big pot of salted water on the stove. Seasoning was typically crab boil, a blend of eye-watering spices that came in a cloth bag. New Orleans's own Zatarain's, Inc., is famous for its herb-and-spice crab boil, both dry and liquid, and it's a concoction so hot it makes New England's famous Old Bay seasoning seem bland.

· ·

Crab Cakes over Spring Greens with Chili-Lime Dressing

Makes 6 first-course or light lunch servings.

· ·

½ cup canola or safflower oil, plus 2 tablespoons
½ teaspoon bottled chili garlic sauce
½ teaspoon grated lime peel

3 tablespoons fresh lime juice
1 tablespoon finely minced onion
1 teaspoon Dijon mustard, plus 1 additional
  tablespoon
1 teaspoon honey
½ teaspoon salt, divided
2 tablespoons mayonnaise
2 tablespoons sour cream
3 tablespoons minced green onion
¼ teaspoon Louisiana-style hot sauce
1 large egg, beaten
1½ cups soft breadcrumbs, divided
1 pound lump crab meat, well-drained and picked
  over to remove shell bits
8 cups mixed spring lettuces

1. Make dressing in a pint jar by shaking together ½ cup oil, chili sauce, lime peel, lime juice, minced onion, 1 teaspoon Dijon mustard, honey, and ¼ teaspoon salt. Set aside or refrigerate.

2. Make crab cakes by mixing together in a large bowl the remaining tablespoon mustard, remaining ¼ teaspoon salt, mayonnaise, sour cream, green onion, hot sauce, and egg. Stir in ½ cup breadcrumbs. Gently mix in crab, being careful to keep lumps from breaking apart.

3. Spread remaining 1 cup breadcrumbs in a plate. Divide crab mixture in half, and divide each half into 6 portions. Form 1½-inch round cakes with each portion, and gently coat cakes with breadcrumbs. Refrigerate at least 1 hour.

4. Over moderately high heat, heat remaining 2 tablespoons oil in a large skillet and sauté crab cakes until golden, about 2–3 minutes per side.

5. Mix lettuce with dressing, divide among 6 salad plates, and top each plate with 2 crab cakes. Serve immediately.

Boiled Redfish Salad with Egg Dressing

Makes 8–10 servings. Recipe is from the files of the late Albertine F. Bigard, and courtesy of her niece Ione Bertrand.

This classic Creole party dish goes back to at least the late 1800s, when recipes for boiled redfish topped with a cream sauce were featured in New Orleans's earliest published cookbooks. The trick to making this show-piece a success is cooking the fish neither too little nor too long. So be sure to test for doneness a few minutes before you think it's done.

1 (4–5 pound) whole redfish, or 3 pounds fillets, or substitute firm, white fish or salmon

3 lemons, quartered, plus 1 lemon

4 medium onions, quartered

4 ribs celery, coarsely chopped

3 bay leaves

1 teaspoon salt

Ground black pepper to taste

Garnish: Shredded lettuce, sliced tomatoes, sliced lemons, pitted and salad olives, sliced pickles, chopped boiled egg whites (reserved from Egg Dressing), and chopped celery

Egg Dressing (recipe page 137)

1. Scale fish and remove entrails, head, and tail. If using fillets, wrap in cheesecloth. Lay fish in a large roasting pan. Add cool water to cover by 1 inch, and toss in the 3 quartered lemons, onions, celery, bay leaves, salt, and pepper.

2. Using medium heat, bring water to a slow boil. Lower to a bare simmer and, uncovered, cook fish thoroughly. (A whole fish is done at about 6 minutes per pound. Fillets are done in about 15–20 minutes.) Remove fish from water and cool until easy to handle.

3. Remove skin and bones. Break fish into 1-inch pieces, and arrange on a large platter. Surround with lettuce, tomato slices, and sliced lemons. Squeeze juice from remaining lemon on top of fish.

4. Decorate top of fish by creating wide rows of olives, pickles, egg white, and celery. Top with Egg Dressing and serve.

> "I'll see you tonight then about seven. Claude says he's gonna come over here. Come pick us up and we'll take us a nice ride out to the lake for some of them good crabs."
>
> —Santa Battaglia, fixing up Mrs. Reilly and Mr. Robichaux on another date.

Oysters Dunbar (Dunbar Restaurant's Artichoke-Oyster Casserole)

Makes 6–8 servings. Recipe is from the files of Maureen Detweiler.

This is the original, authentic recipe for Oysters Dunbar, the most remembered dish from Dunbar's, a restaurant that was housed in a private home on St. Charles Avenue until the 1980s. Dunbar's only had a prix fixe dinner and never had a menu, but this one casserole was served every night. The recipe was given by Dunbar's chef Leonie Victor to one of the restaurant's steady customers, Maureen Simoneaux Reed, who had her husband's secretary decipher and type it up from scribbles on the back of paper napkins. Many versions of this acclaimed dish have popped up over the years, and chef Victor's recipe mostly differs from others in that it calls for a dry roux, roux cooked in a pan without oil.

Egg Dressing

Makes about 1½ cups

1 dozen large hard-boiled eggs
¾ cup olive or vegetable oil
2 tablespoons white vinegar
Salt, ground black pepper, and cayenne to taste

1. Remove egg yolks from whites. (Reserve whites for garnish.) In a medium bowl, mash yolks with a fork. Using a whisk, work a tablespoon of oil at a time into yolks.
2. Whisk in vinegar a drop at a time, and blend until dressing begins to jell. (If necessary, add 1 raw egg yolk for proper consistency. And only use raw eggs you know are safe.) Whisk in salt and pepper. Can be made a day ahead and refrigerated.

4 large artichokes
Juice of 1 lemon
1½ tablespoons flour
8 tablespoons (1 stick) butter, plus 2 tablespoons
3 tablespoons minced green onions
1½ dozen oysters, in their liquid
1 (7-ounce) can mushrooms and liquid, chopped (you can substitute fresh mushrooms, sautéed, and add 2 tablespoons chicken stock or butter for liquid)
Salt and pepper to taste
½ cup breadcrumbs

1. Bring enough water to boil so that artichokes will be covered by 2 inches. Add artichokes and lemon juice, and cook until artichokes are tender. Remove from pot, and cool, making sure all water is drained off.
2. Preheat oven to 350°F. Pull off enough nice-looking artichoke leaves so that each serving has 6, and reserve. Pull remaining leaves off, and scrape the meat into a bowl. Trim artichoke hearts, chop into large pieces, and toss into bowl with artichoke meat.
3. Preheat a dry, heavy-bottomed frying pan over low heat. Add flour, and stir constantly until lightly browned. Set aside.
4. In a medium saucepan, melt stick of butter over medium-high heat. Add green onion, and sauté 5 minutes. Add browned flour to butter, and stir until smooth. Mix in oysters, oyster liquid, mushrooms and liquid, salt and pepper. Simmer 10 minutes.
5. Butter a 2-quart baking dish or individual ramekins, and spoon in the artichoke meat and hearts. Top with oyster mixture; then top with breadcrumbs and dot with remaining 2 tablespoons butter. Bake until brown and bubbles are thick, 15–20 minutes. Serve warm in a ramekin in the center of a salad plate, and surround with 6 artichoke leaves.

. . . .

Tried-and-True Oyster Dressing

Makes 8 servings. Recipe is by Mrs. Octavia Marie Sansovich.

. . . .

Oyster dressing (stuffing) is typically served in South Louisiana during the holidays. For generations, this traditional recipe has been served by the Sansovich family, who are originally from Hvar, Croatia, and who were oyster purveyors in New Orleans from the late nineteenth through early twentieth centuries. During that time, New Orleans processors sent wagons to purchase oysters from the luggers and two-masted schooners that docked at the Old Basin Canal. Another oyster landing site was at Bayou St. John. Yet another, the "Picayune Pier," also known as "Lugger Bay," sat at the foot of Dumaine Street.

1 pint oysters

3 tablespoons butter, divided

1 large onion, chopped

⅓ cup chopped green onions

3 stalks celery, chopped

2 cloves garlic, minced

½ of a 15-inch loaf day-old French bread, cut into ½-inch cubes

¼ cup chopped parsley

¾ teaspoon salt

½ teaspoon black pepper

⅛ teaspoon cayenne pepper

⅛ teaspoon ground thyme

1 large egg, beaten

¼ cup buttered breadcrumbs

1. Preheat oven to 350°F. Drain oysters, reserving liquid. Wash oysters, cut each in half, and return to oyster liquid. Set aside.
2. Melt 2 tablespoons butter in a heavy-bottomed Dutch oven, and sauté onion, green onion, celery, and garlic. Drain oysters again, reserving liquid. When vegetables are tender, add oysters, bread, parsley, remaining 1 tablespoon butter, salt, black pepper, cayenne, and thyme. Heat through thoroughly, then remove from heat.
3. Slowly combine egg with oyster mixture. Add enough re-

served oyster liquid to moisten slightly. (Be careful—too much liquid makes the dressing gummy.)

4. Spoon dressing into a 4-quart casserole dish, and top with breadcrumbs. Bake, uncovered, until deep golden brown, about 1 hour. Serve warm.

Whole Red Snapper Stuffed with Oyster Dressing

Makes 8 servings.

Common in the northern Gulf of Mexico, the red snapper is a rosy-colored fish with large scales and red eyes, and is popular for its mild, sweet flesh. Large "sows" can reach over 20 pounds, but the usual size found in fish markets ranges between 1½ and 10 pounds.

1 whole red snapper (4–5 pounds), scaled and cleaned, head-on
Creole seasoning (purchased, or use recipe on pages 6–7), or salt and pepper
1 recipe Tried-and-True Oyster Dressing (see recipe page 138)
3 tablespoons melted butter

1. Preheat oven to 350°F. Using parchment paper, line a rimmed baking sheet large enough to hold the fish.
2. Season fish thoroughly with Creole seasoning, inside and out. Place fish in prepared pan, and stuff with warm oyster dressing.
3. Bake fish uncovered 15 minutes. Spoon half of butter over fish. Bake an additional 15 minutes, then spoon remaining butter over fish. Bake another 15 minutes, or until fish flakes easily. Serve hot.

P&J Oyster and Brie Soup

Makes 8 appetizer or 16 demitasse servings. Adapted from a recipe by Al Sunseri, general manager of P&J Oyster Company.

P&J Oyster Company was founded in 1876 by Croatian immigrant John Popich, who, around the year 1900, took on a partner, Joseph Jurisich. After a few years, the company expanded into the largest oyster-shucking business in the southern United States and started operating under the name "Popich & Jurisich," or "P&J Oyster Company." In 1921, the company purchased a shucking house at the corner of Toulouse and North Rampart, and P&J, the oldest oyster wholesaler in America, still processes oysters there today.

2 pints shucked fresh oysters
8 tablespoons (1 stick) unsalted butter
2 cloves garlic, minced
1 cup finely chopped green onion, white and light green parts, divided
½ cup all-purpose flour
1 pint heavy cream
3 cups half-and-half
8–12 ounces brie cheese, rind removed and cheese diced
Salt and pepper to taste
Crusty French bread for serving (purchased, or recipe on pages 64–65)

1. Strain oysters, and freeze liquor for another use.
2. In a one-gallon pot, melt butter over medium heat and sauté garlic and ¾ cup green onion until white parts

are translucent. Add flour, and cook until barely brown, stirring constantly, about 1 minute. Add the drained oysters, and simmer until the edges of the oysters curl, 2–3 minutes.

3. Add cream, half-and-half, and cheese, and stir until cheese melts. Add salt and pepper to taste. Remove from heat, cover, and let stand 10 minutes.

4. Ladle into bowls or cups, and garnish with remaining green onion. Serve hot with French bread on the side.

• •

Sal's Oyster Magic

Makes 6 hors d'oeuvre servings. Recipe is by Sal Sunseri, vice-president of P&J Oyster Company.

• •

Not to be outdone, Al Sunseri's brother and business partner Sal came up with his own oyster recipe, his for a sauce and technique that infuse raw oysters with fruity-hot flavor. To achieve optimum seasoning penetration, Sal's recipe calls for marinating the oysters. But the sauce can be served separately for dipping. And, if any oysters are left over, make flavorful poor boys by rolling the marinated bivalves lightly in corn flour and frying.

3 dozen fresh, raw oysters
1 fresh nectarine, stone removed and flesh minced
1 cup ketchup
½ cup minced sweet onion
¼ cup minced celery
¼ cup minced red or orange bell pepper
¼ cup minced parsley
3 tablespoons fresh-squeezed lemon juice
1 teaspoon sugar
1 teaspoon Tabasco brand hot sauce
1 teaspoon Crystal brand hot sauce
1 teaspoon finely minced pickled jalapeño peppers,
    plus 1 teaspoon juice
1 teaspoon finely minced pickled habanero peppers,
    plus 1 teaspoon juice
1 teaspoon siracha chili sauce
¼ teaspoon salt
Pinch cayenne pepper

1. If oysters are still in shell, shuck and discard shells, or save shells for serving. Remove as much liquid as possible by laying oysters on a clean towel or paper towels and gently blotting dry.

2. Combine remaining ingredients in a large bowl. Fold oysters into sauce, and let marinate in the refrigerator 1 hour. (Any longer, and oysters will start to lose their texture.)

3. To serve, spoon oysters and a little sauce into reserved oyster shells that have been nestled into a bed of ice, or into compartments of oyster plates, into martini glasses, or onto salad plates lined with shredded lettuce. Serve immediately.

Pan-Fried Soft-Shelled Crabs with Pecan Butter Sauce

Makes 4 servings.

During spring and summer, local farmers markets carry soft-shelled crabs so fresh they're still kicking. Out of season, frozen ones make good substitutes. A soft-shelled crab is a crab that has outgrown and shed its shell. About 90 percent of a soft-shelled crab is edible.

  4 large, fresh soft-shelled crabs

  ½ cup milk

  1 large egg

  1¼ teaspoons salt, divided

  ½ teaspoon ground white pepper

  ¼ teaspoon hot sauce

  1 cup all-purpose flour

  2 tablespoons corn flour

  ½ cup canola oil, divided

  2 tablespoons, plus 1 stick unsalted butter

  ⅓ cup coarsely chopped pecans

  ¼ teaspoon ground black pepper

  Juice from 1 lemon

  2 tablespoons chopped green onion

1. Preheat oven to 200°F. Remove crab eyes and mouth, and the gills from underneath each side of the carapace, the thick top shell. Snip off the apron, the triangular part of the shell at the base under the crab. With paper towels, pat crabs as dry as possible.

2. In a shallow bowl or pan, beat together milk, egg, 1 teaspoon salt, white pepper, and hot sauce. Mix flour and corn flour together in another bowl.

3. Heat ¼ cup canola oil and 1 tablespoon butter in a large skillet over medium-high heat until hot but not smoking. While oil is heating, dip 2 crabs in milk and egg mixture and shake off excess liquid. Dredge crabs well in flour mixture. With top shell side down first, fry until golden brown, about 3–4 minutes per side. Remove to a plate, and keep warm in oven. Repeat with remaining 2 crabs, using remaining canola oil and butter.

4. To make sauce, melt remaining stick butter over medium heat in a small pan and stir in pecans. Cook until nuts are fragrant, about 30 seconds. Stir in remaining ¼ teaspoon salt, black pepper, and lemon juice. Pour pecan butter sauce over fried crabs, and sprinkle with green onion. Serve hot and eat every part of the crab, even its crispy little legs.

Pan-Fried Speckled Trout with Brown Butter

Makes 4 servings.

Simple is best when it comes to preparing speckled trout, a delicate saltwater game fish that actually isn't a trout, but a member of the drum family. Locally known as a "speck," the silvery, green-speckled fish has black dots on its tail, averages 14–18 inches long, and weighs 1–3 pounds. Speckled trout is a favorite of recreational fishermen, and it seasonally shows up in restaurants, most often in butter-based dishes, including the iconic Trout Meunière and Trout Amandine.

4 fillets speckled trout (8–10 ounces each)

Salt and ground black pepper

1 cup whole milk

1 cup all-purpose flour

3 tablespoons olive oil

6 tablespoons unsalted butter, softened

1 tablespoon freshly squeezed lemon juice

Minced parsley for garnish

1. Dry fish well, and sprinkle with salt and pepper. Place milk in a shallow bowl and flour in another shallow bowl. Dredge fish in milk, then in flour.
2. Heat olive oil in a large, heavy-bottomed skillet over medium heat. When oil is hot, add fish. Cook on both sides until golden brown and cooked through about 4–5 minutes per side. Remove fish to a plate, and keep warm.
3. Add butter to same skillet, and cook over medium heat, stirring constantly, until nut-brown. Remove from heat, and carefully stir in lemon juice.
4. Place fish on serving plates, and top with browned butter and parsley. Serve immediately.

Boiled Crawfish

Makes 30–40 pounds, enough to serve 8. Recipe is by Don Verdicanno.

Waterlogged South Louisiana holds the distinction of being the world's most hospitable region for growing crawfish, a smaller, freshwater relative of the lobster and known elsewhere as a crawdad, mudbug, *écrivesse,* and the more scientific "crayfish." And, although boiled crawfish are now closely associated with the city of New Orleans, it hasn't always been that way.

Habitat is centered west of New Orleans in "Cajun Country," in the Atchafalaya Basin, America's largest river swamp, and where twenty-two million pounds of crawfish are harvested annually. It's also a place that pretty much kept its crawfish to itself until the late 1960s. In the early 1900s crawfish were sold in restaurants, and many New Orleanians caught their own, usually not far from their homes. But that all changed after highway and subdivision construction dried up local crawfish holes, which had been abundant, even in the middle of the city. So, through the 1960s, finding commercially available crawfish became spotty at best, and usually involved knowing so-and-so's Cajun brother-in-law who lived along the Atchafalaya Basin.

Crawfish started becoming plentiful in New Orleans seafood markets and again in restaurants beginning in the late 1960s. One reason for the mudbug's resurgence is that, in 1948, a southwest Louisiana rice farmer commercially rotated a rice crop with crawfish, and by the 1960s, that practice had blossomed throughout the rice-growing region, creating a source that supplemented what was coming out of the Atchafalaya Basin. Also by then, Atchafalaya-area processing plants were aggressively marketing peeled crawfish. Other boosts to the crawfish supply were the start of an official Crawfish Festival in 1960 in Breaux Bridge, about 125 miles west of New Orleans, and the opening of a much faster highway, Interstate 10, that tied crawfish-producing areas with South Louisiana's major cities.

Adding to all that, in 1953 the Bon Ton Café on Magazine Street opened, and there the Cajun-rooted Pierce family started serving crawfish étouffée and sauce piquante, exposing diners to "new" dishes that had been around in Cajun country for as long as anyone could remember. And it would be impossible to talk about crawfish in New Orleans without mentioning Al Scramuzza, the "king" of a seafood market called Seafood City. Mostly remembered for his outlandish 1970s-era television commercials, "Doctor" Scramuzza would bring barely alive patients back to life with a dose of crawfish, and check the health of crawfish with his stethoscope. Scramuzza ran his now-defunct business for forty-five years, and the affable showman likes to give himself credit for teaching modern-day locals how to peel, cook, and eat crawfish.

Beginning in the late 1980s, Chinese crawfish started appearing in Louisiana markets. Over the years, this cheaper product has put a huge dent in the local cleaned-tail market. But live crawfish for local crawfish boils are still virtually all caught in Louisiana. Every year, between December and June, more than sixteen hundred farmers produce crawfish in some 111,000 acres of ponds, and more than eight hundred commercial fishermen harvest from natural wetlands, resulting in this crawfish-obsessed state producing 90 percent of domestically caught crawfish. And it should be no shock that Louisiana's hungry populace also consumes a gigantic portion of that amount.

Although it is certainly possible to boil small batches on a kitchen stove, it's best to cook this messy and highly spiced recipe outside over a propane burner.

1 sack (35–40 pounds) live crawfish
4½ pounds dry, powdered crawfish boil seasoning mix, with salt (available at specialty stores, or use recipe on page 144)
32 small red potatoes
1½ cups Zatarain's liquid concentrated crab boil (available at specialty stores)
⅓ cup cayenne pepper
2 cups Louisiana-style hot sauce
8 cobs fresh corn, shucked and cut in half
1 dozen lemons, cut in half

1. Purge (clean) crawfish by putting the whole, unopened sack in a large ice chest or washtub filled with water. Let them sit 2 minutes, drain the water, pull the sack out, rinse the ice chest and repeat the process until the water comes out clear, about 3–4 more times. When crawfish are clean, dump them out of the sack and into the ice chest. Remove any dead crawfish and debris.
2. In a large pot (at least 80 quarts), bring to a boil enough water to completely cover the crawfish when they are added. Add ¾ of the dry seasoning mix, and boil 10 minutes.
3. Add potatoes, and boil 10 minutes. Add remainder of dry seasoning mix, liquid crab boil, cayenne pepper, and hot sauce.
4. When water returns to a boil, add crawfish and corn, and cover the pot. When water again returns to a boil, boil 2 minutes; then turn off the fire. Squeeze lemons into pot, and add lemon rinds. Let sit at least 10 minutes and up to 30 minutes, uncovered, checking every 10 minutes to see if crawfish have absorbed enough seasoning. Scoop crawfish out of the pot and serve hot.

Crawfish Torte

Makes 8 appetizer servings. Recipe is from Don Verdicanno.

16 tablespoons (2 sticks) salted butter, divided

4 shallots, chopped fine

1 bunch green onions, chopped (separate white bottoms from green tops)

1 large rib celery, finely chopped

8 ounces button mushrooms, sliced

¾ teaspoon Creole seasoning (purchased, or use recipe on pages 6–7)

2 tablespoons brandy

2 tablespoons tomato paste

½ cup heavy whipping cream

¼ cup cream sherry

2 pounds cleaned crawfish tails, with fat

½ cup chopped parsley

18 (17 x 12-inch) sheets phyllo dough, defrosted if frozen

Dry Crawfish Boil Seasoning Mix

Makes enough for 40 pounds crawfish. Great for boiling shrimp and crabs, too.

    2 boxes salt (3 pounds total)
    2 cups dried mustard seed
    ¾ cup crushed hot red pepper flakes
    ½ cup black peppercorns
    ½ cup celery seed
    3 tablespoons whole cloves
    3 tablespoons dried thyme leaves
    12 bay leaves

Add entire amount of salt to water at the beginning of the boiling process. Combine remaining ingredients, and add to water per recipe instructions. Since this mix is not powdered like commercial mixes, parts of it will cling to crawfish. If desired, tie seasoning in muslin or cheesecloth bags before adding to water to keep spices tidily separate from what you're going to eat.

1. Preheat oven to 375°F. Melt ½ stick butter in a large skillet over medium-high heat, and sauté shallots, green onion bottoms, and celery until soft. Add mushrooms, and sauté another 5 minutes. Add Creole seasoning.

2. Carefully add brandy, and stir until liquid is evaporated. Stir in tomato paste, cream, and sherry, and bring to a simmer. Cook 1 minute.

3. Stir in crawfish and fat. Bring just to a boil, and remove from heat. Stir in green onion tops and parsley.

4. Melt remaining 1½ sticks butter. Brush a 13 x 9-inch ovenproof dish with melted butter. Lay a sheet of phyllo on

bottom of dish, allowing to lap over dish sides, and brush with melted butter. Add second sheet of phyllo, and brush with butter. Continue process until dish is lined with 10 phyllo sheets.

5. Spread crawfish filling evenly over phyllo in dish. Fold excess phyllo dough over filling.

6. Cover filling with a sheet of phyllo, and brush with butter. Continue process until filling is covered with 8 sheets of phyllo. Tuck in or cut off overlapping dough, and brush top with butter.

7. Cut slits in the top at 2-inch intervals, and bake until deep brown, about 30–40 minutes. Allow to cool at least 15 minutes before slicing and serving.

Cornmeal-Coated Fried Catfish with Tartar Sauce

Makes 4–6 servings.

Some of South Louisiana's best-eatin' catfish comes from the community of Des Allemands, the French name for "the Germans" who, in 1721, settled some thirty-five miles southwest of New Orleans along Lake Des Allemands and its bayous and canals. Catfish is so important to Des Allemands that in 1975 Governor Edwin Edwards signed a decree declaring the town the "Catfish Capital of the World." The Louisiana legislature topped that proclamation in 1980, when they passed a resolution naming it the "Catfish Capital of the Universe."

When New Orleanians want someone else to fry their fish, they are often likely to take a road trip to Middendorf's on Bayou Manchac, forty miles northwest of New Orleans. This historic restaurant consistently receives national attention for its crispy, thin-fried catfish fillets.

Tartar Sauce
Makes 1½ cups

Something similar to the mayonnaise-based tartar sauce we know today dates all the way back to the Roman Empire. Food historians believe that in the 1800s the French popularized tartar sauce by using it as an accompaniment to steak tartare, finely chopped raw steak. Today, throughout the South, this thick, chunky sauce is a must with fried seafood.

1 cup mayonnaise
¼ cup prepared horseradish, well-drained
½ cup sweet pickle relish, well-drained
2 tablespoons finely chopped green onion
1 teaspoon Creole seasoning (purchased, or use recipe on pages 6–7)
½ teaspoon hot sauce
2 teaspoons fresh lemon juice
1 teaspoon Creole mustard, or any grainy mustard

Combine all ingredients, and chill at least 1 hour to combine flavors. Keeps refrigerated up to 1 week.

2 pounds skinless catfish fillets
½ cup prepared yellow mustard
½ teaspoon cayenne pepper
2 cups finely ground cornmeal
1½ teaspoons salt
½ teaspoon ground black pepper
½ teaspoon garlic powder
Vegetable oil for frying
Tartar Sauce for serving (recipe above)

1. Wipe catfish dry with paper towels. In a large bowl, mix together mustard and cayenne. Add fish to mustard mixture, and gently coat them, using your hands, and refrigerate 1 hour.

2. In a large, shallow bowl, mix together cornmeal, salt, black pepper, and garlic powder. Heat at least 2 inches oil to 350°F in a large, heavy-bottomed pot.

3. While oil is heating, remove fish from refrigerator and wipe off excess marinade. Dredge fish well in seasoned cornmeal, and fry until golden brown, about 3 minutes per side. Drain on paper towels. Continue process with remaining fish. Serve hot with Tartar Sauce.

. . . .

Perfect Fried Oysters

Makes 2 dozen.

. . . .

2 dozen freshly shucked oysters

2 large eggs, beaten

2 tablespoons milk

1 teaspoon salt

½ teaspoon ground black pepper

½ teaspoon garlic powder

¼ teaspoon cayenne pepper

1 tablespoon Creole seasoning (purchased, or use recipe on pages 6–7)

2 cups finely ground cornmeal or corn flour

3 tablespoons cornstarch

Peanut oil for frying

1. Pat oysters dry, and refrigerate until ready to cook.

2. In a shallow medium bowl, beat together egg, milk, salt, black pepper, garlic powder, and cayenne. In another bowl, stir together Creole seasoning, cornmeal, and cornstarch.

3. In a large heavy pot or skillet, heat 2 inches oil to 375°F. Dredge oysters in egg mixture and then in cornmeal. Drop into hot oil, making sure they do not touch. Fry, turning once, until oysters float and are golden and crusty, about 4–5 minutes.

> "Good heavens!" Ignatius leaped up and beat at the bird with his itching paws. What avian menace had depraved Fortuna spun his way? The champagne bottles and the glasses shattered on the floor as he sprang and began staggering to the door.
>
> —Ignatius at the Night of Joy, as he flees an attack from Darlene's cockatoo.

. . . .

Sautéed Flounder with Grapes and Champagne Sauce

Makes 2 servings.

. . . .

It only takes a small amount of Champagne to dress up this sauce for flounder, the flat, bottom-feeding fish common in the Gulf.

2 flounder fillets (6 ounces each)

Creole Seasoning (purchased, or use recipe on pages 6–7)

¼ cup all-purpose flour

4 tablespoons (½ stick) butter, divided

½ cup Champagne, sparkling wine, or white wine

¼ cup heavy cream

1 cup green grapes

Few grindings white pepper

2 tablespoons chopped green onion

1. Rinse flounder, wipe dry, and sprinkle both sides with Creole seasoning. Dredge in flour. Set aside.

2. Heat 2 tablespoons butter in a skillet over medium heat until hot but not smoking. Place flounder in skillet, and cook 3 minutes per side. Remove flounder from pan, and keep warm.

3. Add Champagne to skillet, turn heat to high, and reduce by half. Add remaining 2 tablespoons butter, cream, grapes, and pepper, and simmer until thickened.

4. Spoon sauce over fillets, and sprinkle with green onion. Serve hot.

Paradise Vendors was modeled on Lucky Dogs,
selling hot dogs in New Orleans since 1947.
Photo courtesy Jerry Strahan

12

· · · · · · · · · · ·

Adventures with Paradise Vendors

> Among the afternoon pedestrians who hurried past Paradise Vendors, Incorporated, one formidable figure waddled slowly along. It was Ignatius. Stopping before the narrow garage, he sniffed the fumes from Paradise with great sensory pleasure, the protruding hairs in his nostrils analyzing, cataloging, categorizing, and classifying the distinct odors of hot dog, mustard, and lubricant. Breathing deeply, he wondered whether he also detected the more delicate odor, the fragile scent of hot dog buns.
>
> —Ignatius's first encounter with his future employer, Paradise Vendors.

It would be hard to visit the New Orleans French Quarter without running across at least one seven-foot-long, hot dog-shaped food cart boldly emblazoned with the words "Lucky Dogs." This legendary fleet of rolling wieners has been a fixture in this National Historic Landmark district since 1947, and has since sold more than 21 million hot dogs.

Although they dispense a sought-after product, Lucky Dog carts are also part of what makes the French Quarter quirky. In addition to holding the necessary components of a proper hot dog, these brightly colored weenies on wheels have at one time or another served as impromptu taxis, hand warmers, scavenger-hunt items, and marriage altars. And the carts' gigantic umbrellas have been known to keep tourists dry, and have saved the occasional drunk from an August heat stroke. Cart

vendors, too, are part of the Lucky Dog magic, and have over the years included "occasional" eccentrics, such as fake clergy, sex addicts, ex-accountants, jazz musicians, strippers, bikers, failed doctoral candidates, and con artists, along with run-of-the-mill transients who just don't want to be found. So, although Paradise Vendors Incorporated is fictitious, Lucky Dogs Inc., the impetus for Ignatius's eventual employer, certainly is not.

Jerry Strahan, author of the book *Managing Ignatius,* a tell-all about former Lucky Dog employees, is the real-life Mr. Clyde, Ignatius's fictitious boss at Paradise Vendors. Strahan is also a bona fide historian and has worked for the venerable hot dog vendor since 1968, when Peter Briant and Doug Talbot bought the company from its original owners. In 1976 Strahan was promoted to general manger. And, although he never met John

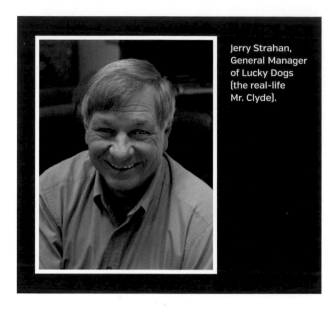

Jerry Strahan, General Manager of Lucky Dogs (the real-life Mr. Clyde).

Kennedy Toole, he loves talking about the impact, both good and bad, the "observational genius" has had on his company.

Strahan admits *A Confederacy of Dunces* has certainly brought Lucky Dogs lots of attention, such as from the starstruck, long-haired gentleman Strahan found bowing to the corporate headquarters' front door and exclaiming, "Hail to Ignatius." There are also those who buy Lucky Dogs strictly because Ignatius ate them. And more than a few tourists just want photos, oftentimes to prove to the folks back home Lucky Dogs actually exists.

But not all the publicity has been good. Before writing *Dunces,* John Kennedy Toole had spent hours at Lucky Dogs headquarters, then at 1304 St. Charles Avenue. While there, he soaked in all he could about the weenie vending business. But although he knew the company's protocol, when writing the novel, Toole obviously took poetic license.

One misconception that "dogs" Lucky Dogs Inc. is that some folks believe that, as in the novel, the company's food safety standards are lax. Ignatius might not have had a problem consuming the "magnified paramecia" that swished about a big pot of boiling water strong as acid. But to the average hot dog lover, an acidic weenie made of "rubber" and "cereal" and "tripe" is not too appealing. In reality, the 450 Lucky Dog pork and beef wieners carried by each cart are not boiled, but steamed on the carts, which, in Ignatius's day would have been run by kerosene pumps. (Beginning in the 1970s, the carts converted to propane.) Modern carts have a wastewater tank, four sinks, and two refrigerator compartments. Lucky Dog rules also strictly forbid vendors from coming in contact with animals, like "rather appealing" cats. More importantly, carts are inspected by both the Louisiana Board of Health and the Louisiana Food and Drug Administration. And if anyone has ever fallen sick after eating a Lucky Dog, they've sure been quiet, since the corporation has never had any product liability lawsuits, nor has anyone sued for food poisoning.

Another difference is that, unlike Ignatius on his aimless routes, Lucky Dog carts sell from set corners. Those spots are the same today as they were in 1947. And modern-day vendors don't have to worry about competition from the city's ever-increasing fleets of food trucks. In 1972, the New Orleans City Council passed an ordinance limiting street vending in the French Quarter to companies who'd been selling there prior to 1964. That decree was challenged by Nancy Dukes, who owned a mobile snack and drink business, and who took her grievance all the way to the U.S. Supreme Court. In 1976, the ruling came down that, due to their historic value, ice cream vendor Oliver Roberts and Lucky Dogs were the only two vendors allowed to sell in the area.

Have you ever wondered if Toole's imagination made up Ignatius's uniform, that white smock that makes him look like a "dinosaur egg" and hat made of a "little rectangle of white paper"? Well, that's pretty much what the outfit looked like back then, minus the cutlass and earring. Today, vendors sport red-and-white-striped uniform shirts.

Since the time Ignatius trudged through the French Quarter pushing his cart, the Lucky Dog menu has changed only a little. New additions include a Cajun sausage sandwich and soft drinks. And today's Lucky Dog is slightly larger, either six or four wieners to a pound, compared to eight to a pound in the sixties. Toppings still include mustard, ketchup, chili, and onion. The eight-inch jumbo topped with the works is the biggest seller, and the weenie business on the whole is most brisk with the after-midnight cocktail crowd.

And what about those whacky vendors? In the old days, many a capricious transient held that job. But the carnie faction is drying up, Vietnam vets are dwindling, and drifters are in the minority. Most, however, still aren't CEO material, and that's more than okay. According to Strahan, it takes a certain off-center personality to put up with the challenges of selling hot dogs on the French Quarter's streets; it's definitely not a job for the timid or the gullible. And if Ignatius were still around? Sure, he'd fit in grandly.

> This vendor was a perfect front man. He would never know what was coming off. He had a good education, though. . . . That was probably what was wrong with him. George had been wise enough to get out of school as soon as possible. He didn't want to end up like that guy.
>
> —George, making plans to hide his pornography in Ignatius's weenie cart.

Paradise Pork and Beef Wieners

Makes 16 (2 pounds of six-inch links).

If you worry that store-bought wieners do contain magnified paramecia, rubber, and tripe, try making your own. It's actually fairly easy using a food processor and the grinding and sausage-stuffing attachments on a standing mixer. To make things even simpler, these dogs are boiled instead of smoked.

The frankfurter was named for the German city of Frankfurt, where the meat specialty also went by the name "dachshund," or "little-dog" sausage. In 1904, German butcher Johann Georg Lahner moved to Vienna (*Wien* in German), and locals started calling his beef and pork sausage a *wiener*. There are claims that the wiener joined forces with the bun either in New York City or on the boardwalk at Coney Island, or even at the St. Louis 1904 World Exposition. But there is strong speculation that Germans had been eating their little-dogs in buns long before setting foot on American soil. The name "hot dog," however, was coined in America, likely when sarcastically referring to the long, thin "dachshunds" eaten by German immigrants.

12 feet of 24–26 mm (1–1 1/16 -inch) sheep casings
    (from your butcher)
1 pound pork loin, cut into 1-inch cubes
1 pound lean beef stew meat, cut into 1-inch cubes
½ pound pork fat, cut into 1-inch cubes (trim from a
    pork shoulder is good)
2 teaspoons salt
1 teaspoon garlic powder
1 teaspoon paprika
½ teaspoon onion powder
½ teaspoon ground white pepper
¼ teaspoon liquid smoke (optional)
1 egg white
¼ cup crushed ice

1. Prepare casings according to manufacturer's directions. (This usually involves soaking and rinsing and may take some time, so be sure to read instructions at least a day ahead.) Freeze pork, beef, and pork fat 45 minutes.

2. In a small bowl, combine salt, garlic powder, paprika, onion powder, white pepper, liquid smoke, and egg white. Cover and refrigerate until ready to use.

3. Put a large empty bowl inside a slightly larger bowl of ice cubes and water. In the scrupulously clean grinding attachment of a standing mixer, use a fine blade to grind together chilled pork, beef, and pork fat, and let it fall into the empty bowl surrounded by ice water. Repeat the grinding process. Stir seasoning mixture into meat, and chill 30 minutes.

4. Put seasoned meat and the ¼ cup crushed ice into the bowl of a food processor. Process until completely emulsified, 4–5 minutes. (If your food processor is small, process in 2 batches.) Place in a clean bowl, and press plastic wrap directly on top of meat. Chill mixture 1 hour.

5. Slip casing onto stuffer attachment. Pull off about 8 inches, make a knot, and slip casing back completely onto the stuffer attachment. Stuff the casing with the chilled meat mixture in one long, coiled rope. Be careful not to overstuff, and if air pockets develop, prick with a toothpick. At 6-inch intervals, twist the rope into links, alternating between clockwise and counterclockwise twists. Tightly tie the open end of the coil.

6. Place the whole coil of wieners into a pot of cold water, covering them by 2 inches. Gradually heat the water until it comes to a bare simmer. Gently cook, uncovered, until the internal temperature reaches 155°F, about 15–20 minutes. Remove wiener coil from pot, and dunk into a large bowl of ice water. Let sit 10 minutes.

7. Drain wieners, dry well, and let air dry on a rack at room temperature 30 minutes. Store tightly covered in the refrigerator up to 1 week, or freeze up to 2 months.

. . . .

BLT Dogs on Fragilely Scented Potato Buns
Makes 8.

. . . .

Wieners were a fantastic 1960s-era budget-stretcher, with a one-pound pack of ten selling for about fifty cents. With the 1980s trends toward fresher foods, however, a shift away from cured, processed meats made this favorite of children fall out of culinary favor. But with markets now offering healthier processed-meat choices, the much maligned frankfurter is definitely worth a second look.

8 skinless beef frankfurters

8 slices bacon

Vegetable oil for frying

8 Fragilely Scented Potato Buns (recipe follows,
    or use purchased buns)

Yellow mustard

Shredded lettuce

Diced fresh tomatoes

1. Wrap each frankfurter with a slice of bacon, and
   secure bacon ends with toothpicks. Refrigerate 30
   minutes.
2. Heat 2 inches oil in a Dutch oven to 350°F. Fry bacon-
   wrapped franks until brown and crisp, 3–5 minutes. Drain
   on paper towels, and remove toothpicks.
3. While franks are frying, slice buns open and toast lightly
   under a broiler. Put one frank inside each bun, and top
   with mustard, lettuce, and tomatoes.

Fragilely Scented Potato Buns   Makes 8

1 envelope (2¼ teaspoons) active dry yeast

2 teaspoons sugar

¾ cup warm water, 105–110°F

¼ cup boiled and mashed potatoes, at room
    temperature

1 teaspoon iodized salt

4 tablespoons (½ stick) butter, melted, divided,
    plus more for brushing on rolls

2–2½ cups bread flour

1. In the mixing bowl of a standing mixer or in a
   large bowl, combine yeast, sugar, and water, and
   let sit until foamy, about 5 minutes.
2. Add potatoes, salt, 2 tablespoons butter, and
   2 cups flour. Attach bread paddle to the mixer,
   and mix on low speed until liquid is absorbed.
   Knead on medium speed 8 minutes, adding
   enough of the remaining ½ cup flour to make
   a soft dough.
3. Roll dough into a smooth ball, and place in a large
   greased bowl. Cover with plastic wrap, and let
   rise 1 hour. Punch dough down, and portion into
   8 equal pieces. Shape each piece into a 2 x 6-inch
   rectangle, and place on a parchment-lined cookie
   sheet. Brush tops with remaining 2 tablespoons
   butter. Cover lightly with a cloth, and let rise until
   doubled, about 30 minutes.
4. Preheat oven to 375°F. Bake rolls until golden,
   about 20 minutes. Remove from oven, and brush
   with additional melted butter. Good for hot dogs
   and as dinner bread.

> "I'm gonna put you down in the French Quarter. . . .
> Take or leave it, you fat bastard. . . ."
>
> "If you insist, I imagine that I shall have to trundle
> my franks down into Sodom and Gomorrah."
>
> —Mr. Clyde, changing Ignatius's weenie route,
>   and Ignatius's reaction.

Bourbon Street Messy Dog
Makes 8.

1 can (12 ounces) beer

2 tablespoons olive oil

8 fresh chicken or turkey sausage links

6 pieces French bread, 6 inches long each (purchased,
    or recipe on pages 64–65)

Mayonnaise mixed with prepared horseradish to taste

Finely shredded cabbage

8 slices tomato

Dill pickle relish

Chicken Gravy (purchased, or Turkey Neck Gravy recipe
    on page 127)

1. Preheat oven to 350°F. Bring beer and oil to a simmer in
   a skillet. Add sausages to beer, and cook over medium
   heat, covered, for 10–12 minutes. Remove cover, and
   cook until beer evaporates and sausages are brown on
   all sides. Internal temperature should reach 150°F. Split
   links open lengthwise almost all the way through, and
   brown the insides in the skillet.

2. Slice French bread pieces open, and spread insides with
   mayonnaise. Stuff bread with sausage, and pile on cabbage, tomato, and relish, and drown everything in gravy.

3. Place filled sandwiches on a large baking tray, and bake
   1–2 minutes. Serve hot.

Weenies Wellington
Makes 8.

This recipe is a cross between two polar opposite dishes
popular during the 1960s, sophisticated Beef Wellington,
a beef tenderloin topped with foie gras and enclosed in a
pastry crust, and pigs in blankets, the easily assembled
wiener-and-canned-biscuit dish many mothers liked to
throw in the oven at the last minute.

2 tablespoons butter

1 small onion, finely chopped

8 ounces fresh mushrooms, finely chopped

1 tablespoon minced parsley

4 ounces cream cheese, room temperature

Prepared yellow mustard

8 jumbo beef frankfurters

Easy Puff Pastry (recipe follows, or 17.3 ounces frozen
    puff pastry, defrosted)

Optional additional fillings: cheese, diced peppers,
    chopped olives, pickles, chow-chow (southern
    tomato relish), chopped boiled eggs, or whatever
    pops into your imagination

1 egg, beaten

1. Heat butter in a skillet over medium heat, and sauté
   onion 2 minutes. Stir in mushrooms, and cook until tender and all liquid is evaporated. Pour mixture into a bowl,
   and cool 5 minutes. Stir in parsley and cream cheese
   until well combined.

2. Preheat oven to 375°F. Line a large cookie sheet with
   parchment paper. Roll puff pastry dough out into a
   14 x 18-inch rectangle, about ¼-inch thick. Slice dough

Easy Puff Pastry

Makes 1 pound, one 14 x 18-inch rectangle

1½ cups all-purpose flour
½ cup cake flour
2 teaspoons baking powder
½ teaspoon baking soda
¾ teaspoon iodized salt
8 tablespoons (1 stick) cold unsalted butter,
    cut into ½-inch pieces
¾ cup buttermilk

1. In a large bowl, use a fork to mix together flours, baking powder, baking soda, and salt. Using a fork or your fingers, rub butter into flour until mixture resembles large peas. Stir in buttermilk, and form into a ball. Cover dough with plastic wrap, and refrigerate 15 minutes.
2. Knead on a floured surface 1 minute. Using flour as necessary to keep from sticking, roll dough into a 14 x 18-inch rectangle and fold it over itself by thirds. Roll into a rectangle again, and fold again. Keep rolling and folding until dough is smooth, 3–4 times total. Wrap the dough rectangle in plastic, and refrigerate at least 15 minutes before using in a recipe.

into eight 9 x 3½-inch pieces. Spread a tablespoon mushroom mixture and any additional fillings lengthwise down each dough rectangle, leaving a ½-inch margin at the ends.

3. Dry each wiener well, and coat with mustard. Place each in the center of a dough rectangle over mushrooms. Bring dough up and over dough all around, pinch seams tight, and turn over, so seam is side down. Brush each Wellington with egg, and bake until golden brown, about 15–18 minutes. Serve hot.

Myrna's Alligator Dogs on Jalapeño Rolls
Makes 6.

As anyone who's ever watched the television series *Swamp People* knows, alligator hunting is alive and well in Louisiana, the state with the honor of being home to the nation's most wild alligators. There are also several alligator farms around, with many offering tours highlighting incubation, hatching, feeding, and housing. For years now, alligator has been popping up all over restaurant menus. Even so, the big money is in the reptile's skin, which brings in ten times more revenue than meat.

Alligator meat is firm and white, and really does taste like strongly flavored chicken. In Louisiana, it's fairly easy to find alligator sausage, and thanks to the Internet, alligator specialties are easy to order online.

> "I don't know why you insisted on living way down there with the alligators."
>
> —Myrna Minkoff, in a letter to Ignatius.

On July 15, 2011, two thousand hungry fairgoers at Paraguay's Expoferia 2011 were served the world's longest hot dog. Measuring more than 668 feet long and weighing more than 264 pounds, the whopping weenie was nestled into an equally long bun. The record-breaking hot dog was created to celebrate Paraguay's 200th anniversary as a country.

2 tablespoons olive oil

4 links smoked alligator sausage, split lengthwise down the center almost all the way through

1 large yellow onion, thinly sliced

6 jalapeño rolls (recipe follows, or use purchased buns)

Creole mustard, or any coarse-grain mustard

Shredded sharp Cheddar cheese

1. Heat oven to 350°F. In a large skillet, heat oil over medium-high heat, spread sliced sausages open, and place insides down in the skillet. Sauté along with onion until sausage is browned on both sides and onion is golden.
2. Slice rolls in half horizontally, and spread insides with mustard. Fill with browned sausages and onion. Top with cheese.
3. Place sandwiches on a cookie sheet, and heat just until cheese starts to melt, 1–2 minutes. Serve hot.

Jalapeño Rolls Makes 6

1 envelope (2¼ teaspoons) active dry yeast

2 teaspoons sugar

1 cup warm water

1 large egg

2 tablespoons vegetable oil

1 teaspoon iodized salt

1 teaspoon garlic powder

2½–3¼ cups bread flour

¼ cup finely minced fresh, seeded jalapeño peppers

4 tablespoons (½ stick) melted butter

1. In a small bowl, combine yeast, sugar, and water. Let sit 5 minutes.
2. In a large mixing bowl, stir together yeast mixture, egg, oil, salt, and garlic powder. Add 2½ cups flour and jalapeños, and stir until combined. If using a standing mixer, attach dough hook and beat on medium speed 8 minutes, adding flour as necessary to form a very soft dough. If kneading by hand, knead 10 minutes and add flour as necessary to keep from sticking.
3. Put dough in a greased bowl; cover with greased plastic wrap, and let sit 1 hour.
4. Divide dough into 6 equal pieces. Shape each piece into a 2 x 6-inch rectangle, and arrange an inch apart on a paper-lined baking sheet. Let rise until doubled in volume, about 30–40 minutes.
5. Heat oven to 375°F. Bake rolls until golden brown, about 20–25 minutes. After removing rolls from oven, immediately brush with butter. Cool on a rack. Good for hot dogs or as dinner rolls.

Pirate's Pompano en Papillote (Pompano baked in a paper bag)

Makes 4 servings.

Pompano en Papillote is an example of grand Creole cooking at its best, and the dish actually has a backhanded connection with Jean Lafitte, Louisiana's most famous pirate, and the scoundrel we have to assume Ignatius is emulating. ("Lafitte" is the common spelling, but the pirate's only authentic signature is spelled "Laffite.") This showy entrée centers on the Gulf pompano, a firm, white fish, which is baked in a savory sauce inside a puffy paper bag, and was created by Antoine's Restaurant's Jules Alciatore for a banquet honoring the aviation pioneer and Brazilian balloonist Alberto Santos-Dumont. In 1958, Cecil B. DeMille was in New Orleans producing a remake of the movie *The Buccaneer,* the sort-of-true story of Jean Lafitte's involvement in the Battle of New Orleans at the end of the War of 1812. DeMille was so taken with Antoine's Pompano en Papillote that he included it in the movie, even though the dish had not been created until more than a hundred years after Lafitte's death.

> "The vendor who formerly had the quarter route wore an improbable pirate's outfit, a Paradise Vendor's nod to New Orleans folklore and history, a Clydian attempt to link the hot dog with Creole legend. Clyde forced me to try it on.... About my cap I tied the red sateen pirate's scarf. I screwed the one golden earring, a large novelty store hoop of an earring, onto my left earlobe. I affixed the black plastic cutlass to the side of my white vendor's smock with a safety pin. Hardly an impressive pirate, you will say. However, when I studied myself in the mirror, I was forced to admit that I appeared rather fetching in a dramatic way."
>
> —Ignatius. writing in his journal about his Paradise Vendors costume.

1 pint oysters, in their liquor

½ pound shrimp, cleaned, and shells and heads reserved

¼ teaspoon salt

4 fillets pompano (5–6 ounces each), or substitute salmon, mahi-mahi, flounder, or red snapper

Creole seasoning (purchased, or use recipe on pages 6–7)

4 tablespoons (½ stick) unsalted butter, divided

2 tablespoons olive oil

1 cup sliced mushrooms

¼ cup finely minced onion

1 clove garlic, minced

2 tablespoons all-purpose flour

¼ cup heavy cream

2 tablespoons brandy

2 tablespoons minced green onion

4 thin lemon slices

Parchment paper for baking

1. Preheat oven to 400°F. Cut parchment paper into four 15-inch squares. Trim off corners so you have 4 roughly round sheets of parchment.

2. Drain oysters, reserving liquid. Using paper towels, pat oysters as dry as possible, and leave between layers of paper towels until ready to use. Pour reserved oyster liquid into a saucepan. Add reserved shrimp shells and heads and salt, and add enough water to just cover. Bring to a boil, and simmer vigorously 10 minutes. Strain and keep ½ cup stock, discarding remainder or refrigerating for another use.

3. Lightly season fish on both sides with Creole seasoning. Melt 1 tablespoon butter in a large skillet, add olive oil, and cook fish over medium heat until just done, about 2–3 minutes per side. Remove fish to a plate. Add mushrooms and onion, and cook until mushrooms have released their liquid and onion is translucent. Stir in garlic, and cook 15 seconds.

4. Add remaining 3 tablespoons butter, and stir in flour. Cook 1 minute. Add reserved ½ cup stock and cream, and simmer until thick and bubbly. Lightly season shrimp with Creole seasoning, add to sauce, and cook 1 minute. Remove from heat, and stir in brandy. Stir in oysters and green onion. Mixture should be very thick.

5. Lay a fish filet in the center of one side of each paper circle, and top each with ¼ of sauce mixture and a lemon slice. Fold the other half of the parchment over the fish, and seal tightly by pinching and crimping edges together. Bake until paper is puffed and slightly browned, about 12–15 minutes. Immediately serve unopened papillotes on dinner plates, allowing guests to slice their own open with a knife.

Toothsome Grilled Rib-Eye Steaks
Makes 4–6 servings.

New Orleans certainly has its share of outstanding steakhouses. But none have risen to the prominence of Ruth's Chris, which was founded in 1965 when single mother Ruth Fertel mortgaged her home for twenty-two thousand dollars to purchase a sixty-seat restaurant on Broad Street. Now a chain revered worldwide, Ruth's gained its lofty status by serving USDA prime cuts sizzling in butter, and which have been broiled at a blistering 1800°F. But since most home broilers don't get that hot, your best bet for cooking a steak at home is outside on a grill. And if you're throwing a thick, handsome piece of meat over those coals, you won't need any embellishment aside from salt and pepper.

"I could only imagine how many haggard and depraved eyes were regarding me hungrily from behind the closed shutters. I tried not to think about it. Already I was beginning to feel like an especially toothsome steak in a meat market."

—Ignatius J. Reilly, journal entry on residents ogling him as he sells hot dogs in the French Quarter.

2 bone-in rib-eye steaks, 1½ inches thick,
    about 1½ pounds each
Salt
Freshly ground black pepper
Vegetable oil for brushing grill

1. Bring steaks to room temperature. Pat dry, and season generously with salt and pepper.
2. Prepare grill at high heat, leaving one side of grill free of coals or, if using a gas grill, keep one side unlit. Oil grill racks, and set 5 to 6 inches over glowing coals.
3. Directly over coals, cook steaks about 3 minutes on one side and flip with tongs. Cook another 3 minutes, and transfer to unlit side of grill. Cover and cook to the following internal temperatures: 125°F for rare, about 2 more minutes; 130°F for medium-rare, about 4–6 more minutes; or 135°F for medium, 8 more minutes.
4. Transfer steaks to a warm platter, and let rest 5 minutes to redistribute juices. Carve and serve immediately.

Broiled Creole Tomatoes

Makes 2 servings.

A great side for steak, and a dish common in local steak-houses.

1 large, ripe Creole tomato
2 teaspoons sugar
2 tablespoons fine breadcrumbs
2 tablespoons freshly grated Parmesan cheese
2 tablespoons unsalted butter, cut into bits
Chopped parsley for garnish

1. Place a rack 5 inches below oven broiler, and heat oven to broil. Cut tomato in half horizontally, and lightly score tops.
2. Spread top of each tomato with 1 teaspoon sugar. Sprinkle on breadcrumbs and cheese, and then dot with butter.
3. Broil on a foil-lined baking pan until tops of tomatoes are deep golden, 4–5 minutes. Sprinkle with parsley and serve.

Rosemary Roasted Potatoes

Makes 4 servings.

And this is a great side for just about any grilled meat.

2 pounds Yukon Gold potatoes, unpeeled
¼ cup olive oil
1 teaspoon salt
½ teaspoon paprika
½ teaspoon ground black pepper
2 tablespoons minced fresh rosemary

1. Preheat oven to 375°F, and line a cookie sheet with parchment paper. Cut potatoes into 1½- to 2-inch chunks. Place in a large pot, cover with water by 2 inches, bring to a boil, and cook 6 minutes. Drain potatoes well.
2. In a large bowl, coat potatoes with olive oil. In a small bowl, mix together salt, paprika, and black pepper. Coat potatoes with seasoning mix and, peeling sides down, lay on prepared pan. Sprinkle with rosemary.
3. Bake potatoes until brown and crispy, 35–40 minutes. Serve warm.

Turnip Soup with Lobster and Lobster Butter

Makes six 1-cup servings.

The turnip came to America with European colonists and has been growing happily in the South ever since. Historically a reliable food for the poor, the lowly turnip's root was eaten by plantation-era elites, while turnip greens were given to slaves. Lobster, of course, has always been plentiful off the New England coast. Ironically, the now relatively expensive crustacean was so dirt-cheap in colonial America, it was considered only fit for slaves, prisoners, and children.

1 boiled lobster (recipe page 161)

8 tablespoons (1 stick) unsalted butter, plus 2 tablespoons

1½ pounds small turnip roots

1 medium Yukon Gold potato

2 cups chopped yellow onion

Leaves from 1 sprig fresh thyme

2 cloves garlic, minced

½ teaspoon kosher salt

¼ teaspoon ground white pepper

5 cups seafood or chicken stock

¼ cup heavy cream

1. Remove tail and claw meat from lobster, reserving shell pieces. Chop meat into ½-inch pieces, and set aside.

2. To make lobster butter, chop reserved shells from the lobster, including legs, into 1-inch pieces. Put shells and 1 stick butter in a food processor or blender, and blend until shells are pureed. Pour mixture into a heavy-bottomed saucepan, and cook over medium heat just until butter starts to turn brown. Strain through cheesecloth, discarding solids, and set aside in a warm place.

3. To make soup, peel turnips and potato and chop into 1-inch chunks. In a large saucepan, melt remaining 2 tablespoons butter and sauté onion over medium heat until translucent, about 5 minutes. Stir in turnips, potato, thyme, garlic, salt, and pepper, and sauté 1 minute.

4. Stir in stock, and bring to a boil. Lower heat to a simmer, and cook, uncovered, until turnips and potatoes are tender, about 20 minutes.

5. Working in batches, puree soup in a blender until completely smooth. Return soup to the pot, stir in cream, and bring to a boil.

6. To serve, ladle hot soup into bowls and top with lobster pieces and lobster butter.

Lobster and Shiitake Risotto with Black Truffle Oil

Makes 3 entrée or 6 side servings.

1 lobster (1½–2 pounds), boiled (recipe below)

3 tablespoons unsalted butter, divided

4–5 cups chicken stock

1 tablespoon olive oil

1 cup coarsely chopped, fresh shiitake mushrooms

½ cup minced onion

1 cup Arborio rice

½ cup dry white wine

¼ teaspoon ground black pepper

¼ cup whipping cream

Boiled Lobster   Makes 1 lobster

1 live lobster

2 tablespoons salt

1. In a large, deep pot, add salt and enough water to cover the lobster by 2 inches, and bring to a boil. Plunge lobster head first into water. When water comes to a boil again, turn heat down to medium and cover pot. Cook 12 to 15 minutes for a small 1¼-pound lobster, and up to 25 minutes for a 3-pound lobster. Shell should be bright red, the meat firm, white, and opaque, and an antennae or small walking leg should pull off easily.
2. Using long tongs, remove lobster from water. Serve warm, or chill up to 2 days.

¼ cup grated Parmesan cheese

2 tablespoons minced fresh parsley

Black truffle oil

1. Remove lobster meat from shell, reserving shell pieces. Chop meat into ¾-inch pieces, and set aside.
2. Chop shells into large pieces. Heat 1 tablespoon butter in a large saucepan over medium-high heat, and sauté lobster shells 3 minutes. Add 3 cups chicken stock, bring to a boil, and simmer 10 minutes. Strain, reserving stock and discarding shell pieces. Measure stock and, if necessary, add additional chicken stock to reach 3 cups.
3. Heat olive oil in a large, heavy-bottomed saucepan. Sauté mushrooms over medium heat until soft, about 3 minutes. Remove mushrooms from pan, and set aside.
4. Using same pan over medium-low heat, add remaining 2 tablespoons butter. Add onion, and cook 1 minute. Add rice, and stir until pale golden, about 2 minutes. Add wine, and stir until it is fully absorbed.
5. Add ½ cup lobster stock to rice, and stir until liquid is absorbed. Continue adding ½ cups of stock and stirring until all liquid is absorbed and rice is creamy and tender, about 20 minutes. Add lobster, black pepper, and cream. Stir until heated through. Remove from heat, and stir in cheese and parsley. Spoon onto 4 serving plates, and drizzle with truffle oil. Serve immediately.

13

....

Vegetables, Orange Juice, Whole-wheat Bread, Spinach, and Such

> "Are you unnatural enough to want a hot dog this early in the afternoon? My conscience will not let me sell you one. Just look at your loathsome complexion. You are a growing boy whose system needs to be surfeited with vegetables and orange juice and whole-wheat bread and spinach and such."
>
> —Ignatius, determined to keep his few remaining hot dogs for himself, trying to convince George they're unhealthy.

Let's face facts: most New Orleans restaurants are not exactly famous for being on the forefront of healthy eating. Although dishes such as sausage jambalaya, poor boys, bread pudding, and seafood drenched in buttery sauces sure taste good, they're not what nutritionists consider heart-healthful or especially kind to the waist. Even most vegetables that arrive are likely to be accompanied with Hollandaise or butter. And we won't even mention alcohol consumption.

In their homes, however, New Orleanians do serve fruit and cook up vegetables, and lots of them. Historically, New Orleans produce is a mix of Creole, Italian, and American southern, with a touch of the tropical. The area's rich produce tradition started with the Germans who settled across the Mississippi River in the 1720s, and who, for years, supplied the city with okra, spinach,

cauliflower, artichokes, onions, garlic, cabbage, and potatoes. Then came steamboats, which funneled down the bounty from the northern states, and sailed up exotic fruits and vegetables from the Caribbean and South America. Right before the Civil War, these sailing warehouses unloaded so much produce in New Orleans it was not unheard of for unwanted mountains of food to be left on the docks to rot.

It was also during antebellum days that southerners moving to the city brought turnips, cowpeas, and sweet potatoes. On plantations, slaves typically planted enough fruit and vegetables for the master's family and were often allowed to plant small plots of land for their own consumption. If there was excess, they might have sold it to their master's family, or the law even allowed them to sell it on Sundays on the streets of New Orleans.

Later waves of immigrants contributed to the region's variety of produce, which increased dramatically beginning in 1880 with the arrival of the Sicilians. Many Italian immigrants settled in the French Quarter, and there, at the Vegetable Market, or *Halle des Légumes,* they sold alongside the Creoles of color who, until then, had dominated the produce business. Sicilians also took to truck farming on the outskirts of town. In time, several became extremely successful wholesale food distributors.

Statewide, Louisiana's top agricultural products are sugarcane, rice, sweet potatoes, pecans, soybeans and corn. Strawberry production thrives north of New Orleans in Independence. Plaquemines Parish to the south has a healthy citrus industry, and peaches rivaling any grow commercially in the northern town of Ruston.

In New Orleans, backyard gardeners grow heat-tolerant produce such as figs, mirlitons, cucumbers, and tomatoes. And just outside of town, small farmers raise cantaloupe, lettuces, purple hull peas, watermelon, okra, and corn, often on only an acre or two. Increasingly, this small-scale produce is showing up at farmers markets, which are also gaining in popularity, as is the so-called "locavore" movement, which advocates eating foods grown from the region. And some of the area's produce does pop up at larger grocery stores, just as it did in the 1960s.

And what about whole-wheat bread: is it really more nutritious for your "system"?

White flour was actually consumed by Ancient Roman and Egyptian elites. But it wasn't until around 1870, at the end of the Industrial Revolution, that the average baker could afford to use anything but stone ground, a brownish flour that didn't have the grain's bran, but did retain the vitamin and mineral-rich germ. The more affordable white flour was being churned out by roller-milling, a process that removes both the bran and the germ, and leaves the starchy endosperm layer, which contains only a fraction of the original grain's nutrients. To make matters worse, early twentieth-century manufacturers started using peroxides to speed up the aging process that creates stronger gluten, and to also make the flour whiter.

Even with machines doing most of the work, stripping wheat germ from grain to make flour white was costly. So, as with those ancient Egyptians and Romans, refined, and therefore more expensive, bread was the favorite of those with wealth and those aspiring to it.

Nutritionists started noting that white bread was not as nourishing as bread made with whole grains as early as the 1820s. Then, following the World War I–era wheat shortages, economists figured out flour supplies could be increased if Americans consumed more whole-wheat and less white flour, so they encouraged nutritionists to convince the public that bread made from genuine whole-wheat flour was one of the most healthful foods on the planet. But that proved hard to do. Factories had long been churning out presliced white loaves that were alluring and seemed modern, and not many minds of the time were changed.

In the 1930s, 90 percent of American families bought industrial white bread. Soon after, specific deficiency disease syndromes were first identified and documented. And, although the government never has required fortification for any food product, in 1940 it did establish the standard for enriched commercial white flour, dictating that it contain the lost nutrients thiamin, niacin, riboflavin, and iron. Folic acid was eventually added to the mix, and in 1943 a federal law was passed requiring that all flour and breads sold across state lines be enriched according to Food and Drug Administration standards.

However, even with "healthier" white bread popping up on store shelves, whole-wheat advocates never gave up.

A big push for whole grain consumption came in the 1960s, when the counterculture started revolting and whole-wheat bread was touted as antiestablishment. But bread made from whole grain really took off during the 1970s farm-to-table movement and, by the 1980s, America was embracing artisanal multigrains. Whole-wheat bread sales finally topped white in 2009, for the first time in U.S. history.

So Ignatius was correct in recommending that the pimple-faced George limit hot dogs and increase consumption of fruit and vegetables, as well as whole-wheat bread. But Ignatius needs to keep in mind, too, that these wholesome foods are also beneficial for the health of hot dog– and pastry-loving adults.

Orange, Honeydew, and Mixed Greens Salad with Spicy Orange Dressing
Makes 4 servings.

Everyone knows the orange is a powerhouse of Vitamin C, but nutritionists also tout the fruit's respectable levels of potassium, Vitamin A, and Vitamin B6, a vitamin that helps maximize energy output and alleviate skin problems.

¼ cup freshly squeezed orange juice

¼ cup sesame oil

2 tablespoons white vinegar

½ teaspoon chili-garlic sauce

½ teaspoon salt

¼ teaspoon ground black pepper

6 cups mixed salad greens

1 orange, peeled and sectioned

2 cups honeydew melon, in ½-inch cubes

4 whole green onions, sliced

1. Make dressing in a pint jar by combining orange juice, oil, vinegar, chili-garlic sauce, salt, and black pepper. Cover and shake vigorously.

2. Divide greens among 4 salad plates. Top with orange slices, honeydew melon, green onion slices, and dressing. Serve immediately.

Thai Sweet Potato Soup
Makes 1 quart.

Ignatius could have also added sweet potatoes to his litany of healthful foods. Sweet potatoes are rich in the antioxidant beta-carotene that the body converts into Vitamin A, a retinoid, which the National Psoriasis

Foundation thinks may discourage the development of acne, the scourge of many teens like George.

½ cup chopped onion

1 tablespoon olive oil

1 clove garlic, minced

½ teaspoon Thai chili garlic paste

1 tablespoon grated fresh ginger

1 tablespoon honey

½ cup tomato sauce

3 cups chicken broth

1½ cups cooked, mashed sweet potato

3 tablespoons fresh lime juice

2 tablespoons fresh chopped cilantro

1. Sauté onion in oil in a large heavy saucepan until onion is translucent. Add garlic, chili paste, ginger, honey, tomato sauce, broth, and sweet potatoes. Bring to a boil. Reduce heat and simmer, uncovered, 10 minutes.

2. Puree mixture in a blender or food processor. (Be careful: mixture will be hot.) Return to saucepan, and bring back to a boil. Remove from heat, and stir in lime juice and cilantro. Serve soup hot.

Minted Beets with Onion

Makes 4 servings.

Mint is native to Louisiana, and was one of the herbs eaten and used for medicine by precolonial Native Americans. Beets are native to the Mediterranean region, where, early on, mostly the leaves were consumed. The bright red root of the plant was elevated to star status by French chefs in the 1800s. Nutritionists say the beet is full of vitamins and minerals that help create a glowing complexion, so maybe George should load up on this vegetable, too.

1½ pounds fresh beets, leaving 1 inch of stem
    attached to roots

¼ cup white balsamic vinegar

1 tablespoon white vinegar

2 tablespoons extra virgin olive oil

1 teaspoon honey

¼ teaspoon salt

¼ teaspoon ground black pepper

½ sweet onion, thinly sliced

2 tablespoons minced fresh mint

1. Set a steamer basket in a saucepan with 2 inches simmering water. Add beets, cover, and steam until tender when pierced with a knife, 25–30 minutes. Chop off stems, and peel skins off roots. Cut roots into ¼-inch slices.

2. Make dressing in a medium bowl by whisking together vinegars, olive oil, honey, salt, and pepper. Stir in onion.

3. Add warm beets and mint to dressing and toss. Serve warm or at room temperature.

Garlic and Ginger Spinach Sauté

Makes 6 servings.

The National Institutes for Health recommend foods high in the water-soluble B vitamin folate, such as spinach, for healthy red blood cells and for maintaining healthy fingernails, hair, and skin.

4 bunches fresh spinach, trimmed
3 tablespoons olive oil
1 tablespoon chopped garlic
5 very thin slices fresh ginger
1 teaspoon salt
¼ teaspoon hot chili sauce
1 tablespoon sesame oil
½ lemon

1. Wash spinach, and shake off excess water. Heat olive oil in a large skillet, and sauté garlic and ginger over medium heat 30 seconds. Stir in salt and chili sauce.

2. Add spinach, and toss well. Cover the skillet, and cook 1 minute.

3. Uncover the pot, raise heat to high, and sauté until spinach is just wilted, 2–3 minutes. Drain, discarding liquid. Place spinach in a bowl, and stir in sesame oil. Spritz on juice from the lemon, and serve hot.

Smothered Okra and Tomatoes

Makes 4 servings.

Okra is rich in Vitamin K, the vitamin needed for proper blood coagulation. The mucilaginous (slimy) vegetable was brought to the French West Indies along with slaves from West Africa, and from there this tall, tropical, flowering herb went to New Orleans. Slaves ate okra dried and ground, and also with rice in a dish called *ya ya,* a stew that was one of the progenitors of today's gumbo.

3 tablespoons vegetable oil

1 cup chopped onion

1 pound sliced fresh or frozen okra

1 tablespoon white vinegar

1½ cups chopped fresh, seeded tomatoes, or
  canned diced or crushed, with liquid

½ teaspoon salt

¼ teaspoon black pepper

1. In a medium, heavy-bottomed pot, add oil and sauté
   onion over medium heat until golden, about 5 minutes.
2. Add okra, vinegar, tomatoes, salt, and black pepper.
   Cover pot. Using low heat, cook until tender, about
   30 minutes, stirring occasionally. Serve hot.

Whole-grain Bread

Makes 1 loaf. Recipe is by Ann Jennings.

Whole-grain bread adds fiber to your diet, which is crucial for elimination of toxins. This nutritious loaf features several different whole grains, and it's great for
slicing for sandwiches.

3½ cups whole-wheat flour, divided

¼ cup wheat bran

¼ steel cut oats

1½ cups warm water, divided

¼ cup olive oil

¼ cup honey

4½ teaspoons yeast

¼ cup flax meal (or grind your own whole
  flax seeds)

1½ teaspoons salt

1. In a medium bowl, combine 1 cup flour, wheat bran, oats,
   and 1 cup warm water. Cover, and let stand 1 hour.
2. In the bowl of a standing mixer, add remaining ½ cup
   warm water, olive oil, honey, and yeast, and allow to
   stand 5 minutes.
3. Add flour mixture to yeast mixture, along with remaining
   2½ cups flour, flax meal, and salt. Using a bread hook,
   mix on low speed 7 minutes. Form dough into a ball,
   place in a greased bowl, cover with plastic wrap, and
   allow to sit in a warm place until doubled in bulk, about
   1½ hours.
4. Punch dough down, and remove from bowl. Knead lightly
   and shape dough into an 8-inch loaf. Place in a greased
   9-inch loaf pan, cover lightly with a clean dish towel, and
   let sit until bread rises about 1 inch above pan rim, about
   30 minutes.
5. Position a rack in the middle of the oven, and preheat
   oven to 350°F. Bake bread until dark brown, about 30–35
   minutes. Remove from pan immediately, and allow to
   cool at least 30 minutes before slicing.

Whole-wheat Parmesan Sage Drop Biscuits

Makes 12.

These quick biscuits are delicious with soup. And feel free to make them with all whole-wheat flour. The biscuits will be denser, yet still tender, and certainly more nutritious.

1 cup whole-wheat flour

1 cup all-purpose flour

¾ cup freshly grated Parmesan cheese

2 tablespoons minced fresh sage (or substitute parsley or chives)

1 tablespoon baking powder

1 teaspoon garlic powder

½ teaspoon iodized salt

½ teaspoon baking soda

¼ cup olive oil

1 cup buttermilk, room temperature

1. Adjust oven rack to center position, and preheat oven to 425°F. In a large bowl, use a fork to combine flours, cheese, sage, baking powder, garlic powder, salt, and baking soda.
2. In a separate bowl, whisk together oil and buttermilk. Pour into the dry ingredients all at once, and stir just until a moist dough forms.
3. Drop biscuits by heaping rounded tablespoons onto a parchment-lined cookie sheet, and bake until golden brown, about 10–12 minutes. Serve warm.

Skinny Fruit Salad

Makes 6–8 servings.

This fruit salad tastes decadent with only a fraction of the calories and fat of traditional recipes. The secret is nutmeg, which gives the yogurt its bold taste.

1 cup plain low-fat yogurt

1 tablespoon honey

1 tablespoon freshly squeezed lime juice

¾ teaspoon freshly grated nutmeg

1 pint hulled and sliced strawberries

1 banana, sliced

1 orange, peeled, seeded, and sectioned

2 cups grapes

1 small apple, seeded and coarsely chopped

1 cup blueberries

In a large bowl, stir together yogurt, honey, lime juice, and nutmeg. Gently stir in fruit, and serve immediately.

No-booze Hurricane Cocktail

Makes 1 tall drink.

The world-famous hurricane cocktail gets its distinctive flavor from a trio of fruit juices, including orange juice, and this festive, nonalcoholic version is a good party option for all "growing boys." For the original alcoholic version, substitute the club soda with 2 tablespoons each dark and light rum.

The hurricane was invented by French Quarter bar owner Pat O'Brien during World War II, when bars were forced to buy as many as fifty cases of rum in order to qualify for one case of scarce whiskey. To use his excess rum, O'Brien huddled with a liquor rep and the two came up with a fruity cocktail and served it in a glass shaped like a hurricane lamp. The distinctive glass has, for years, been one of New Orleans's most coveted souvenirs.

Half a lime
¼ cup passion fruit juice
3 tablespoons fresh-squeezed orange juice
2 tablespoons sweet cherry juice
2 tablespoons red grenadine syrup
1 tablespoon simple syrup
Chilled club soda or lemon-lime soda
Orange slice and maraschino cherry for garnish

1. Fill a shaker with ice, and squeeze in lime. Add passion fruit juice, orange juice, cherry juice, grenadine, and simple syrup. Cover shaker, and shake vigorously 1 minute.
2. Strain into a hurricane glass filled with ice, and fill glass to top with club soda. Stir well. Garnish with orange slice and cherry.

Dining in That Whirlpool of Despair, Baton Rouge

"The only excursion in my life outside of New Orleans took me through the vortex to the whirlpool of despair: Baton Rouge."

—Ignatius J. Reilly, journal entry.

You just gotta feel sorry for a guy who, in his thirties, has only ventured out of his home city once. But the single time Ignatius dared wander, he was left scarred. What caused such everlasting distress? Was it the bouncing around on a Greyhound Scenicruiser through the abysmal swamps? Maybe it was the fear of rural rednecks. Or, as Myrna Minkoff keenly observes, he might be transferring guilt for blowing the interview for a teaching position at Louisiana State University. Whatever the reason, Ignatius is supremely sour on Louisiana's state capital, the city of Baton Rouge.

Although Baton Rouge and New Orleans were settled by the French at the same time, the two cities grew culturally in different directions. *La Nouvelle-Orléans,* New Orleans, was founded in 1718 by the explorer Bienville and named for the Regent of France, the Duke of Orléans. Baton Rouge was settled by the French in 1719, but had been named in 1699 by Bienville's brother, D'Iberville, who had come upon a Native American settlement along the Mississippi River known as Istrouma. There the explorer spotted a hunting-ground boundary marker made from a blood-soaked cypress tree, so he named the area *le baton rouge,* red stick.

In the early years, Baton Rouge, like New Orleans, was home to whichever Catholics the French and Spanish rulers allowed in, along with African slaves governed by the laws of the *Code Noir,* or black code, which required them to be baptized Catholic. But Baton Rouge was established as a military post, while agricultural and economic development centered on the strategic port city of New Orleans. For that reason, New Orleans attracted every social level of the human spectrum. Soon, it grew into a cosmopolitan and boisterous, yet laid-back metropolis that, today still, is described as America's most European city. Baton Rouge, on the other hand, developed a reputation as a genteel, family-oriented college town, with customs leaning more toward the American South than to France.

Unlike Ignatius, most Baton Rouge residents don't think twice about leaving behind their relative tranquility and driving an hour to reach their sister city, New Orleans. And on that woeful day he suffered through his "pilgrimage" to Baton Rouge, Ignatius would have probably fared better had he taken a moment to seek out something comforting and familiar to eat. Although he would not have had much luck finding Lucky Dogs or wine cakes, he would have had an easy time locating eateries that served a variety of pizzas, poor boys, and steaks, and fried chicken and seafood rivaling any. And who knows, he might have stumbled upon one of the city's many doughnut shops, where he would have certainly found an item or two to remind him of home. Then maybe he would have been less fearful—and in turn he wouldn't have been nauseated, or had to pay that cab forty dollars to drive him back to New Orleans.

Airline Motors Turtle Soup

Makes 6 servings. Adapted from a recipe from the files of Elouise R. Cotham, an owner and the café manager of Airline Motors until the early 1980s.

Before Ignatius had gotten very far out of town, his Scenicruiser would have likely made a scheduled stop at Airline Motors on Highway 61 in LaPlace, about twenty-five miles west of New Orleans. This popular restaurant actually started out in 1937 as a Chevrolet dealership and service station. The Great Depression put an end to the company's car sales, so in 1939 the still-spiffy building was opened by the Cotham and Woods families as a twenty-four-hour café that also included slot machines, a service station, wrecker services, and an automobile repair garage.

Famous for its flashing neon and glass bricks, Airline Motors and its original Cajun/Creole menu attracted droves of diners from New Orleans. The original restaurant closed in 1993 but has since reopened under new ownership.

Turtle soup is a New Orleans specialty going back to the early colonial period. This thick, savory dish is also known by the Creole name *caouage*, referring to the alligator snapping turtle typically used. Many old-line restaurants, such as Commander's Palace and Galatoire's, are celebrated for turtle soup.

1 gallon water

3 pounds turtle meat

2 dried bay leaves

2 large onions

1 large bell pepper

3 stalks celery

6 cloves garlic

8 tablespoons (1 stick) butter

½ cup all-purpose flour

¼ cup tomato paste

¼ cup Worcestershire sauce

2 lemons, thinly sliced, divided

Salt and pepper to taste

6 tablespoons sherry, optional

4 hard-boiled eggs, peeled and chopped

3 tablespoons minced parsley

1. Bring water to boil, and add turtle and bay leaves. Simmer until turtle is tender, about 45 minutes, skimming off any fat and foam that rises. Remove turtle meat. Strain and reserve stock. Remove meat from bones, and chop into ¼ to ½-inch pieces. Discard bones.

2. In a food grinder or food processor, grind together onions, bell pepper, celery, and garlic.

3. Make a roux in a heavy-bottomed Dutch oven by first

melting butter over low heat. Add flour, and stir constantly until dark brown, about 10–12 minutes.

4. Stir in ground vegetables, tomato paste, Worcestershire sauce, and reserved stock. Blend well, raise heat, and bring to a boil. Reduce heat to medium, and add turtle meat and ¼ of lemon slices. Season with salt and pepper, and simmer over low heat 1 hour.

5. Right before serving, remove lemon slices and add sherry to pot, or to taste in bowls. Garnish hot soup in bowls with remaining lemon slices, eggs, and parsley. Serve immediately.

· ·

Airline Motors Oysters Rockefeller

Makes 8 appetizer servings. Adapted from a recipe from the files of Elouise R. Cotham.

· ·

Oysters Rockefeller was the brainchild of Jules Alciatore, owner of Antoine's Restaurant on St. Louis Street in the French Quarter. During an 1899 European snail shortage, Alciatore ground together a secret recipe for a hodgepodge of local greens that he dolloped on top of oysters and broiled. The elegant appetizer tasted so rich it was named after one of the wealthiest men in the country at the time, John D. Rockefeller. The popularity of Oysters Rockefeller has endured, and even though the original recipe is still a secret, the dish is thought to be the single greatest contribution of the United States to haute cuisine.

Some versions of Oysters Rockefeller use fennel to provide the dish's distinctive kick, but this recipe, probably written in the 1940s, relies on absinthe. That's interesting since the United States halted sales of the liquor in 1912. The concern was over hallucinations caused by the compound thujone found in the wormwood used to make absinthe. The ban was, however, lifted in 2007, and the bright green spirit once again sits prettily in American bars, including at the French Quarter's Absinthe House Bar, where the famous Absinthe House Frappé was invented back in 1874.

4 dozen oysters and shells

2 bunches green onions

1 bunch parsley

1 stalk celery

2 packages (10 ounces each) frozen spinach, cooked and well-drained

16 tablespoons (2 sticks) unsalted butter, melted

⅓ cup toasted breadcrumbs

¼ cup Worcestershire sauce

2 ounces (¼ cup) absinthe, or substitute Pernod, Herbsaint, or Pastis

1 teaspoon salt

1 teaspoon ground black pepper

Cayenne pepper to taste

Rock or ice cream salt for filling baking pan and serving

Fresh lemon wedges for serving

1. Shuck the oysters, or have your fishmonger shuck them. Reserve shells.
2. Make Rockefeller Sauce in a blender or food processor by grinding together the green onions, parsley, celery, spinach, and butter. Transfer to a bowl, and mix in breadcrumbs, Worcestershire sauce, absinthe, salt, black pepper, and cayenne.
3. Preheat a broiler. Fill a large baking pan with rock salt, and place 48 oyster half-shells on top of the salt. Put one oyster in each half-shell. Broil just until edges start to curl, about 2–3 minutes. Remove from oven, and pour liquid from each shell.
4. Top each oyster generously with Rockefeller Sauce; then place under broiler and cook until sauce begins to brown. Serve hot on salt-lined plates, and garnish with lemons.

Rustic Cajun Chicken and Sausage Jambalaya

Makes 8 servings.

Aside from Airline Motors, the town of LaPlace is noted for its andouille, a German smoked-pork sausage, earning the town the nickname "Andouille Capital of the World." And andouille from LaPlace regularly finds its way to the town of Gonzales, some sixty miles north of New Orleans and another stop Ignatius would have made on the way to Baton Rouge.

Every year Gonzales holds its Jambalaya Festival and Cooking Contest to honor the one-pot rice dish that has come to be identified with the area. The big difference between Cajun/Gonzales-style jambalaya and the kind cooked in New Orleans is tomatoes; New Orleans jambalaya has historically been cooked with the fruit, and the finished dish is therefore red, while Cajun-style jambalayas usually don't call for tomatoes and are therefore brown. Also, New Orleans jambalaya often has shrimp, while Cajun jambalaya centers on chicken and andouille and heavily smoked sausage, and typically has lots more cayenne pepper. In the old days, Cajuns cooked jambalaya outdoors in large cast-iron pots over wood fires, and this technique is still used by many purists.

8 chicken thighs, with skin and bones, or 1 cut-up
  whole fryer or hen

Salt, black pepper, and cayenne pepper

¼ cup vegetable oil

1 pound andouille or smoked pork sausage, sliced into
  ½-inch pieces

3 cups chopped onion

1 large green bell pepper, chopped

2 stalks celery, chopped

2 tablespoons minced garlic

6 cups chicken stock, divided

3 cups raw long-grain white rice

½ cup chopped green onion

¼ cup chopped parsley

1. Season chicken liberally with salt, black pepper, and cayenne. In a large, heavy-bottomed Dutch oven, heat oil over medium-high heat and brown chicken well on all sides. Remove chicken. Add andouille, and sauté 5 minutes. Remove andouille with a slotted spoon, and take out all but 2 tablespoons oil from pan.

2. Add onion, bell pepper, and celery to Dutch oven. Cook, stirring often, until everything is well-browned and a brown crust starts appearing on bottom of pan, about 5–7 minutes. Add garlic, and cook 30 seconds.

3. Add ½ cup chicken stock, and cook until liquid has evaporated, the whole while stirring and scraping up the browned bits. Add chicken and andouille and remaining 5½ cups stock, and bring to a fast boil. Stir in rice, let liquid come to a boil again, then lower heat to a bare simmer. Cover pot tightly, and cook 10 minutes. Uncover and gently fold rice over, scraping up from the bottom. Cover tightly again, and cook until liquid is completely evaporated and rice is tender, about 10–20 minutes more.

4. Taste for seasoning, and stir in green onion and parsley. Take pot off heat, top tightly with cover, and let sit at least 15 minutes (and no peeking). Can be made up to 1 hour ahead and kept warm, covered, in a 200°F oven. Serve with salad or the traditional Gonzales-area side dish, creamy white beans.

> "Only the most flamboyant offal would be seen in a miscarriage like that."
>
> —Ignatius's reaction to Dorian Greene's mauve cashmere sweater.

Beausoleil's Sweetbreads with Beurre Blanc and Capers

Makes 4 appetizer servings. Adapted from a recipe by chef Nathan Gresham of Beausoleil Restaurant, Baton Rouge.

Offal, also known as variety meat, is the internal organs of a butchered animal, excluding skeletal muscle. Examples include liver, sweetbreads (thymus gland), chitlins (small intestine), heart, kidney, tongue, and brain. When these various insides come from a bird, they're called giblets. Although Ignatius means to belittle Dorian, cuts known as offal can be pretty tasty. And they are increasingly popping up on upscale restaurant menus, including in Baton Rouge.

1 pound veal sweetbreads

4 tablespoons olive oil, divided

2 stalks celery, medium dice

1 small onion, medium dice

1 small carrot, medium dice

3 garlic cloves, peeled and smashed

2 bay leaves

5 black peppercorns

2 sprigs fresh thyme

2 cups white wine

3 cups water

Salt and ground black pepper

All-purpose flour for dusting

2 tablespoons capers for serving

2 tablespoons minced parsley for serving

Beurre Blanc Sauce (recipe at right)

1. Soak sweetbreads in cold water 3–24 hours.
2. In a large pot, heat 2 tablespoons olive oil over medium-high heat and sauté celery, onion, and carrot 2 minutes. Add garlic, bay leaves, peppercorns, and thyme, and stir 1 minute. Add wine and water, and bring to a simmer. Add sweetbreads, and simmer 10 minutes. (If sweetbreads are not completely covered with liquid, add more water.) Sweetbreads should be plump and firm to the touch, and bounce back when touched.
3. Remove sweetbreads from liquid. Using your fingers, remove any visible veins and gristle, along with the thick exterior membrane. Place sweetbreads between two baking dishes. Place heavy weights, such as a few canned items, a pot of water, or a brick, on the top pan to press the sweetbreads. Refrigerate until completely cool, about 1 hour.
4. Remove sweetbreads from pan, and slice ¼-inch thick on the bias. Season medallions with salt and pepper. Dust with flour.
5. Add remaining 2 tablespoons olive oil to a sauté pan, and place over medium heat. Sauté sweetbreads, turning frequently until brown on both sides, 3–5 minutes. Place on paper towels to drain.
6. To serve, divide hot sweetbread medallions among 4 plates, placing in a spiral pattern, and top with capers, parsley, and Beurre Blanc Sauce.

Beurre Blanc Sauce — Makes about ⅓ cup

Recipe is by chef Nathan Gresham, Beausoleil Restaurant, Baton Rouge.

1 teaspoon diced shallot

1 teaspoon diced garlic

1 sprig fresh thyme

1 bay leaf

1 cup white wine

2 tablespoons Champagne vinegar

5 black peppercorns

½ cup heavy cream

4 tablespoons (½ stick) cold unsalted butter, cut into ½-inch pieces

1 teaspoon fresh lemon juice

1. In a small saucepan, stir together shallot, garlic, thyme, bay leaf, wine, vinegar, and peppercorns. Bring to a simmer, and reduce until *au sec* (almost dry), about 5 minutes.
2. Add cream, bring to a boil, and reduce until bubbles are thick, about 1 minute. Remove from heat, and whisk in butter a piece at a time until completely incorporated and smooth.
3. Strain through a wire mesh, and stir in lemon juice. Use sauce immediately, or place in a thermos to retain heat.

Dirty Rice

Makes 12–14 servings.

1 large bell pepper, finely chopped

2 stalks celery, finely chopped

2 cloves garlic, chopped

1 teaspoon salt

½ teaspoon ground black pepper

3 cups beef stock

8 cups cooked rice, at room temperature

¼ cup chopped parsley

½ cup chopped green onion, green and white parts

1. Grind chicken livers in a food processor or meat grinder. (Don't worry if livers get mushy; they're only added for flavor.) Over medium-high heat in a Dutch oven, sauté chicken livers, ground beef, sausage, onion, bell pepper, celery, garlic, salt, and black pepper until meat has browned well.

2. Add stock, and cook at a brisk simmer, uncovered and stirring occasionally, until liquid has almost totally evaporated, down to 2–3 tablespoons, about 20 minutes.

3. Fluff rice up with a fork, and stir it into meat mixture. Stir slowly and gently, until everything is heated through and liquid has totally soaked into rice. Stir in parsley and green onion. Serve hot.

One of the Baton Rouge/New Orleans area's most popular recipes that contains internal organs is dirty rice, which gets its distinctive taste from chicken livers or gizzards. Dirty rice is so named because, after the browned meats are stirred into the rice, the dish looks "dirty." This rich side dish often shows up in some form at large gatherings, such as family reunions and funerals and, for many, it's mandatory at barbecues. Once you're out of Baton Rouge and travel west into the Acadian parishes, this same dish is a little moister, it might contain only ground beef and no chicken innards, and the Cajuns there call it rice dressing.

1 pound chicken livers

1 pound ground beef

½ pound hot bulk sausage

1 large onion, finely chopped

Classic Spinach Madeleine

Makes 6 servings. Recipe is by Madeline Wright.

In 1956, Madeline Wright of St. Francisville, a small town just north of Baton Rouge, needed to make a luncheon dish for her bridge club. So the former bed-and-breakfast owner cooked up a pot of creamed spinach and tossed in a roll of jalapeño cheese that had been hanging around in her refrigerator. Wright's new recipe received rave reviews, so she submitted it for inclusion in the 1959 inaugural edition of the Baton Rouge Junior League's *River Road Recipes* cookbook. Soon, the spicy, creamy spinach concoction became famous regionally. Today, Madeline's stroke of genius is known all over the United States and even beyond, easily making Spinach Madeleine the most recognizable dish from the Baton Rouge area.

The difference in the spelling of the dish and Wright's first name was intentional; she has said she thought the French spelling was more sophisticated. Also, Madeline's original creation called for a roll of Kraft Jalapeño Cheese, which was discontinued in 1999. One good substitute is a cheese roll made by Parkers Farm, and creative cooks have also concocted their own cheese substitutes with various processed cheeses and dried or fresh peppers. Although the cheeses in today's markets will not produce the exact result as the original, the dish is still outstanding, and is a regular on many South Louisiana holiday tables.

2 packages (10 ounces each) frozen chopped spinach

4 tablespoons (½ stick) unsalted butter

2 tablespoons flour

2 tablespoons chopped onion

½ cup evaporated milk

½ teaspoon black pepper

¾ teaspoon celery salt

¾ teaspoon garlic salt

1 teaspoon Worcestershire sauce

6 ounces pepper cheese, cut into ½-inch cubes

Salt and cayenne pepper to taste

Optional buttered breadcrumbs for topping

1. Cook spinach according to package directions. Drain well, and reserve liquor.
2. Melt butter in a large saucepan over low heat. Add flour, stirring until blended and smooth, but not brown. Add onion and cook, stirring constantly, until onion is soft, but not brown, about 2–3 minutes.
3. Add ½ cup reserved vegetable liquor and evaporated milk slowly, stirring constantly to avoid lumps. Cook while still stirring until smooth and thick. Add black pepper, celery salt, garlic salt, Worcestershire sauce, and cheese, and stir until melted. Combine with spinach. Check for seasoning, and add salt and cayenne to taste.
4. Serve immediately, or put into a 1-quart casserole, top with buttered breadcrumbs, and bake at 350°F until brown and bubbly, about 35 minutes. Can also be made ahead and refrigerated overnight or frozen.

Sensation Salad

Makes 6 side salads.

When Ignatius was in Baton Rouge, he could have stopped for a meal at Bob and Jake's restaurant on Government Street and sampled the hottest salad in town, Jake Staples' Sensation Salad. Created in the 1950s, this cheesy, garlicky salad grew to be so popular it became a regular menu item throughout South Louisiana, and it's still a fixture in many restaurants. Back in the 1950s–60s, iceberg lettuce was, of course, pretty much the only thing around. But go ahead and give iceberg a try; the salad needs this lettuce's crunch and heft to complement the bold dressing.

⅓ cup olive oil

⅓ cup canola oil

3 tablespoons freshly squeezed lemon juice

2 tablespoon red wine vinegar

2 tablespoons finely minced fresh parsley

1 teaspoon mashed or finely minced garlic

½ teaspoon salt

¼ teaspoon ground black pepper

1 large head iceberg lettuce, chopped

⅔ cup freshly grated Romano cheese

Combine olive oil, canola oil, lemon juice, vinegar, parsley, garlic, salt, and pepper in a pint jar, and shake well. For best flavor, refrigerate 24 hours. When ready to serve, toss lettuce with dressing and cheese.

....

Incredibly Tender Italian Cream Cake

Makes a 9-inch, 3-layer cake.

....

Ignatius would surely take comfort in this special-occasion confection, also commonly known as Italian Wedding Cake, and one of the most popular desserts at Piccadilly, the home-style cafeteria chain of sixty restaurants that started back in 1932 as a tiny restaurant on Third Street in Baton Rouge.

No one is sure who invented Italian Cream Cake, but its building blocks of sponge cake, cream, nuts, and flavorings have been common in Italian baking for hundreds of years. Because of the inclusion of coconut and pecans, it's speculated that an Italian baker in America's South may have created this masterpiece and given it its name. Compared to traditional recipes, this one calls for cake flour instead of all-purpose flour, in addition to one more egg, resulting in a richer, yet lighter crumb.

16 tablespoons (2 sticks) unsalted butter

2 cups sugar

6 eggs, at room temperature, yolks and whites
    separated

1 cup buttermilk, at room temperature

1 teaspoon baking soda

½ teaspoon iodized salt

1 teaspoon vanilla extract

½ teaspoon almond extract

2¼ cups cake flour

1 cup shredded coconut

1 cup finely chopped pecans

Italian Cream Cake Icing (recipe follows)

1. Preheat oven to 350°F. Grease insides of three 9 x 2-inch round cake pans, line bottoms with parchment paper circles and grease them, and dust insides of pans with flour.

2. In a large bowl, with an electric mixer using medium speed, cream together butter and sugar until light and

fluffy, about 3 minutes. Add egg yolks, one at a time, beating well after each addition.

3. In a small bowl, stir together buttermilk, baking soda, salt, vanilla, and almond extract. Alternate adding flour and buttermilk mixture into batter, beginning and ending with flour. Stir in coconut and pecans.

4. Beat egg whites until stiff, and gently fold into batter. Divide batter among prepared pans, and smooth tops. Bake until center bounces back when lightly touched, about 30 minutes.

5. Remove layers from oven, and cool in pans on a rack 5 minutes. Remove cakes from pans, and cool completely on racks.

6. To frost, spread ½ cup icing on top of bottom layer and sprinkle with ⅓ cup pecans. Place second layer over bottom layer, and spread with ½ cup icing and ⅓ cup pecans. Place third layer on top, and spread icing on top and sides of cake. Decorate with remaining chopped pecans and pecan halves. Can be made up to 3 days ahead and refrigerated.

Bread Pudding with Meringue and Caramel and Vanilla Bourbon Sauce
Makes 6–8 servings. Recipe is from the files of Ray Sonnier.

Creole cooks actually get excited about stale bread, the key ingredient to bread pudding, a dessert that certainly wasn't invented in New Orleans or Baton Rouge, but one which locals long ago turned into something sublime. This is also one dish many home cooks still cobble together without a recipe, and their various soufflé-like versions can show up studded with raisins or nuts, dolloped with a variety of sauces or toppings, or served just

Italian Cream Cake Icing

Makes enough to frost a 3-layer cake.

- 12 ounces cream cheese, at room temperature
- 12 tablespoons (1½ sticks) butter, at room temperature
- 2 teaspoons vanilla extract
- 6 cups sifted confectioners' sugar
- 1½ cups shredded coconut
- 1⅓ cups finely chopped pecans, plus pecan halves for garnish

In a large bowl using medium mixer speed, beat together cream cheese and butter until completely smooth. Beat in vanilla and confectioners' sugar until smooth. Stir in coconut. Use pecans for sprinkling between layers and for garnish.

plain. Bread pudding has always been popular in Louisiana, including that wasteland of Baton Rouge.

    10 slices white bread, or ¾ of a standard French
        bread loaf, cut into 1-inch pieces
    2½ cups whole milk, scalded
    5 large eggs, yolks separated from whites
    1 (12-ounce) can evaporated milk
    1 teaspoon cinnamon
    3 teaspoons vanilla, divided
    1½ cups, plus 6 tablespoons sugar
    Caramel and Vanilla Bourbon Sauce (recipe follows)

1. Soak bread in scalded milk 30 minutes to 2 hours (longer
   is better).
2. Preheat oven to 350°F. In a large bowl, beat egg yolks
   with a fork. Beat in evaporated milk, cinnamon, 2 teaspoons vanilla, and 1½ cups sugar.
3. Stir bread into egg mixture, and pour into a well-buttered
   9 x 13-inch baking pan. Place dish in a hot-water bath
   made by placing the custard-filled pan in a larger pan
   and adding enough boiling water to reach halfway up the
   side of the smaller pan. Bake until deep brown and center is set, about 1–1¼ hours.
4. About 5 minutes before bread pudding is ready, make
   meringue by using medium-high mixer speed to beat
   egg whites until foamy. Add remaining teaspoon vanilla.
   Gradually add remaining 6 tablespoons sugar, and continue beating until stiff, glossy peaks form.
5. Remove pudding and water bath from oven, and turn
   oven up to 375°F. Spread meringue over top, and return
   to oven (not in the water bath). Bake until meringue is
   lightly browned. Cool on a rack at least 20 minutes before serving. Ladle tops of servings with Caramel and
   Vanilla Bourbon Sauce.

> After Santa had left, Mrs. Reilly filled
> her glass with bourbon and added a
> jigger of Seven-Up.
>
> —Irene Reilly at Santa's house, waiting to meet
>   Mr. Robichaux for the first time.

Caramel and Vanilla Bourbon Sauce
Makes about 1¼ cups

    1 cup sugar
    ¼ cup water
    4 tablespoons (½ stick) unsalted butter
    ⅔ cup heavy cream
    1 vanilla bean, sliced open lengthwise and seeds
        scraped, or 2 teaspoons vanilla extract
    ¼ cup bourbon

1. In a heavy-bottomed saucepan, bring sugar and
   water to a boil and cook over medium heat, stirring
   constantly, until mixture just reaches a light caramel color, about 6–7 minutes. (Be careful. Caramel
   turns dark fast.)
2. Remove from heat and whisk in butter. Slowly and
   carefully add cream (mixture will bubble). Stir in
   vanilla bean seeds and pod halves. Bring to a simmer, turn heat down to low, and cook 1 minute.
   Remove from heat, cover, and set aside up to 1
   hour, or refrigerate.
3. When ready to serve, remove vanilla pods and
   bring sauce to a simmer. Cook 30 seconds, stirring
   occasionally. Remove from heat, and stir in bourbon. Serve warm.

John Kennedy Toole's Muses

It's fairly obvious that most characters in *A Confederacy of Dunces* are drawn from John Kennedy Toole's perceptions of everyday life around him. Exhaustive studies have been done on the literary works and lofty authors who may have also been possible influences, and hints of Chaucer, Edmund Spenser, Cervantes, and T. S. Eliot can certainly be found throughout. But it can't be argued that this novel gets its life from the bar owners, housewives, homosexuals, policemen, Italians, African Americans, Irish, the well-heeled and the stone-broke and, of course, the hot dog salesmen who touched Toole's life at one time or another.

Toole's mother, the former Thelma Ducoing, had grown up in a faded stretch of Elysian Fields Avenue in the Faubourg (suburb) Marigny, just outside the French Quarter. Seeking to upgrade her social status, the oftentimes caustic and judgmental Thelma insisted that her car-salesman husband, John Dewey Toole Jr., rent a house in the genteel Uptown area. There, Kenny, or Ken, as he was known to close friends and family, was born on December 17, 1937.

Starting when Toole could barely walk, his mother coached him in the finer things, including how to act in high society and recite on stage. More than a performer,

however, Toole proved exceptionally bright, and by ninth grade, he was already entering and winning writing contests. By sixteen, he had completed a novel, *The Neon Bible*, which, like *Dunces*, took a long and torturous road to publication.

Early on, Toole also proved a natural mimic, and this gift for parodying dialects clearly shows through in *A Confederacy of Dunces*. The city's lower-class Irish and Italian "yats," African Americans, garish homosexuals, wealthy factory owners, lowly street vendors, and barflies—the jargon of very few groups was off-limits.

Some of Toole's inspiration came from within a few blocks of his home. But much of his exposure to the city's expansive reservoir of colorful characters occurred on visits to far-flung neighborhoods. Although Toole was famously controlled by his mother, as a sponge-brained teenager he secretly wandered sections of New Orleans she deemed beneath him. And, according to Cory Mac-Lauchlin, author of the Toole biography *Butterfly in the Typewriter,* it was in these forays that Toole sought, observed, and learned, gathering information for literary character models.

Behind the city's main boulevard, Canal Street, begins the French Quarter, and there Toole could not have

As with the Reilly's ragtag home, many tiny houses on Constantinople Street moved into the twentieth century "carelessly and uncaringly." But by the time the twenty-first century rolled around, most had been lovingly renovated.

escaped the sight of scantily clad "exotic" dancers like *Dunces*'s Darlene, along with the drunks, shysters, bookies, unconcerned cops, and hookers, who were all tied together by the Mafia and bar owners like Lana Lee. MacLauchlin writes that it was in the French Quarter that an uncomfortable Toole and a casual acquaintance attended a gay party, an event where Toole met "thoughtful guests," but also a "lot of silly people." And, of course, interspersed throughout the Quarter's flash and alcohol, Toole would have found the eccentric vendors who sold hot dogs from the city's famed Lucky Dog carts.

In the blue-collar Irish Channel section butting to Uptown were musicians and brewery and dock workers descended from the area's original immigrant Irish, Germans, and Italians, along with African Americans. Jazz and beer would have been flowing. Open windows would have spilled out scents of garlic and onion, and chatting neighbors would have ended questions with the words "sugar," "precious," "honey," "dahlin'," or "baby." And from that neighborhood's potholed streets, he would have also heard homemakers like Santa Battaglia fret about undercooked daube or overcooked jambalaya, all screeched out in "yat," the area's distinctive dialect ("ersters" and "grammaw"), and a jargon that, in reality, is not an actual speech pattern, but resistance from a population from the "old country" that likes to keep the status quo.

The historic Carrollton district where Burma Jones sought advice from Mr. Watson is part of Uptown, and only a few miles from where Toole grew up. Carrollton Avenue ends at the Mississippi River, and the area where the street meets St. Charles Avenue forms the Black Pearl, a neighborhood surrounding Pearl Street and historically mostly occupied by African Americans. Like most parts of the city, this area was awash with corner grocery stores, where customers not only bought beer and sausage, but also caught up on the latest news.

On Canal Street, there roamed bumbling, yet notoriously no-nonsense policemen who protected the bustling blocks of upscale department stores and well-dressed patrons. Streetcars clanked down the neutral ground (the local term for a street median), and movie theater marquees flashed titles of the latest features. And at the area's numerous lunch counters, just about anything a typical Creole enjoyed eating could be bought, by whites, that is, including wine cakes that, at the time, were known almost exclusively to New Orleans.

After receiving a full academic scholarship, Toole graduated at the age of twenty-two from Tulane University, only blocks from his home. During this time as a student, he would fill in for a friend who made extra cash selling the Fiesta company's hot tamales from a pushcart. Then there was the summer job at the Haspel Brothers men's clothing plant, the stint there his inspiration for Gus Levy and his wife.

Toole eventually ended up teaching at New Orleans's all-female Dominican College. But before that he'd been drawn to New York, where he studied twice at Columbia and taught classes at Hunter College, where a strong-willed brand of coed could have served as models for Ignatius's girlfriend, Myrna Minkoff.

Inspiration for the book's main character may have taken root back in 1959, and not in New Orleans, but in Lafayette, the heart of Louisiana's French-speaking Cajun country, where Toole had a short stint as an English professor at Southwestern Louisiana Institute, now called the University of Louisiana at Lafayette. There, he made friends with a quirky and overweight fellow professor named Bob Byrne, who refused to drive and wore mismatched clothes. Byrne was an expert in

Photograph of John Kennedy Toole.

the medieval period, and regaled in discussing Boethius, the wheel of Fortuna, and theories of theology and geometry. The eccentric professor also wore a deerstalker hat, played the lute, and adored hot dogs. Sound familiar? There's also a theory that part of Ignatius came from Toole himself, who, when he worked selling tamales, was known to gobble up more than a few.

Through much of his adult life, Toole downed gallons of coffee and café au lait, as well as a fair amount of alcohol at watering holes such as the Napoleon House and the Roosevelt Hotel's Sazerac Bar. Often he cavorted with acquaintances whom he captivated with his high IQ and knowledge of literature, along with an ability to dance, a knack at making people laugh, and that talent of mimicking the real-life eccentrics of New Orleans. From all indications, Toole's life was rich with a coterie of genuine friends. But apparently these ties weren't enough.

In 1961, Toole was drafted into the U.S. Army, and he ended up teaching English to Spanish-speaking recruits in San Juan, Puerto Rico. It was there that he dove headlong into *A Confederacy of Dunces*. The book's title came from the 1706 essay "Thoughts on Various Subjects, Moral and Diverting" by Irish-born satirist Jonathan Swift, who divined that, "when a true genius appears in the world, you may know him by this sign, that the dunces are all in confederacy against him." Toole's novel eventually attracted serious attention from Simon & Schuster editor Robert Gottlieb. But, after two years of deliberation, that potential partnership ended. And on March 26, 1969, after failing to attract another publisher, and in poor health and dogged by paranoia, John Kennedy Toole ended his life by asphyxiation in a car parked on a lonely road in Biloxi. It was not until eleven years later, when the strong-willed Thelma convinced the writer and Loyola University professor Walker Percy to

intercede, that Toole's masterpiece found a home at LSU Press. Posthumously, the book was awarded the 1981 Pulitzer Prize for Fiction.

The Neon Bible, written in 1954, was finally published in 1989. But it's *A Confederacy of Dunces* that hasn't stopped capturing accolades, with critics still crowning it "the quintessential New Orleans novel." Toole clearly based his work on his home, the most European of American cities in the most eclectic of the American states, and through parodies based on outrageous characters whose arguments, speech patterns, eating habits, hopes, and schemes are so wildly exaggerated they're clearly fictitious. Or maybe not.

· ·

Sazerac Bar's Sazerac

Makes 1 drink. Recipe is from bartender Matthew Steinvorth of the Sazerac Bar in the Roosevelt Hotel.

· ·

Toole liked to chill out at the Sazerac Bar in Canal Street's old Roosevelt Hotel, which, after changing hands in 1965 and renamed as the Fairmont, reopened again as the Roosevelt in 2009. The drink known as the Sazerac is heralded as the oldest known American cocktail. The basic recipe for the cognac/whiskey-based beverage was created in the 1830s by Antoine Amedie Peychaud, a New Orleans apothecary who had immigrated from the West Indies and created his own brand of bitters. Named for the cognac originally used to make it, Sazerac de Forge et Fils, in the beginning was known as a breezer and was a "medicinal" toddy consumed in the morning. On June 23, 2008, the Louisiana Legislature designated the Sazerac as the official cocktail of the City of New Orleans.

2 ounces (4 tablespoons) rye whiskey

¼ ounce (1½ teaspoons) demerara syrup (recipe
   follows), or simple syrup

3 dashes Peychaud's Bitters

Big splash absinthe or anise-flavored spirit

Lemon twist for garnish

1. Fill a rocks glass with ice, and set aside.
2. In a separate glass, mix whiskey, demerara syrup, and
   bitters. Add a couple of ice cubes.
3. Discard ice in chilled rocks glass. Add absinthe, and
   swirl around until glass is thoroughly coated. Pour out
   excess.
4. Strain whiskey mixture into the chilled and coated glass,
   and garnish with the lemon twist.

Demerara Syrup   Makes 1½ cups

Demerara sugar is an unrefined sugar with large,
irregular crystals and a golden color. Full of natural
molasses flavor, demerara is popular for sweetening
both alcoholic and non-alcoholic drinks.

   2 cups demerara or turbinado sugar
   1 cup cold water

Stir sugar and water together in a high-sided saucepan, and bring to a boil over medium heat. Reduce
heat to a bare simmer, and cook 3 minutes, stirring
occasionally. Remove from heat, cool, and refrigerate
in a covered glass container up to 1 month.

Napoleon House's Corsican Salad with Balsamic-Raspberry Vinaigrette

Makes 4 side salads, or 2 entrées. Recipe is from Sal Impastato, owner, Napoleon House Bar and Café.

Another place Toole was known to hang out at was the Napoleon House Bar on Chartres Street in the French Quarter. Built for Mayor Nicholas Girod in 1797, in 1821 the home was supposedly offered as a retirement hide-out to Napoleon Bonaparte. Only problem was that, at the time, the emperor was jailed on the island of St. Helena. It's rumored that Girod and the pirates Jean Lafitte and Dominique Youx plotted Napoleon's escape, but the exiled general died before the plan could be executed.

   3 cups crisp red leaf lettuce
   ½ cup kalamata olives
   12 cherry tomatoes
   ½ cup toasted walnuts
   ½ cup thinly sliced red onion

½ cup crumbled gorgonzola cheese

Balsamic-Raspberry Vinaigrette (recipe this page)

Divide lettuce among plates, and top with olives, tomatoes, walnuts, onion, and cheese. Drizzle with Balsamic-Raspberry Vinaigrette, and serve immediately.

Ninth Ward Hot Tamales
Makes 40.

When John Kennedy Toole pushed a tamale cart as a student, he was working for Fiesta, a tamale company based in the Ninth Ward near the Industrial Canal, and which closed in the 1980s. An even bigger name in tamales in New Orleans was Manuel's, a Mid-City business shut down by Hurricane Katrina. Even with these legendary manufacturers no longer in business, it's still easy to find outstanding tamales all over town. And most of today's tamales, as with their predecessors, are typical of what you'll find in the Deep South—smallish with hardly any cornmeal, and greasy, peppery, and addictive.

Balsamic-Raspberry Vinaigrette
Makes 1¼ cups

Recipe is from Sal Impastato, owner, Napoleon House Bar and Café.

½ cup canola oil

½ cup fresh or frozen raspberries

¼ cup freshly squeezed orange juice

3 tablespoons balsamic vinegar

2 teaspoons sugar

1 teaspoon kosher salt

1 teaspoon coarsely ground black pepper

Puree all ingredients in a blender, and strain. Keeps up to 4 days covered in the refrigerator.

¾ pound ground beef chuck

¼ pound ground pork

1 large onion, chopped

2 cloves garlic, minced

2 tablespoons tomato sauce, plus
    1 (8-ounce) can

3 cups finely ground cornmeal, divided

6 teaspoons chili powder, divided

3 teaspoons ground cumin, divided

1½ teaspoons salt, divided

½ teaspoon paprika

½ teaspoon ground black pepper

¼ teaspoon cayenne pepper, or to taste

40 (5 x 7-inch) paper tamale wrappers (or make
    your own from parchment paper)

1. In the bowl of a food processor, combine beef, pork, onion, garlic, 2 tablespoons tomato sauce, 3 tablespoons cornmeal, 4 teaspoons chili powder, 2 teaspoons cumin, 1 teaspoon salt, paprika, black pepper, and cayenne. Process until meat and onion are finely ground.

2. Fill a shallow bowl with warm water. Dip one tamale paper into water, lay it flat horizontally, and sprinkle ½ teaspoon cornmeal up the center 3 inches of the paper. Roll a heaping tablespoon of meat mixture into a 3-inch log, then roll the log in remaining cornmeal. Place the meat log onto the center edge of the paper, and roll it up, tucking the sides underneath. Repeat process for remaining tamales.

3. In a large Dutch oven, lay rows of tamales on their sides, making each row go in opposite directions. In a bowl, combine 1 quart water with remaining can of tomato sauce, remaining 2 teaspoons chili powder, remaining teaspoon cumin, and remaining ½ teaspoon salt. Carefully pour over tamales in Dutch oven until liquid reaches the bottom of the top layer of tamales.

4. Bring liquid to a boil. Reduce heat to a bare simmer, cover tightly, and cook until meat is completely cooked through, about 1–1½ hours. Serve hot. If freezing tamales, first allow to come to room temperature.

> "Many's the week we lived
> on red beans and rice."
> "Red beans gives me gas."
> "Me, too."
>
> —Mrs. Reilly and Santa Battaglia.

Parasol's Roast Beef Poor Boys

Makes 12–18 sandwiches. Recipe is from Thea Hogan, owner, Parasol's Bar and Restaurant.

Toole was known to enjoy poor boys at Parasol's, the historic Irish Channel bar and restaurant that also serves as headquarters for the city's annual St. Patrick's Day Street Festival.

6 cloves garlic, divided
1 inside round (top round) of beef (4–6 pounds)
Salt
Black pepper
½ teaspoon onion powder
½ teaspoon garlic powder
2 tablespoons vegetable oil
1–2 cups beef broth
2 large onions, chopped
1–2 tablespoons all-purpose flour
Poor boy French bread

Mayonnaise

Shredded lettuce

Tomato slices

Dill pickle slices

1. Preheat oven to 325°F. Thinly slice 3 cloves garlic. Make slits in beef and insert sliced garlic. Season outside of beef with salt, pepper, onion powder, and garlic powder.

2. Heat oil over medium-high heat in a Dutch oven, and sear beef until browned well on all sides. Remove pot from heat, and add enough broth to reach ¼ way up the roast. Add remaining garlic and onion to the pot. Cover and bake 2–3 hours, or until extremely tender.

3. Remove meat from pot, and strain stock. Return stock to pot, bring to a boil, and thicken with flour mixed with a little water. Slice beef thin, and add to gravy.

4. To make sandwiches, slice 6-inch pieces of French bread horizontally. Spread bread with mayonnaise, and layer on lettuce, tomatoes, pickles, and sliced beef. Cover beef with gravy, and put bread top on, pressing slightly to soak up the juices. Serve immediately. (This sandwich is even better when heated in an oven a few minutes before serving.)

Monday Red Beans and Rice

Makes 6–8 servings. Recipe is by Dr. Willard Dumas.

Growing up in New Orleans, Toole could not have escaped what has become this city's unofficial official Monday dish. The old story goes that back before the time of washing machines housewives kept a big pot of economical dried beans boiling on the stove while they did laundry on Mondays; hence the modern connection with eating the dish that day.

Dr. Dumas adds a layer of flavor to his signature dish with smoked turkey necks, which are not that difficult to find in New Orleans. If your corner grocery is fresh out, substitute smoked sausage. And, like many busy local cooks, Dumas makes his beans in a slow cooker. But this recipe can also be cooked the traditional way, on top of the stove. And the beans need to soak overnight, so plan on starting the day ahead.

1 pound dried red beans

16 ounces (2 cups) Creole seasoning vegetable mix (purchased, or use recipe on page 190)

4 cloves garlic, minced

4 large bay leaves

1 (1½- to 2-pound) package smoked turkey necks

6–8 cups water

2 pounds smoked beef or pork sausage, sliced into ½-inch rounds or serving-sized portions

¼ teaspoon salt

Ground black pepper and cayenne to taste

Hot, cooked brown or white rice

Chopped green onion for garnish

1. The night before cooking, place beans in a large bowl, rinse well, and cover with 2 inches water. Allow to sit overnight. The next morning, drain beans before cooking.

2. Place drained beans, seasoning vegetables, garlic, bay leaves, and turkey necks into a slow cooker. Stir in 6–8 cups water, using less water for a thicker finished dish, and more water for thinner. Cook on high temperature 6 hours. Alternatively, simmer in an uncovered pot, stirring occasionally, until beans are just tender and liquid starts to thicken, about 2 hours.

3. Remove turkey necks, and add sausage. (To remove some of the fat from sausage, lightly sauté before adding to beans.) Cook another hour. Smash some of the beans against the side of the slow cooker to thicken the sauce. If cooking in a slow cooker, cook another hour. If cooking on top of the stove, simmer a few more minutes. Remove bay leaves, stir in salt and pepper, and the dish is done.

4. Serve beans and sausage hot over rice, and garnish with green onion.

Creole Seasoning Vegetable Mix

Makes 2 cups

A commercial mixture of pre-chopped onion, bell pepper, and celery is available fresh or frozen in most local grocery stores. This Louisiana version of the French mirepoix (chopped onion, carrot, and celery) is known in this historically Catholic state as the "holy trinity." For extra punch, many suppliers, as well as home cooks, also make green onion, parsley, and garlic part of this standard seasoning mix.

¾ cup chopped onion
½ cup chopped bell pepper
⅓ cup chopped celery
¼ cup chopped green onion
2 tablespoons chopped parsley
2 cloves garlic, minced

Combine all ingredients in a bowl. Cover and refrigerate up to 3 days.

Crawfish Étouffée

Makes 4 servings. Recipe is by Kathy Comeaux.

When Toole spent a year teaching in Lafayette, he made close friends who liked to entertain. At one of these Cajun soirees he was no doubt served crawfish étouffée, a savory mudbug stew served over rice, and a specialty of the area.

8 tablespoons (1 stick) butter
2 cups chopped onion
½ cup chopped green bell pepper
1 large clove garlic, minced
2 tablespoons all-purpose flour
1½ cups seafood stock or water
½ cup tomato sauce
Salt, ground black pepper, and cayenne to taste
1 pound peeled crawfish tails, with fat
2 tablespoons minced fresh parsley
¼ cup chopped green onion
Cooked rice for serving

1. In a large skillet over medium-high heat, melt the butter and sauté onion and bell pepper until vegetables are tender, about 10 minutes. Add garlic, and cook 1 minute.

2. Lower temperature to medium, add flour, and cook, stirring constantly, until medium brown, 7–8 minutes.

3. Add stock, tomato sauce, salt, black pepper, and cayenne. Lower to a simmer, and cook 30 minutes, stirring occasionally to prevent sticking.

4. Stir in crawfish tails and fat, and simmer 12–15 minutes, or until crawfish is cooked through, but not overcooked. Stir in parsley and green onion, and serve hot over rice.

Ruby Sharlow's Chicken and Sausage Gumbo

Makes 6–8 servings. Recipe is by Ruby Sharlow.

While in Lafayette, Toole would have also surely been served lots of bowls of the dark, heavy Cajun version of gumbo. Unlike traditional New Orleans gumbo, gumbo served in southwest Louisiana uses lots of roux and shuns the use of tomatoes and the ubiquitous heavy dose of thyme. Ruby Sharlow is the retired owner of Ruby's Creole restaurant in Lafayette, Louisiana, the heart of Cajun country and the region where many food historians believe gumbo was perfected. Served with chicken still on the bone and smelling of heavily smoked sausage, this recipe won her many fans.

3½ quarts water

1½ cups roux (recipe this page)

½ cup chopped onion

½ cup chopped celery

½ cup chopped bell pepper

¼ cup minced fresh garlic

1 (2½–3-pound) fryer, cut into 8 pieces

Salt, ground black pepper, and cayenne pepper

2 links (½ pound) smoked pork sausage, sliced

2–4 chicken bouillon cubes, depending on
   saltiness desired

Chopped fresh parsley and green onion,
   optional

4 cups hot cooked rice for serving

1. Bring water to a boil in a large, deep pot. Stir in roux. (Be careful when adding hot roux. If pot is not deep enough,

Ruby Sharlow's Roux — Makes 2¼ cups

This recipe calls for a relatively large amount of flour, and anything made with it will have a pronounced nutty roux flavor. Ruby reminds us that in South Louisiana there's no making gumbo or stew without the region's famous thickener. Because of the time and patience involved in making roux, she advises making it in bulk. Roux keeps two months stored in the refrigerator.

1½ cups vegetable oil

3 cups all-purpose flour

1. In a large, heavy-bottomed saucepan, heat oil over medium heat. Slowly mix in flour, and cook, stirring constantly, until mixture turns the color of dark caramel, about 15–20 minutes.
2. To prevent further coloration, immediately pour hot, cooked roux into a clean pot or metal bowl.

mixture may boil over.) Stir in onion, celery, bell pepper, and garlic. Simmer 30 minutes, stirring occasionally.

2. Season chicken liberally with salt, black pepper, and cayenne. Add seasoned chicken and sausage to stock, and simmer 15 minutes. Add bouillon cubes, and cook 30 more minutes, or until chicken is tender. Check for seasoning. If gumbo gets too thick, add more water.

3. Stir in optional parsley and green onion. Place ½ cup rice in the middle of a soup bowl, and ladle gumbo over rice. Serve hot.

Elysian Fields Blueberry and Pecan Banana Bread

Makes 1 loaf.

Former neighbors of John Kennedy Toole's mother recall sending bunches of bananas to the house on Elysian Fields Avenue where the aged and ailing Thelma lived with her brother Arthur, and then getting a loaf of banana bread in return. Bananas were apparently a favorite of Arthur, who worked the docks unloading bananas and who could easily eat the fruit without his dentures.

2 cups all-purpose flour

1 teaspoon baking soda

1 teaspoon baking powder

½ teaspoon iodized salt

1 teaspoon cinnamon

¼ teaspoon freshly grated nutmeg

8 tablespoons (1 stick) unsalted butter, room temperature

½ cup light brown sugar, packed

2 large eggs, room temperature

⅓ cup honey

1 teaspoon pure vanilla extract

2 cups mashed overripe bananas

1 cup frozen blueberries

½ cup chopped pecans

1. Preheat oven to 325°F. Lightly oil the insides of a 9 x 5-inch loaf pan.
2. Sift together flour, baking soda, baking powder, salt, cinnamon, and nutmeg. In a separate large bowl, use medium mixer speed to beat together butter and brown sugar for 3 minutes. Beat in eggs, one at a time. Stir in honey, vanilla, and bananas.
3. Add flour mixture to butter/banana mixture, and use a spoon to stir until just moist (don't over mix). Quickly and gently fold in frozen blueberries and pecans.
4. Pour batter into prepared pan, and bake until golden and a knife inserted into the center comes out clean, or when a probe thermometer registers 195–200°F, about 1½ hours. If top browns too quickly, cover with foil.
5. Cool in pan 10 minutes; then remove from pan and cool on a rack. Serve warm, or wrap tightly when cool and freeze up to 1 month.

Vanilla Bean Ice Cream

Makes 1 quart.

Tucked into John Kennedy Toole's estate was a napkin from a Howard Johnson's he'd visited while living in New York. Throughout the 1960s, the hotel chain was also the largest restaurant chain across the United States. Foodwise, the well-recognized brand with the orange roof was known for its clams, hot dogs, and "28 Flavors" of ice cream. In 1962, those ice cream choices included banana, black raspberry, butter pecan, butter crunch, butterscotch, caramel fudge, chocolate, chocolate chip, coconut, coffee, cherry vanilla, frozen pudding, fudge ripple, lemon, macaroon, maple walnut, mint chip, mocha chip, orange pineapple, peach, pecan brittle, pineapple, peppermint stick, pistachio, strawberry, strawberry ripple, Swiss almond, and vanilla.

1 whole vanilla bean

1¼ cups sugar

2 tablespoons cornstarch

¼ teaspoon salt

2 cups whole milk

3 egg yolks

1 (12-ounce) can evaporated milk

1 cup whipping cream

1 tablespoon vanilla extract

1. Split vanilla bean lengthwise, and scrape seeds into a large saucepan. Add scraped vanilla bean pod, sugar, cornstarch, salt, and whole milk. Whisk over medium heat until boiling, and reduce heat to low. Simmer 1 minute. Remove from heat.

2. Whisk egg yolks in a small bowl; then slowly whisk in 1 cup of hot milk mixture. Whisk egg mixture into remaining milk in saucepan. Cook mixture over low heat 2 minutes, whisking constantly. Remove from heat, remove vanilla bean pod, and stir in evaporated milk. (If lumps have formed, strain mixture.)

3. Stir in whipping cream and vanilla extract. Chill custard at least 4 hours, or preferably overnight.

4. Freeze custard in an ice cream maker according to manufacturer's directions. Spoon ice cream into a container, cover, and freeze until proper scooping texture, at least 2 hours.

> "We are going to have the most fantastic time in New York. Honestly."
>
> "I can't wait," Ignatius said, packing his scarf and cutlass. "The Statue of Liberty, the Empire State Building, the thrill of opening night on Broadway with my favorite musicomedy stars. Gab sessions in the Village over espresso with challenging, contemporary minds."
>
> —Myrna and Ignatius, as they prepare to sneak Ignatius out of New Orleans.

Chambord Espresso Jellies with Cream

Makes 4–8 servings, depending on size of dessert bowls.

While living in New York, Toole obviously enjoyed drinking espresso. At the time, sipping these little shots of thick coffee was a favorite pastime in the coffee houses of Greenwich Village, where poets and intellectuals discussed politics and philosophy and where, on America's East Coast, the stage was set for the 1960s rebellion against tradition.

If she finds time between writing letters to the editor, picketing, producing "bold and shattering" movies, and leeching money from her father, Myrna can easily whip up this espresso-based dessert for her "Ig."

1¾ cups brewed, cold espresso

1 package (.25 ounces, or 2½ teaspoons)
   unflavored gelatin

3 tablespoons sugar, divided

4 tablespoons Chambord liqueur, divided

1 cup chilled whipping cream

Fresh raspberries for garnish

1. In a small saucepan, stir together espresso and gelatin, and let sit 1 minute. Stir in 2 tablespoons sugar. Put saucepan over a low flame and heat, stirring constantly, until mixture just comes to a full boil, about 5 minutes.

2. Remove pan from heat, and let sit at room temperature 2 minutes. Stir in 3 tablespoons Chambord. Divide mixture among clear dessert glasses or bowls, and refrigerate up to 1 day ahead.

3. Up to 1 hour before serving, use a whisk attachment and medium-high mixer speed to beat together the whipping cream, remaining tablespoon sugar, and remaining tablespoon Chambord until stiff. Spoon whipped cream over jellied espresso. Top with raspberries, and serve chilled.

Afterword

Does Ignatius find a rich inner peace in New York with Myrna? Does Burma Jones get a decent job, and does Darlene get to dance in a respectable nightclub? How high does Patrolman Mancuso rise in the ranks? And what about Santa—is she successful in marrying Mrs. Reilly to Claude Robichaux, or does Mrs. Reilly miss her boy Ignatius too much and track him down? We'll never know the answers. That it's hard to let go of these remarkable characters is a tribute to the power of a masterpiece.

—Cynthia LeJeune Nobles

ACKNOWLEDGMENTS

Thanks to Susan Lipsey, Joan Berenson,
Linda Cannon, Brenda O'Connor, and to my husband,
Howard, and stepson Trey, my official taste-testers. Also
to Alisa Plant at LSU Press, and especially to Maureen
Detweiler, Greg Morago, and Cheramie Sonnier for their
expert editing and advice, and to Marjo Easley and
Melinda Winans for testing recipes.

SELECTED REFERENCES

Alexander-Bloch, Benjamin. "The Louisiana Seafood Industry's History, from Start in 1700s to Present." *Times-Picayune,* February 27, 2013.

Baker, Richard A. "Seersucker Thursday." *The New Members' Guide to Traditions of the United States Senate.* www.senate.gov. Retrieved March 30, 2014.

Baudier, Roger, Sr. "A General Review of Origin and Development of the Baking Industry in Old New Orleans, 1722–1892." Tulane University Library Special Collections.

Berendt, Joachim Ernst. *New Orleans Jazzlife 1960.* Los Angeles: Taschen, 2006.

Blue Plate Mayonnaise History. www.blueplatemayo.com /history. Retrieved January 29, 2014.

Bourg, Gene. "New Orleans History Explored through its Restaurants." *Times-Picayune,* July 18, 1989.

"Bowling Alleys." Rediscovering America's Roadside! www.vintageroadside.com. Retrieved February 8, 2014.

Brunet, René, Jr., and Jack Stewart. *There's One in Your Neighborhood: The Lost Movie Theaters of New Orleans.* Mandeville, La.: Arthur Hardy Enterprises, 2012.

Burnham, Ted. "American History Baked Into Loaves of White Bread." www.npr.org. Retrieved August 9, 2014.

Cable, Mary. *Lost New Orleans.* Boston: Houghton Mifflin, 1980.

Christian Woman's Exchange of New Orleans. *The Creole Cookery Book.* 1885. Rpt. Gretna, La.: Pelican Publishing, 2005.

Curtis, Wayne. "Big Train in the Big Easy." *Imbibe Magazine,* May–June 2014.

Delaup, Rick. "Vintage Bourbon Street Burlesque." www.frenchquarter.com. Retrieved January 23, 2014.

"Dr. Nut, Popular Local Soft Drink in 1930s, '40s." *Times-Picayune,* June 23, 2012.

"Early Times Kentucky Whisky." earlytimes.com. Retrieved February 2, 2014.

Fazzio, Sam. Telephone interview, February 27, 2014.

Fitzmorris, Tom. *New Orleans Food.* New York: Stewart, Tabori & Chang, 2006.

Fletcher, Joel L. *Ken & Thelma: The Story of A Confederacy of Dunces.* Gretna, La.: Pelican Publishing, 2005.

Folse, John. "Natchitoches Meat Pies." www.jfolse.com. Retrieved January 3, 2014.

"Freedom March in New Orleans" and "New Orleans Boycotts and Sit-ins." crmvet.org. Retrieved March 26, 2014.

"George Crum, Inventor of Potato Chips." www.black-inventor.com. Retrieved March 4, 2014.

Grady, Bill. "Confederacy of 2 Recalls Stealing Holmes Clock." *Times Picayune,* June 23, 2002.

Gurtner, George. "Farewell to St. Henry's." www.mynew orleans.com. Retrieved January 31, 2014.

Hearn, Lafcadio. *Creole Cook Book.* 1885. Rpt. Gretna, La.: Pelican Publishing, 1990.

"History of Brownies." www.thenibble.com. Retrieved February 9, 2014.

"History of the French Market." www.frenchmarket.org. Retrieved April 23, 2104.

Hochman, Karen. "The History of the Macaroon." thenibble.com. Retrieved November 17, 2013.

"Hurricane." Pat Obrien's Bar, patobriens.com. Retrieved August 26, 2014.

Irwin, Sam. *Louisiana Crawfish*. Charleston, S.C.: American Palate, 2014.

Kroeper, Al. Personal interview. February 27, 2014.

LaBorde, Peggy Scott, and Tom Fitzmorris. *Lost Restaurants of New Orleans*. Gretna, La.: Pelican Publishing, 2012.

LaBorde, Peggy Scott, and John Magill. *Canal Street: New Orleans' Great Wide Way*. Gretna, La: Pelican Publishing, 2006.

——. *Christmas in New Orleans*. Gretna, La.: Pelican Publishing, 2009.

Leighton, H. Vernon. "Evidence of Influences on John Kennedy Toole's *A Confederacy of Dunces*, Including Geoffrey Chaucer." Version 2.0, July 1, 2011. Digital source on "the Library," Winona State University, www.course1.winona.edu. Retrieved October 16, 2014.

"Louisiana Industry." About Louisiana-History and Culture. www.doa.louisiana.gov. Retrieved April 5, 2014.

"Louisiana Seafood Facts." www.louisianaseafood.com. Retrieved March 5, 2014.

Louisiana Sweet Potato Commission. www.sweetpotato.org. Retrieved February 16, 2014.

MacLauchlin, Cory. *Butterfly in the Typewriter: The Tragic Life of John Kennedy Toole and the Remarkable Story of A Confederacy of Dunces*. Boston: Da Capo Press, 2012.

Marks, Gil. *Encyclopedia of Jewish Food*. New York: Wiley, 2010.

Mason, Laura. *Sugar-Plums and Sherbet: The Prehistory of Sweets*. Devon, U.K.: Prospect Books, 2004.

McNulty, Ian. "New Orleans Bakeries on the Rise." *Gambit*, July 23, 2013.

Miller, Hanna. "American Pie." *American Heritage* 57, no. 2 (April–May 2006).

Nevils, René Pol, and Deborah George Hardy. *Ignatius Rising: The Life of John Kennedy Toole*. Baton Rouge: Louisiana State University Press, 2001.

"New Orleans, Gateway to the Americas." nutrias.org. Retrieved February 2, 2014.

Reckdahl, Katy. "Sit-ins at Canal Street Lunch Counters 50 Years Ago Sparked a Civil Rights Case That Went All the Way to the Supreme Court." *Times-Picayune,* September 16, 2010.

"Rich Gay Heritage." www.neworleansonline.com. Retrieved April 22, 2014.

Robinson, Jancis. *Vines, Grapes, Wines*. New York: Knopf, 1986.

"Spotlight on Business: Howard Johnson's—Father, Son, and Grandson Give Three Cheers for the Old Orange and Blue." *Newsweek,* August 13, 1962, 66–67.

Stanforth, Deirdre. *The New Orleans Restaurant Cookbook*. New York: Doubleday, 1967.

Strahan, Jerry. *Managing Ignatius: The Lunacy of Lucky Dogs and Life in New Orleans*. New York: Broadway Books, 1998.

——. Personal interview. February 11, 2014.

Trillin, Calvin. "An Attempt to Compile a Short History of the Buffalo Chicken Wing." *New Yorker,* August 25, 1980.

Tucker, Susan, ed. *New Orleans Cuisine: Fourteen Signature Dishes and Their Histories*. Jackson: University Press of Mississippi: 2009.

Ursuline Academy. *Recipes and Remembrances of New Orleans*. New Orleans, 1971.

Van Kraayenburg, Russell. *Haute Dogs*. Philadelphia: Quirk Books, 2014.

Van Syckle, Katie. "Preserving the Louisiana Heritage Strawberry." bestofneworelans.com/gambit. Retrieved December 28, 2013.

Varney, James. "History of Cuba-Louisiana Relations." *Havana Journal,* www.nola.com. Retrieved March 31, 2014.

Williams, Elizabeth M. *New Orleans: A Food Biography*. Lanham, Md.: AltaMira Press, 2013.

WYES Television. "Where New Orleans Shopped." Videotape. New Orleans, 2002.

York, Michael Y. "Happy Birthday, Bloody Mary!" www.epicurious.com. Retrieved April 2, 2014.

GENERAL INDEX

· ·

Note: Page numbers in *italics* refer to illustrations and captions. For recipes, see Recipe Index.

Big Chief writing tablets, xv, *38*
biscotti, 86
biscuits, 66
bison, 56–57
bistro craze, 55
Blackened Redfish, 9
black-eyed peas, 67
Black Pearl, 183
Blange, Paul, 121
Blue Horse paper, xv
Blue Plate mayonnaise, 83
Bob and Jakes' restaurant, Baton Rouge, 177
Boethius, xv, 39, 40
boiled redfish, 136
Bon Ton Café (Magazine St.), 77, 143
The Boston Cooking-School Cook Book
    (Farmer), 50
Bourbon Street
    Café Lafitte in Exile, 52
    clean-up of, 17
    history of, 15
    Madame Francine's nightclub, *16*
    name of, 15
    recent changes to, 17
    strip clubs on, 15–17
    strippers of, 17
    See also Night of Joy nightclub and bar
bourbon whiskey, 15
Boursin, 72
Boursin, François, 72
bowling and bowling alleys, 91–93, *92*, 96,
    97–98
braciole, 82
brandy, 45
bread pudding, 179–80
breads, 62–63, 64, 75, 163–64
Breaux Bridge, 143
Brennan, Owen, 50
Brennan's Restaurant, 50, 121
Briant, Peter, 149
Brocato's Bakery, 21, 104
Brown-Forman Distillers, xvi
brownies, 50
Brown's Velvet ice cream, 129

Brunet, René, Jr., 91
Bruning's, 134
bruschetta, 77
The Buccaneer (film), 157
Bucket of Blood Club, Chicago, 40
Bucktown, 134
buffalo, 56–57
Bumper, Betty, xiv, 53
Burma. *See* Jones, Burma (character)
Butterfinger candy bar, 37
Butterfly in the Typewriter (MacLauchlin),
    181–83
Byrne, Bob, 183–85
Bywater, 120

café au lait, *23*, 24
Café du Monde, 24
Café Lafitte in Exile (Bourbon Street), 52
café noir, 24
cafeteria at D. H. Holmes, 3, 5, 8
Cajun food
    about, x, 3
    crawfish, 142–43
    gumbo, 30, 191
    jambalaya, 78, 173
"Cajun," meaning of, 3
Canal Street
    about, 183
    as fashionable retail district, 1
    Palace Café, xviii, *2*, 3
    Vitascope Hall, 89
    Werlein's, xviii, *2*, 3
    See also D. H. Holmes Department Store
Canary Islands fishermen, 134
candy shop at D. H. Holmes, 3, 10–11
Cangelosi, Robert, 85
canned foods, 62, 64, 66, 70
caouage, 171
Capital One Financial Corp., xvi
Caribbean immigrants, 3
Carrollton district, 183
Carver, George Washington, 59
Carver Theater, 91
Casbarian, Katy, 121

cashews, 27, 28
casket girls, 71
Castro, Fidel, 46
Castrogiovanni, Nick, 20
catfish, 145
Catholic Church
    Cuba and, 46
    slavery, *Code Noir*, and, 170
    St. Louis Cathedral, xviii
cattle drives, 29
Cazenave, "Count" Arnaud, 121
Celentano Brothers, 43
céleri-Rave rémoulade, 6
character development, food trends and, x
Charity Hospital, xv, 40
Chateau Sonesta Hotel, 4
chayote (mirlitons), 120
cheese balls, 56
cheese dips, 55
chewing gum, 93–94
Chicago deep-dish pizza, 43
chicken hot-wings, 56
chicken Pontalba, 121
chicken salad at D. H. Holmes, 7
chicory, 24
Child, Julia, ix, 53
chili, 96
Chinese crawfish, 143
chocolate chip cookies, 106
choux, 112
Chrysler Plymouth, 117
Chunky candy bars, 101
citrus growers in Plaquemines Parish, 130, 163
civil rights movement, 27–28
Civil War, American, 24, 46
clock at D. H. Holmes, 4
Club, Frieda (character), xiv, 53
Clyde, Mr. (character)
    description of, xiv
    pirate outfit and, 157
    real-life version of, 149–50
    route discussion with Ignatius, 154
cochon de lait (suckling pig), 32–33
cocktails at parties, 53

pralines (*pralinières*), 71
prime rib, 125
processed foods in the 1960s, ix
produce, 162–63
Professional Bowlers Association, 93
profiteroles, 112
Prudeaux, Victoria B., 30
Prudhomme, Paul, x, 3, 9
Prytania Theatre, xvii, 89–91, *90, 102*
Puerto Rico, 185
puff pastry, 104
Pulitzer Prize for Fiction, 185
Punch Jelly, 20
purple hull peas, 31–32
pyloric valve. *See* "valve" of Ignatius

quail, 35
quingombo, 76

recipes. *See Recipe Index*
red beans and rice, 188, 190
redfish, 9
redfish, boiled, 136
red gravy (tomato sauce), 75, 84
red snapper, 139
Reed, Maureen Simoneaux, 137
Reeves, Sally, 4
refrigerators, 62, *63*
Reilly, Ignatius J. (character)
  1960s food trends and, x
  attacked by Darlene's cockatoo at Night of
    Joy, 146
  auto accident and, 119
  beans grown in ice cream cartons at Levy
    Pants, 129, 130
  brownies and, 50
  café au lait in Shirley Temple mug, *23*
  under the clock at D. H. Holmes, 1, 4, 5
  in cookie jar, 73
  Darlene and, 17
  descriptions of, xiii, 47
  Dixie 45 beer and, 19
  at Dorian Greene's party, 52
  Dr. Talc's memories of, 46
  frozen pizza and, 43

George's plans to hide pornography in hot-
  dog cart of, 151
habits of, 39–40
hot-dog vending uniform and pirate outfit,
  151, 157
hunting and, 47
inspirations for, 185
junk food and, 94
at Levy Pants, 119–20
luncheon meat sandwiches and, 124
Mancuso's attempt to arrest, 116
Milky Way candy bars and, 100
Miss Annie on hearing Myrna and, 51
on Miss Trixie's turkey, ham, or roast, 125
mother's family, thoughts about, 112
Mr. and Mrs. Levy trying to visit at mental
  hospital, 132
Mrs. Reilly remembers conception of, 102
at Night of Joy, 15, 17
out of place at D. H. Holmes, 1
at Paradise Vendors, 149, 154
at Penny Arcade, 1
philosophy and influences on, 39
Santa's advice to put Ignatius away, 40
statue of, 4
threatening note to Dr. Talc, 40
valve of, 50
at Werlein's, 1
writing of, xv, 39
Reilly, Ignatius J., quotations from
  after auto accident, 41
  on brandy, 45
  on cheese dip, 55
  on chicory coffee and instant coffee, 24
  Dorian Green, conversations with, 107,
    174
  on food and comfort, ix
  journal entry on the Prytania theatre, 89
  Levy Pants discussion with Mrs. Reilly, 62
  on macaroons, 12
  on Miss Trixie and luncheon meat, 124
  to mother about her wine, 42
  on moving to New York, 193
  on Mrs. Reilly going bowling, 96
  on Mrs. Reilly's cooking, 66

over want ads with Mrs. Reilly, and "those
  bowling Sicilians," 99
on Paradise Vendors weenie pot, 160
on pirate outfit, 157
on selling hot dogs in French Quarter, 154,
  158
"tasteful and decent king . . . ," 39
telephone conversation with Mr. Levy, 106
on trip to Baton Rouge, 170
on wholesome food, to George, 162
Reilly, Irene (Mrs. Reilly) (character)
  1960s food trends and, x
  auto accident (1946 Plymouth), 41, 70, 117,
    119
  in back yard, 72
  bowling and, 91, 96
  coffee and, 24
  cooking of, 66, 67
  crabs at Lake Pontchartrain and, 136
  description of, xiii
  at D. H. Holmes, 1, 10
  family of, 112
  on German's Bakery, 103
  Ignatius's philosophy and, 39, 40
  kitchen of, 62
  at Night of Joy, 15, 20, 45
  over want ads with Ignatius, 99
  remembering Mr. Reilly, the Prytania, and
    conception of Ignatius, 102
  at Santa Battaglia's party, 79, 80, 180
  Santa's advice to put Ignatius away, 40
Reilly, Irene, quotations from
  on cooking, 67
  on daiquiris, 17
  at D. H. Holmes bakery, 1
  on Gallo muscatel, 42
  king conversation with Ignatius, 39
  on lady selling pralines, 71
  Levy Pants discussion, 62
  ordering Dixie 45 beer, 19
  on red beans and rice, 188
  on wine cakes to Darlene, 20
Reilly, Mr. (father of Ignatius), 102
Reilly, William B., III, 83
Reilly house on Constantinople St., 49, *182*

remoulade, 6
restaurants and the 1960s way of life, x–xi.
    See also specific restaurants
ribs, 34
rice, 69
Rihner, Tony, 4
Rite Aid, 14
River Road Recipes (Baton Rouge Junior
    League), 177
Rizzo, Sofia, 77, 82
Roberts, Oliver, 150
Robichaux, Claude (character)
    arrest of, 27
    on "communiss," xiii, 27, 116
    on cooking, 80
    crabs at Lake Pontchartrain and, 136
    description of, xiii
    on electric stove ("letrit range"), 62
    in jail with Jones, 27
    at Santa Battaglia's party, 79, 80
Rockefeller, John D., 172
Rock 'n' Bowl (Mid-City Lanes), 93, 98
rolls, 65
Roosevelt, Franklin, 19
Roosevelt Hotel, 185
roux, 30
Ruby's Creole restaurant, Lafayette, 191
rum, 169
Russian cake, 116
Ruth's Chris Steak House, 158

sabotage, 28
San Giuseppe, 75–76
Sansovich, Octavia Marie, 138
Santa. *See* Battaglia, Santa
Santos-Dumont, Alberto, 157
Sarrat, Ben, 32
Sarrat, Ben, Jr., 32
satire, ix
Saturday Hop (TV show), 40
savarin, 21
Savings and Loan. *See* "Homestead"
Sazerac, 53, 185
Sazerac Bar, Roosevelt Hotel, 185
Schnering, Otto, 37

school lunchrooms, 65
Schwabe's Bakery (Magazine St.), xvi, 103
Schwegmann's supermarket, x, 63
Scramuzza, Al "Doctor," 143
seafood industry, 76, 133–35
second line, 35
seersucker suits, 119
segregation, 27
Sephardic Jews, 67
Sewell, Ike, 43
Sharlow, Ruby, 191
Shell Beach, 134
Sherman, William T., 67
S&H Green Stamps, 63
Shirley Temple mug, xviii, *23*
S. H. Kress, 1
shopping trends in the 1960s, x. *See also* gro-
    cery stores and supermarkets
shrimp, "barbecued," 36
shrimp remoulade, 5
Sicilian cooking, 75–88
Sicilian immigrants, 75–76, 133, 163
sit-in lunch counter protests, 27–28
slaves, African and African-American, 3,
    170
Smirnov, Vladimir, 40
smoked turkey, 125
snoballs (snow cones), 18
Sno-bliz machine, 18
Sno-Wizard, 18
soft-shelled crabs, 141
Sonnier, Ray, 179
sorbet, 51
soul food in the 1960s, ix
Southeast Louisiana Hospital. *See* Mande-
    ville State Mental Hospital
southern peas, 31–32, 67
Southwestern Louisiana Institute (now
    University of Louisiana at Lafayette),
    183–85
spaghetti, 83, 84
Spain, Louisiana under, x, 72, 98, 104, 133,
    134, 170
Spanish influences on New Orleans
    Creole, 3

Spanish Rice, 22
spareribs, 34
speckled trout ("speck"), 142
spices mixes, Creole, 6–7
spinach, 166
Spinach Madeleine, 176–77
Standard Fruit Company, 49
standing rib roast, 125
Starr, Blaze, 17
St. Charles Theatre, 89
steamboats, produce on, 162
steamship era, 46
Steele, Liz (character), xiv, 53
Steinvorth, Matthew, 185
Stern, Justin, 19
Stewart, Jack, 91
St. Joseph's Altars, 75–76, 88
St. Louis Cathedral, xviii
St. Louis ribs, 34
St. Odo of Cluny Parish (fictitious), xviii
Storyville Brothel District, 15
stoves, electric, 62
St. Patrick's Day Street Festival, 188
Strahan, Jerry, 149–50, *150*, 151
strawberries, 11
street vending limitations in the French
    Quarter, 150–51
strip clubs in New Orleans, 15–17, *16*. *See also*
    Night of Joy nightclub and bar
stroopwafel, 131
suckling pig (*cochon de lait*), 32–33
Sunseri, Al, 139
Sunseri, Sal, 140
Super Bowl Sunday, 44
supermarkets. *See* grocery stores and
    supermarkets
Swamp People (TV), 155
sweet potatoes, 74, 164–65
Swift, Jonathan, 185
Swiss Bakery, 103
Swiss Confectionery, 103

"Take Me Out to the Ballgame" (Norworth),
    94
Talbot, Doug, 149

RECIPE INDEX

· ·

Macaroni, *See also* Pasta
  Ignatius Eatery's Mac 'n' Cheese with
    Fried Shrimp, 100
Macaroons, Coconut and Macadamia,
  Dipped in White Chocolate, 12–13
Malt, Grasshopper Cocktail, 13
Marinade, Pork, 33
Marinated Garlic Olives, 76
Marshmallows
  Effortless Heavenly Hash Candy, 10–11
Meat and Spinach–Stuffed Pasta Tubes,
  85–86
Meatballs
  Buffalo Meatballs with Blue Cheese Dip,
    56–57
  Daube and a Big Pot of Meatballs with
    Boiled Eggs and Spaghettis, 84–85
Meat Pies, Rock 'n' Bowl, 98
Meringue
  Bread Pudding with Meringue and Cara-
    mel and Vanilla Bourbon Sauce, 179–80
  Deep Dark Chocolate Cream Pie, 110–11
Messy Dog, Bourbon Street, 154
Milk
  Café au lait, 23–25
  Creole Cream Cheese, 73
Milky Way Soufflés, 100–101
Mimosa Sorbet, 130–31
Mint
  Blueberry, Mint, and Rosemary Sorbet, 51
  Figs and Proscuitto with Boursin, 72–73
  Minted Beets and Onion, 165
  Mint Juleps for a Crowd, 60–61
  Pineapple, Ginger, and Mint Snoballs, 18
  Promising Watermelon Salad, 41
Mirlitons, Shrimp and Ham–Stuffed, 120–21
Miss Trixie's Orange-and-Bourbon-Glazed
  Ham, 120
Mixed Greens Salad, with Orange, Honey-
  dew, and Spicy Orange Dressing, 164
Mocha Chocolate Ice Cream, 129–30
Mojo Sauce, Cuban, 33
Molasses Coated Popcorn and Peanuts,
  Grownup, 94
Monday Red Beans and Rice, 189–90

Muffins, Orange and Pecan, 11–12
Muscatel Braised Lamb Shanks with Sour
  Cream Mashed Potatoes, 42–43
Mushrooms
  Braised Venison Round Steak, 47–48
  Crawfish Torte, 144–45
  From-Scratch Pizza, 43–44
  Lobster and Shiitake Risotto with Black
    Truffle Oil, 161
  Oysters Dunbar, 137–38
  Pirate's Pompano en Papillote, 157–58
  Pork Chops with Brandy Mustard Sauce,
    45–46
  Weenies Wellington, 154–55
Mustard
  Barbecued Pork Spareribs with Pineapple
    Bourbon Sauce, 34–35
  Lemon Vinaigrette, 99
  Pork Chops with Brandy Mustard Sauce,
    45–46
  "Potatis" Salad, 83
  Remoulade Sauce, 6
Mustard Seed
  Dry Crawfish Boil Seasoning Mix, 144
Myrna's Alligator Dogs on Jalapeno Rolls,
  155–56

Napoleon House's Corsican Salad with Bal-
  samic-Raspberry Vinaigrette, 186–87
Nectar Ice Cream Soda, 14
Nectar Syrup, 14
Newfangled Crispy Buttermilk Fried
  Chicken, 8–9
New Orleans French Bread, 64–65
New Orleans–style Vegetable Beef Soup, 29
Nice Glazed Jelly Doughnuts, 105–106
Ninth Ward Hot Tamales, 187–88
No-booze Hurricane Cocktail, 168–69
No-cook Creole Tomato Soup, 67

Occasional Chipotle Goat Cheese Dip, 55–56
Offal
  Beausoleil's Sweetbreads with Beurre
    Blanc and Capers, 174–75
  Dirty Rice, 176

Okra
  Creole Okra-Filé Gumbo, 30–31
  Refrigerator Okra Pickles, 76–77
  Smothered Okra and Tomatoes, 166–67
Olives, Marinated Garlic, 76
Onion, Minted Beets and, 165
Oranges
  Cuban Mojo Sauce, 33
  Duck Breast with Fig Sauce, 49
  Lemon and Double-Orange Jell-O Shots,
    20
  Orange and Pecan Muffins, 11–12
  Orange, Honeydew and Mixed Greens
    Salad with Spicy Orange Dressing, 164
  Mimosa Sorbet, 130–31
  Miss Trixie's Orange-and-Bourbon-
    Glazed Ham, 120
  No-booze Hurricane Cocktail, 168–69
  Skinny Fruit Salad, 168
Organic Banana's Frozen Tropical Daiquiri, 18
Oysters
  Airline Motors Oysters Rockefeller,
    172–73
  Oyster Patties, 54–55
  Oysters Dunbar, 137–38
  P&J Oyster and Brie Soup, 139–40
  Perfect Fried Oysters, 146
  Pirate's Pompano en Papillote, 157–58
  Sal's Oyster Magic, 140
  Tried-and-True Oyster Dressing, 138–39
  Tujague's Oysters en Brochette, 53–54
  Whole Red Snapper Stuffed with Oyster
    Dressing, 139

P&J Oyster and Brie Soup, 139–40
Pan-Fried Soft-Shelled Crabs with Pecan
  Butter Sauce, 141
Pan-Fried Speckled Trout with Brown But-
  ter, 141–42
Paradise Pork and Beef Wieners, 151–52
Parasol's Roast Beef Poor Boys, 188–89
Parmesan, Whole-wheat and Sage Drop Bis-
  cuits, 168
Passion fruit
  No-booze Hurricane Cocktail, 168–69